More Praise for *Improvisational Negotiation*

"Jeff is a mediator who cares deeply about his craft, and every page of this book shows it. It deserves to be read by all professional mediators who aspire to his level of excellence, by lawyers who advise clients in the mediation process, and also by students of human nature. His stories are full of warmth and the characters skillfully drawn. The insights into negotiation theory are profound."

—Tony Willis, Brick Court Chambers, London, England

"The reason this book is so important is because it allows the reader to feel and sense what the mediation of conflict is really about. Beyond technique, at core, the success of a mediator is his or her authenticity— that's not necessarily the same as honesty and goes beyond mere empathy—it is the ability to connect and develop an essential level of trust with the parties. That's why Krivis has been so successful in his mediation practice and it's what permeates through his words and stories. Every mediator, novice or advanced, practicing in any area of conflict management, would reap great benefit from reading this book."

—Robert Benjamin, senior mediator, Mediation and Conflict Management Services, Portland, Oregon

"All conflicts are an alchemy of strong emotions, deep hurts, great perils. Always, there is the prospect of finding something bigger and transformational around the corner if we can find our way through it. Krivis shows us the way. A skilled mediator and master communicator, he demonstrates the patient power of story as a strategy for overcoming anger, pain, and sadness. More important, he renews hope that all of us can do the same when we are dealing with our own problems or helping others with theirs."

—Peter S. Adler, president, The Keystone Center

"*Improvisational Negotiation* is a road map to mediation ingenuity. It inspires us all to be creative and persistent in seeking resolution."

—Richard Chernick, managing director, JAMS Arbitration Practice

"*Improvisational Negotiation* is a must-read for all mediators. Jeff Krivis, a world-class mediator, brings the reader into the conference room and provides amazing insights that are both practical and useful. This wonderful book is like attending a superior advanced mediation training in the comfort of your living room."

—Eric Galton, mediator and author, Lakeside Mediation Center, Austin, Texas

"Jeff Krivis has once again demonstrated why he is one of the premier mediators in the world by writing an easy-to-read yet sophisticated treatment of what actually happens in mediation. The post-story sections of 'What Happened?' and 'What Strategies Can We Learn?' are helpful for practitioners from the novice to the master levels. The conversational tone, rather than a research approach with footnotes and case authority, is refreshing yet is still an invaluable way of telling the mediator's story!"

—Robert A. Creo, founding member and past president, International Academy of Mediators

"After decades of negotiating and mediating some of the toughest cases around, Jeff Krivis has written a book explaining how he gets the job done. Well-written and entertaining, this is a book every lawyer should read."

—Richard H. Friedman, trial lawyer and author of *Rules of the Road: Proving Liability in Bad Faith and Other Complex Cases*

"This is a valuable and accessible resource for anyone interested in knowing about commercial mediation. And it is fun to read."

—Arlen Gregorio, Gregorio, Haldeman & Piazza, Mediated Negotiations

"Without compromising the mystical interaction of human touch with high skill, Krivis delivers a treasure trove of methods to discover the 'art of the deal.'"

—Tracy Allen, trainer and private mediator

"Jeff Krivis's stories of masterful mediation are perfect for promoting the kind of moment-to-moment creativity that characterizes the great mediators—and the great jazz musicians. For mediators at any stage of their careers, *Improvisational Negotiation* is a treasure of illustration, illumination, and inspiration."

—Leonard L. Riskin, C. A. Leedy Professor of Law, University of Missouri-Columbia School of Law; director, Center for the Study of Dispute Resolution

IMPROVISATIONAL NEGOTIATION

A Mediator's Stories of Conflict About Love, Money, Anger—and the Strategies That Resolved Them

Jeffrey Krivis

Foreword by Jim Melamed

For Kirk —
a terrific lawyer
and friend!
Best
Jeff Krivis

JOSSEY-BASS
A Wiley Imprint
www.josseybass.com

Published by Jossey-Bass
A Wiley Imprint
989 Market Street, San Francisco, CA 94103-1741   www.josseybass.com

Jossey-Bass books and products are available through most bookstores. To contact Jossey-Bass directly
call our Customer Care Department within the U.S. at 800-956-7739, outside the U.S. at 317-572-3986,
or fax 317-572-4002.

Jossey-Bass also publishes its books in a variety of electronic formats. Some content that appears in
print may not be available in electronic books.

Library of Congress Cataloging-in-Publication Data

Krivis, Jeffrey, date.
  Improvisational negotiation : a mediator's stories of conflict about love, money, anger—and the
strategies that resolved them / Jeffrey Krivis ; foreword by Jim Melamed.
     p. cm.
  ISBN-13: 978-0-7879-8038-2 (alk. paper)
  ISBN-10: 0-7879-8038-2 (alk. paper)
  1. Conflict management. 2. Mediation. I. Title.
  HM1126.K76 2006
  303.6'9—dc22
                              2005021192

Printed in the United States of America
FIRST EDITION
HB Printing 10 9 8 7 6 5 4 3 2 1

Contents

Foreword   vii
    Jim Melamed
Introduction   1

PART ONE: HUMAN V. HUMAN: HEALING RELATIONSHIPS   5

1	Independence Day	7
2	Paintball Pranks	19
3	Step-by-Step	29
4	A Sweet Deal	44
5	Reading Minds	55
6	Rock Star	66
7	Gratitude Is the Attitude	75
8	Memories	84
9	Working at the Car Wash	92
10	Transforming the Journey of Revenge	103
11	A "Hats-On" Approach	114

PART TWO: "SHOW ME THE MONEY (OR SOMETHING OF EQUAL VALUE)!": CREATIVE SOLUTIONS   125

12	Liar, Liar!	127
13	The Handicap	138
14	Legally Blind	147
15	The Slow Drip	158
16	Death Takes a Holiday	167
17	If the Shoe Fits . . .	175
18	The Staggered Approach	185
19	Time-Share	198
20	The Silent Mover	207

21	A Small Deception	214
22	The Laddered Approach	225
23	The Confidential Listener	233
24	Dropping the Bombshell	247
25	Worth the Wait	255
26	Creating Value	267

PART THREE: GETTING TO THE BOTTOM LINE   **279**

27	Too Many Cooks	281
28	Bottom-Line Negotiating	291
29	The "Fishy Calculator" Method	296
30	The Crossover	303

PART FOUR: THE MEDIATOR'S HIP-POCKET GUIDE TO STRATEGY   **311**

About the Author	323

FOREWORD

I first met Jeff Krivis nearly fifteen years ago. For the first couple of years, our relationship was exclusively online. Jeff was jkrivis@igc.org, and I was jmelamed@igc.org. We both had my cofounder at Mediate.com, John Helie, to thank for having set up the ConflictNet network that allowed so many in the conflict resolution field to initially meet. In the era of 9,600-baud modems, text only, and monochrome monitors, we exchanged information about getting our mediation practices going, about legal and policy issues, and about ways to expand the field of mediation. Jeff was one of the first to recognize that we needed to develop a mediation industry.

When I finally met Jeff in person in the early 1990s at a Southern California Mediation Association (SCMA) conference in Malibu, I remember thinking, "He's not as imposing as I'd imagined." We developed an immediate rapport. From our first meeting, I have always enjoyed looking Jeff in the eyes and listening to his thoughts on "taking the next steps" and "making a bigger difference." I remember Jeff saying that "small things can make a big difference" years before the publication of *The Tipping Point*.

Jeff has contributed mightily to the field of mediation. At our first meeting in Malibu, I remember Jeff being honored as the outgoing SCMA president. SCMA was in the middle of a substantial growth spurt, in great part due to Jeff's leadership. When it came to the formal honoring ceremony, most of the discussion revolved around Jeff's love of baseball. Jeff was relaxed and not out to impress, and he offered himself with humor and humility. Jeff's lack of pretense was noticeable.

Over the years, Jeff went on to become one of the founders and an early president of the International Academy of Mediators (IAM), a group of approximately two hundred elite civil and commercial mediators. Jeff's dominant interest with IAM was to elevate mediator education and collegiality. Whether online or at SCMA or IAM, I have regularly seen Jeff pushing the envelope. Jeff has been an outside-the-box thinker and entrepreneur in a field that, paradoxically, is perhaps too often conflict averse if not downright conservative. Mediators tend not to want to rock the boat too much. We tend to seek calmer waters. Jeff offers a huge service to our field by insisting that we mediators rock our boats and ask ourselves whether we might bring benefit to all waters, calm and raging.

A simple review of Jeff's nearly two dozen articles on Mediate. com reveals his activism and openness of thought. Here are a few sample article titles: "Stand-Up Comedy: Lessons for Mediators"; "Preventing the Death of Mediation"; "The Truth About Deception in Mediation"; and "The End of the Cold War: The Marriage of Mediation and the Court System." In a refreshingly honest and clear way, Jeff asks the hard questions, challenging each of us to be at our best.

I am now coming to understand how my personal relationship with Jeff mirrors many of Jeff's other professional relationships and his mediation work generally. Jeff is a creative thinker and motivator. He is a catalyst and communicator of imaginative solutions. Jeff brings this spirit and capability wherever he goes.

Most noteworthy are his flexibility and transparency, his insights and imagination. Through his stories, he helps us explore his treasure chest of techniques and approaches. This is really valuable stuff for mediators! No matter how experienced we may be (or think we are), the navigational tools that Jeff offers in *Improvisational Negotiation* are of immense value as we head into the storm. More important than any of Jeff's specific techniques is the multidimensional awareness that he describes and offers. His is an intuitive and eclectic approach, assisting parties in most capably resolving their unique differences.

Whether offering services in the mediation room or reviewing our new online mediation technology, Jeff recognizes the many dimensions of conflict: substantive, relational, and psychological. He is open to any and all new approaches, with only one requirement: that the approach works. Jeff operates beyond any designated style of mediation practice (evaluative, facilitative, transformational, problem solving, narrative . . .), always asking himself, "What will work here and now?" Then he acts on his intuition with confidence and purpose. Perhaps the most important thing we can learn from Jeff is to trust our instincts in our own mediation work and not to be afraid to take risks. Surely it is worth reading all the books and taking all the courses, but mediation work is so complex, so human, and so fraught with variables that there simply is no linear recipe for success. What Jeff so capably demonstrates is that we are at our best in performing our noble work as mediators when we are genuine, imaginative, and self-trusting. Through our creativity and resourcefulness, we stimulate those around us to be at their best.

So thank you, Jeff, for your personal friendship and even more for bringing your creativity, thoughtfulness, and energy to the field of mediation. Although there is surely no simple recipe for success in mediation, in *Improvisational Negotiation* you have given mediators and conflict resolution professionals a unique and valuable opportunity to experience how your mind and heart work as you place yourself at the center of heated battles. Thank you for your authenticity and for modeling mediation at its best, both in and beyond the mediation room.

Jim Melamed
CEO, Mediate.com
Eugene, Oregon

For Amy, Hannah, and Rachel

Improvisational Negotiation

INTRODUCTION

As a young trial lawyer, I learned early on that there's nothing like a good story to get your point across simply, effectively, and memorably. When I made the transition into mediation full-time, the importance of the story in my daily work soon became strikingly clear. The narrative of a case can be elusive, changing according to the point of view of each party. Often, if I simply gave both sides in the negotiation the opportunity to tell me their story, and made sure they felt listened to and heard, I had an excellent chance of helping them break the deadlock that had brought them to my office in the first place. In other cases, I found that the crucial factor was the *timing* of the stories about my own experiences that I would share during the meetings. In every case, however, it became clear that my role as mediator made me the person in charge of shaping the negotiation's narrative so that it reached the happy ending all parties hoped for: settlement.

Mediators must follow the law, of course, and must strive to be ethical. But beyond that, there are no set rules. Reaching settlement is the goal. How you get there is up to you. Each new day presents a new case, a new set of parties, and a unique combination of factors. I wake up knowing that I will have to take these various factors into account, direct the flow of the negotiation toward settlement, be prepared for the unexpected, and deal with it. With thousands of mediations under my belt, and after teaching countless seminars and workshops, I know one thing for sure: when it comes to negotiation, we all have to use our improvisational skills to make deals happen. This is why the power of the story is so compelling, and why *Improvisational Negotiation* skips the long discussions of philosophy and the step-by-step programs found in other books and goes straight to the point: telling entertaining true stories that show a mediator using the skills and tools of the trade to direct a successful negotiation. Most of these tales are taken from my own experience; others I have gratefully borrowed from friends and students. In all cases the names (and sometimes the genders) have been changed to protect the privacy of the parties, but all of the stories happened pretty much the way I tell them here.

Being a mediator is a great job. I love waking up in the morning, knowing that anything might happen during my day at work. I mediate a wide variety of cases—from class action and mass torts to entertainment to insurance, business, and catastrophic injury—and I teach mediation workshops as an adjunct professor of law at the Straus Institute for Dispute Resolution at Pepperdine University. I have learned from experience that no two stories are the same. Still, I have found that most revolve around one of two issues: personal relationships or money.

Some negotiations are over relatively quickly, but many continue for hours and hours—and hours. My work doesn't leave me as much free time as I'd like, and I'm betting yours doesn't either. That's why I've kept these thirty stories short and to the point. Life is messy—often it's up to the mediator to clean up. And just as life conflicts don't always fall neatly into categories, the cases you deal with every day cover a lot of ground. One case may be about repairing communications, a second may involve parties who have strategic incentives for using information to achieve a better deal, a third may be strictly about finding ways to split the financial pie. Some cases may involve all these factors, and any one of them may require you to come up with a creative solution on the fly. To make it easy for you to learn, the stories are organized into three categories. The stories in Part One are about rebuilding communication breakdowns and healing broken relationships. The stories in Part Two may involve relationships, but they are concerned more with financial negotiations, finding other kinds of value, and parties who are likely to have strategic incentives for using information to achieve a better deal. The stories in Part Three offer some useful and proven techniques that can get you through knotty technical negotiations. Each story is capped by a deeper exploration of what the mediator did (or might have done better) to reach a successful conclusion, and a brief discussion of the specific strategies highlighted in the case. Finally, for quick reference, Part Four is a brief guide to advanced techniques that you can use to quickly shift the energy when a negotiation is locked down (or to prevent it from getting locked down).

Do I expect you to follow these stories slavishly? Of course not! No two mediators work the same way, and no two cases are the same. In fact, mediators need to change their approach not only from case to case but also *within* the same case, as many of the stories in this book make clear. That's one of the things that makes being a mediator such an interesting profession. Every mediation is a fresh challenge. With your tools and skills and wits about you, you just jump into the center of the conflict and try to bring it to a successful conclusion. Hockey great Wayne Gretzky used to say that he liked to skate to where the puck is going, not to where it has been. I hope the stories in this book encourage you to follow a similar path: to search the length and width of the field, anticipating the direction of the case, constantly maneuvering the parties toward the deal.

ACKNOWLEDGMENTS

Each day my work brings out a variety of responses from people, ranging from utter helplessness to a gentle calm. At the conclusion of some days, I am lucky enough to feel as though I've received a standing ovation from the parties, which I attribute to an appreciation of the mediation process. It is with this in mind that I humbly turn the tables to salute and offer my own standing ovation to the many people who have supported my work over the years and who have contributed to this book.

Without the vision of my editor, Alan Rinzler, this book might never have been born. He worked with me tirelessly to shape and encourage the manuscript through every phase of the process, from idea to finished product. His old-school ethic and sixties' spirit helped shape my thinking tremendously.

Not surprisingly, I am indebted to several women who have shone a bright light around me personally and professionally, and without whom this book would never have been realized. Naomi Lucks, an editor extraordinaire, was my shadow for several months, taking my random thoughts and concepts and helping me frame sentences and narrative that came to life. Mariam Zadeh, my friend and student, allowed me to serve as her mentor but has been more of a mentor to me on this project and many more. Christine Goedert, who has artfully kept my practice moving forward for many years, laid the foundation for many of the cases in this book. Last but not least is my wife, Amy, an incredible editor in her own right and a true collaborator in every way.

Many of my good friends in the mediation community and members of the International Academy of Mediators submitted story ideas, for which I am grateful. Unfortunately I couldn't use them all. There are a few special people whose own experiences and inspirational stories were included in this book: Cliff Hendler, Jay Rudolph, Bob Creo, Judy Meyer, Pat Coughlan, Deborah Rothman, and Mike Young.

Finally, much of this work has been inspired by my friends, colleagues, and students at the Straus Institute for Dispute Resolution at Pepperdine Law School, with whom I have enjoyed a wonderful relationship.

Jeffrey Krivis
Los Angeles, California

PART ONE

HUMAN V. HUMAN

Healing Relationships

CHAPTER ONE

INDEPENDENCE DAY

When Dan was suddenly fired from his job as a systems analyst "due to a reduction in workforce," he felt as if he'd been kicked in the stomach. He had worked at the high-tech firm Expantec for more than ten years—from the very beginning of the company. But for Dan, this was more than a good job: he thought of his coworkers as his family. Now he felt that he'd been betrayed and abandoned by that family, and he was ready to go to court for wrongful termination.

Before the case went to trial, however, the court encouraged both sides to try mediation. Now the parties found themselves staring at each other across the polished expanse of a green marble conference table in the office of a downtown law firm, wondering what went wrong. Although they had an outside mediator, they agreed to meet in the offices of Expantec's law firm because it was more convenient for Dan and offered all the room they would need. Settling into the dark red leather chair, and taking in the opulent scene, however, Dan began to wonder if he'd put himself at a disadvantage by coming into the "enemy's" camp.

On the other side of the table, the company's three representatives looked pretty comfortable. Bill, Dan's ex-boss and old friend (he'd thought), Expantec's corporate attorney, and the head of human resources were huddled together, probably discussing strategy. Displayed prominently in front of them was a laptop and projector for the PowerPoint presentation they'd prepared to detail Dan's supposed failings in the workplace.

Dan got tired of waiting for the meeting to start, took out his cell phone, and called his fiancée, Jennifer. He wished she were there with him now.

The Mediator sized up the young man sitting rigidly in his chair. His buzz cut, tightly knotted tie, and buttoned-up suit gave Dan a military look that was somewhat incongruous in the high-tech world. *I wonder if he has many friends,* the Mediator thought.

As soon as Dan got off the phone, the Mediator explained that they would begin by making their opening statements. This would give them a base from which to proceed.

Dan's lawyer was blunt: "We intend to make Expantec pay for firing my client. They didn't fire him because of a 'reduction in force.' This was nothing less than a cold and calculated effort to ruin a life's work."

Dan nodded vigorously in agreement. "That's right," he said, looking fixedly at Bill. "If only they had talked to me first, I would have been able to do things differently before I was let go."

Dan's clear anger, and the anger behind his lawyer's message, took Bill by surprise. Until this moment he had not realized the lawsuit was personal. Ex-employees had taken him to court before. It was almost expected.

Expantec's attorney explained that they had planned an extensive presentation, including a computerized summary of the case presented by a large accounting firm, intending to prove statistical support for their reduction in force. They intended to back it up with aggressive legal support by the litigation team, confirming Expantec's right to lay Dan off.

The Mediator, sensing Dan's fragile emotional state, was concerned about the impact this presentation would have on the settlement discussions. He knew it would be a potential minefield if the mediation went forward with this agenda, so he called a time-out to talk to the parties. First, he wanted to learn more about how Dan perceived his relationship to the company. In today's volatile economy, high-tech employees were let go all the time. Why was he taking this so hard?

—⁓—

As the Expantec team went to get coffee, the Mediator turned to Dan and his lawyer. "Let's go outside for few minutes and get some air. I'm curious about a few things, and maybe you can clue me in." They sat down on a stone bench under some trees in the courtyard of the office complex, and the Mediator began. "Dan, I'm trying to understand where you're coming from here. Can you tell me a little bit more about yourself and your work?"

"I loved my job," Dan said simply. "I helped get that business up and running, and I helped it grow. Over the years they gave me more and more responsibility, and I never let them down." Dan's jaw muscles tensed reflexively as he tried to hold back his tears. "The last ten years have been amazing. I would actually wake up every morning excited about going to work. In fact, sometimes I would sleep at the office in order to get a quick start on a project."

"And when you were let go? How did you feel?" asked the Mediator.

"Like they had abandoned me. They hung me out to dry!" Now Dan was shaking. "Why does this keep happening to me? I know I'm good at my work. What have I done to deserve this kind of treatment?"

The Mediator felt that Dan's reaction was a little extreme. There must be something else going on here, beyond the job itself. "I'm puzzled," he said. "What do you mean, 'Why does this keep happening to me?' Your records don't show that you've been fired from other jobs. In fact, you have a stable work record."

Dan looked down at the ground as he spoke, his voice suddenly quiet and matter-of-fact. "My mother died when I was five, and my father disappeared. He never called, he never wrote. For all I know he's dead. If he's not, he might as well be." Dan had been shuttled from one foster home to another, raised by people who cared more about the money they got for his care than for him. When he turned eighteen, the state abandoned him too. He worked at a number of jobs to put himself through school, and soon after college he'd landed at Expantec. For the first time in his life he'd found himself surrounded by a group of people who laughed together, played together, and worked hard for a common goal. He'd grown to adulthood at Expantec, and it had been great. Until now. Dan laughed sardonically. "You know what's really ironic? I'm getting married in a few months. Who am I going to invite to the wedding now?"

The Mediator was taken aback. Dan's coworkers were not only *like* his family; in his mind they *were* his family. He had no one else.

Dan was clearly wrung out, but he still held himself proudly. But the Mediator's new understanding of the depth of Dan's anguish resonated deeply. This was more than the loss of a job; it was a personal rejection, a profound loss similar to what he'd experienced as a child. The Mediator now saw that honoring Dan's story would be paramount in a successful mediation. They'd already put in a few hours and the real negotiations hadn't even started yet. But what the Mediator had learned would shape the course of what would follow.

"Thanks for sharing your story with me, Dan; I know that must have been difficult for you. Take a few minutes to get yourself together, and let's go back in."

—∞—

When they went back inside, the Mediator put Dan and his lawyer in a small office and went to have a private chat with the company's lawyers. "While I'm in there," he said to the lawyer, "you might want to talk to Dan about some of his options, and when I come back we'll discuss those."

The Mediator walked down the long hallway, the plush carpet muffling his footsteps. As he pushed open the door to the large conference room, he noticed that the Expantec team had turned on the laptop and projector and were waiting to get on with their presentation. Bad idea. "Look," he said, "I know you have a well-organized case. But if you make this type of presentation in front of Dan, it will likely sabotage this mediation before it gets started. Right now, Dan is emotionally invested in his case. Any evidence you provide is going to seem like an attack on him, and any attack is going to be counterproductive."

Expantec's lawyer was not ready to back down. "Dan's all wet here. We have proof that a reduction in force was necessary. If you look at the bottom-line numbers for Dan's department, you'll see that they were terrible."

"Numbers are only as good as the person who inputs them into the computer," responded the Mediator. "If you can verify them, then okay—I'll agree that Dan would have to admit there's been a problem. Do you have any support for those numbers?"

"Well," the lawyer admitted, "they're preliminary, but we believe they will be borne out as we get into the case." The Mediator could see the group's disappointment. They really wanted to present their case. "I'll tell you what," the Mediator said. "Let's leave Dan out of this for the moment. Why don't you show me what you've got right now, and I'll see what I can do?" This would allow them to be heard and would also let the Mediator evaluate what kind of case they really had.

They all sat down and watched the presentation, which went on for some time but seemed to lack corroborating detail. When it was over, the Mediator thought hard. *I didn't see any numbers to back up their claim. What's the deal here? Did they really have a good financial basis for terminating Dan, or are they just trying to get rid of him because he was too expensive and they didn't like him as much as he liked them?* But when he spoke, he chose his words carefully. "Thank you. I really appreciate you showing me all the work you've done in preparation for this meeting. It seems to me from what I've just seen, though, that those statistics haven't been confirmed. Is that right?"

The team members looked at each and agreed that no, they hadn't been confirmed, but . . .

"If they haven't been confirmed," the Mediator continued, "then how could they be the basis of a decision to terminate Dan?" He let that thought hang in the air for moment. The skills he'd honed in his years as a litigator were coming in handy now.

"Do you suppose that Dan will argue that your motivation to lay him off was really financial because of his high salary?" The Expantec group exchanged glances.

"And if he makes that argument, what conclusion do you think the jury would come to? Is it possible the jury might be angry with you once they see his sterling performance record?" The Mediator looked at Expantec's attorney, waiting for his response.

"That's certainly possible," admitted the attorney. Now Dan's ex-employer, who had sat quietly through most of this exchange, was becoming alarmed. "Wait," he said. "Could we be exposed to liability if we can't verify the poor performance of Dan's department?"

"Well," said the Mediator, "your attorney knows as well as I do that trying to predict what a jury will do is like looking into a crystal ball to see the future. However, I would certainly want to know that there was sufficient documentary support for such a decision—especially in light of Dan's terrific personnel record.

Also, the fact that Dan was one of the most highly paid executives in the company will be presented as a motivating factor in the company's decision to dismiss him. Expantec is clearly saving a lot of money by letting Dan go." *Interesting,* thought the Mediator. *With as much time and energy as they had expended on putting this case together, they don't seem to have seriously considered this point.*

The Mediator felt they had enough food for thought. He decided to let the company stew while he returned to the small office to discuss the situation with Dan and his lawyer.

—〰—

"Dan," he began, "I need to hear more about your relationship with your employer. Why do you feel things got to this point?"

"I don't know," Dan replied, clearly at a loss. "They never gave me any reason to think there was a problem. In fact, they just kept giving me more responsibility." He shook his head in angry bewilderment. "Expantec has been my family for ten years! To suddenly be told they don't want me anymore is beyond anything I can explain."

"Have you ever had the chance to discuss these thoughts with the company?"

"Not really. They just gave me the pink slip, had me box up my desk, and escorted me out the door. It was surreal. Ten years of work, and I was gone in ten minutes. The only person who really knows what I've gone through is my lawyer—and now you."

The Mediator could see that Dan felt he had been rejected without any explanation and had not had the chance to defend himself. He simply did not understand what led to the decision to fire him. The company line was not enough for him. After a solid seven hours of negotiation, Dan still felt utterly and inexplicably rejected. The Mediator also had some information that Dan didn't know about: the company reps were feeling just a little less sure of their position. Maybe they were just enough off balance now to listen to what Dan had to say. He decided it was time to get the two sides together to do the one thing they hadn't done: talk.

"Dan," he said, "here's what I think we need to do next. Let's get you and the company together so you can find out once and for all what happened. Maybe the company will also appreciate that they need to think carefully about their position and try to come up with a settlement opportunity that has some teeth. I hope you'll feel comfortable telling them what the company meant to you."

Dan stared at the wall for a few moments, his jaw muscles working. Finally, he nodded his head and said, "Let's do it."

"Okay," said the Mediator. "Wait here for a few more minutes while I tell Expantec what's going on."

"What is this, a settlement negotiation or a group therapy session?" The idea of a meeting with Dan had clearly caught Bill off guard. Expantec had laid off several employees over the years, but nothing remotely like this had ever happened before. Then the human resources director, who had sat quietly beside Bill for the last few hours, spoke up.

"Look," she said, "let's just listen to what Dan has to say. Maybe we can figure out why this happened." Expantec's attorney agreed. This case might not be going the way they had planned. What did they have to lose by listening?

"Okay, okay," sighed Bill. "I give up. Bring them back here, and let's find out what the hell's going on."

Once again, both parties sat quietly around the marble table, waiting for someone to begin what promised to be an uncomfortable conversation.

The Mediator wanted to make sure that the power of Dan's narrative got through without putting Expantec on the defensive, so he began mildly. "Dan, from our brief conversations this morning, I've gleaned that Expantec was more to you than just a company to work for. Would you mind expanding on that a bit?"

Dan looked miserable but determined to soldier on. "The company has been my life," he said, looking directly at Bill. "They've been my family, the air I breathe. I would have taken a bullet for them." Bill was shocked. This was a little over the top. Dan had always seemed like such a one-pointed worker bee. Bill had no idea that all this emotion was just under the surface.

"What was it about your job that was so meaningful?" The Mediator gently nudged Dan into his story.

"A lot of things," said Dan. "Knowing they'd be there for me every day, knowing they appreciated the work I did—a lot of things."

"Can you give us an example?" the Mediator asked.

"Sure, okay. Having people say hello in the morning, or calling to make sure I was okay when I called in sick. Growing up as an orphan, I never had a Thanksgiving or a Christmas or any other holiday with my real family. Since coming here, to Expantec, I've come home. They always had cake for my birthday, every year. They'd take me out to lunch. Everybody would sign a card. Hell, most of my foster families never even knew it *was* my birthday!"

The room was dead silent. The Mediator thought, *Well, this can go two ways. Either Expantec jumps up and leaves right now, or they actually take in what Dan is saying.* The silence went on so long that he began to get worried, but he sat still and let Dan's words resonate a little.

Bill's first response was anger—this wasn't his problem!—but it was quickly replaced by guilt. He owed Dan more than this boot out the door, and he knew it. He and Dan had spent a lot of time together when they were first building the company. They'd gone to bars, a few parties, had some fun, but they'd never had this kind of personal conversation. Who knew Dan's life was so screwed up? As the years went by and Expantec grew powerful and prosperous, Bill worked harder and harder, got married, and started a family, and his relationship with Dan became all business. At least for Bill. Apparently, Dan had other ideas. Damn. Deep down, Bill knew he had been trying to avoid just this kind of personal confrontation.

The human resources head was also surprised. She had had no idea of the depth of Dan's feelings for the company, or what it had meant to him. Of course, she really didn't know Dan very well. She'd only been with Expantec for the last few years, and she had a lot of employees to keep track of. Layoffs were tough, in her experience, but everybody understood that this was life, and they moved on. But after seven hours of negotiation, the raw emotion of Dan's story had broken down some of her habitual ways of thinking about her job. She felt drained.

Dan leaned back in his chair, exhausted but ready to proceed. The fact that everyone was still sitting there seemed to him a positive sign that maybe they'd heard him. He took heart and assumed a more businesslike attitude. Damn it, he was good at what he did. He really hated wearing his heart on his sleeve like that. "I understand the need to reduce costs," Dan told the company's general counsel. "But I know this company inside out. I'm confident that my experience and understanding of how this company works cannot be duplicated."

The general counsel was willing to pay Dan a modest settlement, but he also began to realize that the company was letting go of a valuable employee who could significantly contribute to the bottom line. "I'd like to talk to Bill for a few minutes, if you don't mind." The two men went out into the hall, and when they came back the attorney spoke directly to Dan.

"Look," he said, "corporate won't let us rehire you as an employee. That's just how it is. But as you well know, we've used the services of people like you as consultants from time to time. Would you be interested in that kind of arrangement with Expantec? You might even decide to start your own consulting business, and we would be your first client."

Dan was overwhelmed by the offer and excited about the possibilities. A new marriage, a new business . . . it could be a new start. "I've never had my own business," he said, "but it does sound appealing—especially if I know I can get business from Expantec."

Corporate counsel said that he would talk to Bill about guaranteeing a certain amount of consulting work for a period of two years. This would allow Dan to set up his own business while maintaining a steady stream of income in an industry to which he was already accustomed. And with a nationally known client like Expantec, he should do well with other clients.

When they finally hammered out a settlement, Dan got both monetary compensation and the promise of an ongoing relationship, including a consulting agreement. The Mediator was elated: this was the best possible outcome.

Dan later thanked the Mediator for his work in getting the settlement. "Maybe getting fired wasn't the greatest thing that ever happened to me, but I have to admit that it was for the best. The negotiations forced me to take a good look at myself. I have some complicated personal issues to work through. I have to learn to keep my work and personal lives more separate. Anyway," he laughed, "sleeping in the office doesn't make much sense now that I'm going to be married!"

WHAT HAPPENED?

In some ways, this "sudden" turnaround seemed magical, even to the Mediator. But this negotiation didn't take fifteen minutes. It took at total of ten hours, a lot of pacing, and a lot of effort on the part of the Mediator in trying to create an environment where everyone would feel comfortable. Just the Mediator's talking to Dan wasn't enough; Dan needed the audience with the other side.

Dan was a good-looking guy who dressed well, worked out every day, and got the job done. Because he carried all his feelings inside, no one knew how emotionally vulnerable he was. And because his coworkers really *weren't* his family, they didn't try to find out.

This mediation could have failed before it even began. If the Mediator had allowed the company to present its case to Dan, it's likely that he would have been offended and deeply wounded, and not open to any more negotiation. Fortunately for both parties, the Mediator was fully engaged in the case.

He realized that the two lawyers were mistaking the conference room for a courtroom. A negotiation is a very different environment, with no judge or jury to preach to. Taking an aggressive position with someone so emotionally distraught would just alienate him further. As mediator, he saw the impediment. He wouldn't let them present the PowerPoint to Dan, but he did let them present it to him. This way they could follow through with what they intended, and the Mediator could act as a filter for the information. Then, instead of accusing them, the Mediator used his litigating skills to ask them questions that got to the truth of their numbers. Challenging the employer's claim in this way showed real grit and real skill.

He also went with his instinct that there was more going on beneath the surface, and teased that information out of Dan in a way that was nonthreatening and empathetic. He questioned Expantec about their figures and got them to see that maybe their case wasn't as strong as they thought it was. He persuaded the employer to listen to what Dan had to say without putting the employer on the defensive. Finally, he created an atmosphere in which everyone felt free to express himself or herself without fear of negative consequences.

It was key that Dan told his story when he did, two-thirds of the way into the mediation. It was the right solution, and it came at the right time. It's good to remember, as Pepperdine University Professor Randy Lowry always says, that *the right solution at the wrong time is the wrong solution.* Dan had to feel rejected, to understand that it was really over, and then to have the chance to tell his story. He was floored by the result.

The timing led to a compromise in which both sides felt that they achieved value in the transaction. Dan felt heard, maybe for the first time. Expantec realized that this wasn't just about group hugs: Dan still had something to offer the company. They gave him some respect, made him feel needed, and also offered a consultancy, which gave him the confidence to stay out on his own and start a new business.

What Strategies Can We Learn?

1. **Look for clues to deeper psychological issues.**
   Unresolved conflicts from a client's childhood development may play a powerful role in the current situation. Addressing the internal conflict will eliminate the obstacles to resolving the external conflict.
2. **Create an atmosphere where both sides feel free to open their hearts, listen, and have compassion for each other.**
   Make an extra effort to be sure that all parties are fully informed and respectful about the other parties' feelings and desires (where they're coming from, so to speak). In this way you allow room for new information, as yet unrevealed, that would help resolve the conflict.

3. Consider your audience.

Adjust your approach according to the situation. You can act as a coach to help the parties understand what's going on. Sometimes lawyers are so intent on just presenting their case—hardboiled aggressive advocacy—that they forget they are in a conference room, not a court. In other circumstances, you can use headstrong maneuvers if you believe they will move the negotiations forward. Mediators who began as lawyers need to remember that they are not in a trial situation. In court, your audience is the judge and jury—the time for negotiation is over, and you need a powerful position. In mediation, this mindset can backfire. A skilled mediator knows which approach to use when.

4. Be transparent when you need to be.

Being transparent is sharing with the parties what you the mediator believe is the best task to focus on next and why you believe that task is the most appropriate. Letting people know where you're coming from helps them feel included in the process and offers you immediate feedback about strategic decisions. It saves time in the long run by reducing delays created by uncertainty about the process, and gives the parties a window into your thinking.

CHAPTER TWO

PAINTBALL PRANKS

It was the opening session of mediation, the lawyers were gearing up to present their cases, and tensions were high. It didn't help that the primary figures in the case were all younger than eighteen. On one side of table sat the plaintiffs: Steven, his jaw clenched tight, was sitting next to his eight-year-old daughter, Danielle, who was concentrating on drawing and seemed to be trying to make herself as small as possible. The defense side of the room was more crowded: four seventeen-year-old boys—Harvey, Justin, Devin, and Noah—who were alternately slouching and twisting in their chairs, and two anxious, defensive parents for each boy. *It's going to be a long day,* thought the Mediator.

As the Mediator listened attentively, each lawyer told his version of the small drama that had unfolded on a warm afternoon a few months earlier in Lader, a small suburban town. It was quite a vivid picture.

Lader was a relatively affluent suburb, with nice parents and nice kids and not much crime. But teens didn't have much to keep them occupied, so the town had its fair share of cars and houses being egged during Homecoming and trees that were festooned with toilet paper. On this particular afternoon, the four boys, all friends since grade school, were hanging out after school with nothing to do. As luck would have it, Harvey's parents had recently bought him four paintguns and some paintballs. The boys were planning to go to the local paintball field for a full-out tournament, but that wasn't until the weekend. They were bemoaning their sad fate and staring longingly at the guns—which looked just like handguns and fired paintballs at up to two hundred miles per hour—when they all seemed to have the same idea at the same time: let's drive around town and fire these things at people! They couldn't wait to see paintballs explode red paint all over their targets. Excellent.

So, their adrenaline already pumping, they jumped into Justin's pickup truck and drove around town firing paintballs at cars and pedestrians. It was everything they had imagined, and more. No one seemed to know what had hit them, and the red paint really stood out on the cars. But as they passed by Lader Elementary School and fired a few balls at the after-school kids on the playground, the mood of the afternoon changed completely. They heard a long, bloodcurdling scream like something from a horror movie, and turned to see a young girl covered in red paint, down on the ground, screaming and crying hysterically. Danielle had been hit in the chest by the paintball, and when she saw the red paint she thought she had been hit by a real bullet. Even after her teacher came running out to comfort her, it took her a while to calm down. The boys were long gone by then, but it was a small town, and several of the kids on the playground knew who they were.

The teacher had to call Steven at work to pick up Danielle. He was relieved to find out that she was not seriously injured, but he was irate when he found out what happened. Danielle's mother had passed away a couple of years earlier from cancer, and Danielle was his only child. It terrified him to think that she was not even safe at school in a town like Lader. He didn't think he was going to have to worry about boys until Danielle was at least in junior high, but he was wrong. The more he thought about what had happened, the angrier he became. He called his lawyer and filed suit against the four boys and their parents. He demanded that the boys pay $100,000 to cover therapy and other expenses related to Danielle's trauma.

Danielle's physical suffering was minor, but Steven claimed that she suffered profound emotional distress that would have long-term effects. He was enormously upset over the incident, and he wanted to punish the boys as much as he wanted to obtain a recovery for Danielle. He viewed the lawsuit as a means to exact this punishment.

Steven sat quietly throughout the lawyers' presentations, but the Mediator could see that he wanted to talk. He decided to let Steven speak, curious to see what would happen if he gave him the space to vent some anger.

"Steven," he said, "you look like you have something to say. What is it?"

"I'd like to know what the hell these boys thought they were doing! Do they think it's *funny* to terrorize young girls into thinking they've been shot? There's enough real violence in the world without this. Guns are not toys! Shooting people is not a game!" He brought both fists down on the table so hard that a glass of water fell over and spilled onto the floor.

The Mediator looked at Danielle. She seemed frozen. He decided that was enough venting. "Steven, if it's all right with the defendants, I'd like to talk to you and your lawyer privately and hear a little more." He asked the boys and their families to wait, and told them he'd be back to hear their side in a little while.

⚬⚬⚬

In their private session, Steven told the Mediator that his family doctor had told him that Danielle was fine and not to worry, but he couldn't leave it there. "Sure, she wasn't physically harmed, but she was really upset." So he had had Danielle evaluated by a social worker to determine the extent of the emotional harm the boys had caused.

"What was her report?" asked the Mediator.

"It was unbelievable!" replied Steven, shaking his head. "She said that Danielle was traumatized by the event, but that no further treatment was necessary. Anyone could see she was traumatized. She needs therapy! Social workers don't know about trauma; they're not shrinks. So I hired a psychiatrist to evaluate Danielle, and he determined that she had been *profoundly* traumatized and would require two years of therapy at a cost of $14,000. These boys need to pay for all of it, and more."

"Okay, Steven, it's obvious that you and Danielle have had a pretty rough time lately. Wait here while I talk to the boys and their parents and determine what they're willing to do."

⚬⚬⚬

The first thing the Mediator noticed was that these parents were puzzled rather than angry.

"Anyone can see that Danielle's not really hurt," said Justin's mother. "My youngest son is in her third grade class, and he says she's just the same as usual—laughing, playing with her friends, keeping up with her homework. I know Justin and the other boys acted like jerks"—she shot her son a withering look—"but Steven's reaction just seems over the top." The other parents nodded as she spoke and voiced their agreement.

"Look at his so-called medical evidence," said the defense lawyer. "First of all, the first medical examiner, Danielle's own family doctor, gave her a clean bill of health. Then this psychiatrist he hired says she's 'profoundly disturbed' by what happened. But when you examine his own notes—I have a copy right here—they completely contradict his conclusion. Among other things, they say, and I quote, 'Danielle did not feel she suffered a significant psychological injury.' And his credibility is suspect for other reasons."

"What do you mean?" asked the Mediator.

"He's a frequent participant in litigated cases—a professional courtroom witness who's willing to tailor his testimony depending on who's paying the bills."

"Look," Harvey's father chimed in. "The boys admit they're at fault, and we're not particularly proud of what they did. We've already discussed this and told the boys that they will need to pay the damages out of their own pockets—our insurance companies won't even cover the claim because of the intentional character of the acts. But $100,000 is ridiculous any way you cut it. We're offering Danielle a total of $7,500, and we think that's fair compensation."

"We have a big gap to close," said the Mediator. "Let me talk to Steven, and I'll get back to you."

—⟳—

"They're offering $7,500?" said Steven. "That's ridiculous." *Well at least they agree on something*, thought the Mediator. "Danielle's therapy alone was almost *twice* what they're offering. Go back and talk to them again."

When the Mediator presented the $100,000 offer to the boys and their parents, they were astonished. The boys thought the whole thing was crazy. "It was just a prank!" said Noah. "Her dad is blowing this whole thing way out of proportion. Look at her! Danielle is fine."

"Besides," added Harvey, "with what we earn at our after-school jobs we could never come up with $100,000, or even half of that."

So they were at a standstill. The Mediator instinctively recognized that the large settlement demand was simply a way for Steven to express his immense anger. He felt that the only way to get past it was to bring everyone together again and let Steven tell them what the boys' actions had really meant to him as the father of this girl. "If it's all right with you," he said, "I'd like to let Steven try to explain how this whole incident has affected him."

They looked doubtful, and clearly weren't eager to be subjected to Steven's rage yet again.

But the Mediator pressed on. "I really think this is going to help us reach a settlement today," he said firmly. "I'd like to give this a try."

"Okay," they finally agreed. "Do what you think is best."

—◦◦◦—

Back at the plaintiffs' room, Steven jumped at the offer to let them know how he felt. "But," said the Mediator, "I don't want to make this any more painful for Danielle then it already has been. I recommend that she not be in the room." He made sure she was occupied with her drawing and had some snacks. He thought she was beginning to look tired, and he wasn't surprised.

—◦◦◦—

Steven made no attempt to hide his hostility. "You've done permanent damage to Danielle," Steven told the boys angrily. "I don't know if she'll ever feel safe again. I know I don't. How can she ever feel okay about playing on the playground in her own school? I feel like you four boys have destroyed her childhood with your stupid game." He glared at each of them in turn.

"Danielle is my only child. She means everything to me. Since her mother passed away a couple of years ago, I've been her only parent. I wish I could be home all day to take care of her, but I have to go to work. The only thing that makes it possible for me to do that is the belief that she will be safe and well taken care of at school and after school, until I can pick her up and take her home. Your little prank makes that impossible now.

"I'm pretty discouraged, if you want to know the truth," Steven continued. "I know you probably won't be able to come up with the money. I just want you to understand why I'm so upset."

"Thank you, Steven," the Mediator said as Steven trailed off. "I think we all have a better sense of how you feel and what you are going through as a single parent. Please allow me to go in the other room and speak to the boys and their parents privately."

—⁓—

The boys wasted no time in telling the Mediator they felt that Steven was over the top. "We really understand what we did was wrong, and we've all been grounded for our actions. But come on. Steven is pushing this too far. We really don't want to hear any more of what he has to say," they said.

"I understand your point of view," the Mediator said quietly. "It was just a prank—you weren't out to hurt anybody."

"Exactly," they agreed.

"But put yourself in his shoes," the Mediator continued gently, looking at the boys and past them to their parents. "Put aside your personal feelings about the situation and think about your choices. Letting this whole mess go to court is going to hurt all of your reputations. It will be on your records. I know you're all applying to colleges next year—believe me, this is not what you want the admissions people to see. And if you let a judge or jury decide this case, you may easily end up paying even *more* than Steven is asking. Or you can try to come up with something that acknowledges Steven's anger and his feelings."

The boys looked down at the ground. Their parents looked at one another. *Endgame,* the Mediator thought.

"I'll give you guys some time alone to sort this all out with your lawyer," said the Mediator. "Let me know what you decide."

In the end, the boys and their parents decided that they didn't want to risk losing even more money and possibly their college prospects. They just wanted this nightmare to end. They calculated how much they could earn if each of them worked full-time over the summer.

"We're willing to offer Steven $17,000," their lawyer reported.

"That makes more sense. Let me take that to Steven and encourage him to put this behind him," the Mediator replied.

—⌘—

By this time, some of the anger had gone out of Steven. Having been given the chance to speak his mind one more time, he realized that there was only so far he could take this thing. At this point his primary concern was his daughter's health and happiness, and right now she just wanted to go home. Playing on this, the Mediator said, "Steven, if we don't settle this case, it's going to go to trial, and Danielle is going to have to testify."

Danielle looked up from her drawing. "Dad, I don't want to go to court. I just want to forget about what happened. Let's just go home."

That did it. "Okay, baby," said Steven. "We're almost done here."

He talked to his lawyer for a minute and then turned to the Mediator. "Look, we're going to get this settled, but they have to feel more pain. We need them to pay $20,000." He was ready to compromise, but was not quite ready to accept what they had offered.

"I'll take it back to them, but you need to know that the $17,000 represented their entire earnings for the summer. I think that represents an acknowledgment that their actions were stupid," the Mediator said, sighing quietly.

—⌘—

"He offered *what?*" the boys exclaimed. "We offered him as much as we can possibly make working at minimum-wage jobs. He's just jerking us around. What's wrong with that guy?"

Wearily, the Mediator said, "Let me talk to him again."

—⟨ψ⟩—

Alone with Steven and his lawyer, he said, "Steven, what's going on? We're so close to a settlement, and your demand for an extra $3,000 is creating another impasse. What can we do?"

"They can afford another few thousand dollars," mumbled Steven. "I've got to pay my lawyer, and we need enough for Danielle's medical treatment." Then he stopped, looking at Danielle, who was staring at him hard. "Okay, okay. I just want to make sure they feel remorse, and I want them to promise never to do anything like that again. Here's my deal. I'll take the $17,000 on two conditions: first, they each have to give me a written apology for what they did and describe the lesson they learned. Second, they each have to complete a gun safety course. Finally, I expect to talk to each of them individually after the meeting."

—⟨ψ⟩—

The boys took Steven's offer, but they weren't happy about it. They would have a long, hard summer ahead of them, and on top of that they had to say they were sorry and take some classes. But they also knew things could have been much worse, and they were relieved to have the incident behind them.

Steven was satisfied too. He told each of the boys how he felt and got an apology; he paid for Danielle's therapy and had a little left over. And Danielle was content too, because her father finally relaxed and just let her get back to the business of being a kid.

WHAT HAPPENED?

In every mediation there is an intermediate step between the initial claims and the final settlement. The intermediate step usually involves some communication gap, possible a stray emotion or a misunderstanding that hasn't been addressed. If you don't identify the issue and take that step, you won't reach settlement. The truth is that the nature of the step is different in every case, and the challenge is to understand it. In this case, the issue of the intermediate step turned out to be the communication between Steven and the boys, in which he was allowed to tell them exactly how their actions affected him as a father.

The Mediator framed this intermediate step in a structured approach that actually took four separate stages. In the first stage, he opened the door by having the boys and their parents acknowledge Steven's anger. Even if they didn't agree with it, they were forced to listen attentively. The second stage occurred when the Mediator invited Steven in by expressing how he understood his perspective. It didn't take many words to do that; in fact, a simple hand gesture or body movement is sometimes enough to make someone feel heard. The third stage occurred when the Mediator asked nonjudgmental questions of the parties in order to clarify issues and get to the bottom of things. The fourth and final stage, which resulted in closure, was when the Mediator showed them that he understood each party, setting the stage for moving toward a cooperative resolution. This happened when the boys agreed to use their entire earnings for the summer to fund the settlement, and Steven was made aware of this effort.

WHAT STRATEGY CAN WE LEARN?

1. **Recognize when it's time to use a communication tool known as "VECS."**

   A simple way to understand the approach described in "What Happened?" is through the mnemonic VECS: Validate, Empathize, Clarify, and Summarize. This is an important tool that you can use over and over again, not only in emotionally driven cases like this one but also in cases that revolve around money. People or companies who feel that their proposals are fair also need to feel understood. Here's a quick overview of the VECS process:

   - *Validate.* Acknowledge the parties for talking even if you disagree. This opens the door to further communication.
   - *Empathize.* Understand their perspective and help them evaluate their own concerns. This is when you invite them in to keep talking.

- *Clarify.* Make sure you understand by asking nonjudgmental or open-ended questions to get to the bottom of
  things.
- *Summarize.* Review the progress in the negotiation by list-
  ing the key points that have transpired thus far in the
  case. By showing the parties you understand, you can
  bring a case to resolution.

CHAPTER THREE

STEP-BY-STEP

The Mediator watched the ten-year-old twins, Ben and Gary, as they sat in silence next to their uncle Frank, thumbs moving rapidly on their handheld games, and wondered what they thought of all this. In premediation telephone conferences, he had learned that they were both bright kids who had always played sports and done well in school, but that everything had changed over the course of the last year, when they lost both parents, one to a traffic accident and the other to suicide—maybe. And that lingering uncertainty had brought them all to mediation this morning.

The Mediator had had a crash course on the basics of this case, thanks to an extensive PowerPoint presentation the plaintiffs' attorney sent him. The presentation detailed how they would approach this case if it went to trial, complete with research and interviews with psychiatrists. The Mediator had learned quite a bit: the previous year, the boys' father had been killed instantly in a car crash. Their mother, Maria, was distraught—she had lost the love of her life, her rock and her soul, her sweetheart since junior high school. She had depended on him for everything since the age of fourteen, and she was struggling to continue—emotionally, financially, and in every other way. But, for the sake of her sons, she kept going.

Then, one bitter October day, on the first anniversary of her husband's death, she drove out to the seashore and walked into the chilly Atlantic, hoping to be swept away to sea. According to the note she left, her dream was to "meet up with her husband again, somewhere, somehow."

But the waves pushed her back to shore, still breathing. She was found by local police, who took her to the hospital, where she was treated for hypothermia. During her stay in the hospital, she was evaluated for depression and received psychiatric care. She made a pact with her psychiatrist that she would look forward, not backward, and would never again try suicide. The psychiatrist was satisfied with her progress, felt that she was no longer a danger to herself, and discharged her.

On the day she was to go home, Maria overheard the nurses talking about the possibility that she needed more treatment—that maybe they would be sending her to another medical facility to deal with her depression. Frightened, Maria panicked and tried to get away. It was an old hospital, and her seventh-floor room had a small ledge. She unhooked the window, climbed out onto the ledge, and screamed, "No, it's over! I'm not going!" One of the nurses went after her and climbed out the window to comfort her and bring her back inside. She reached out to take Maria's hand, and Maria reached out her hand too. But just before their fingers touched, Maria fell seven stories to her death.

Did she slip or did she jump? Either way, Ben and Gary were now orphans. Their father's brother Frank and his wife, who lived on the other side of the country, agreed to care for them. But the family had very little money. Their uncle sued the hospital and doctors who had cared for Maria, but a jury decided there had been no negligence. The only other possibility of providing a financial future for the boys rested in a life insurance policy Maria had purchased a couple of years before she died. The policy provided $1 million in coverage on the condition that the policyholder did not commit suicide within two years of the policy inception date. Because Maria's death occurred within the two-year period, the insurer denied payment.

This time, Uncle Frank found a law firm that believed Maria's fall was accidental: she had only gone out on the ledge to avoid being taken to a medical facility; she did not mean to jump to her death. If they could prove it, the boys would be entitled to the policy benefits. The law firm specialized in this type of case. Their services would cost the uncle nothing because they were willing to work on a contingency fee: they had the potential to wind up with 40 percent of at least $1 million, plus legal fees and punitive damages.

The case was a murky mix of emotions and money. For the boys and their guardians, their future was hanging on the outcome of the case. Their lawyers made a sizable initial demand of $5 million before the mediation to capitalize on the boys' sympathetic position. Privately, the lawyers had told the Mediator that they realized the demand was a bit extreme and that they would come down dramatically if the insurer offered their policy limits. The Mediator was virtually certain from premediation discussions that the insurance company lawyer was not authorized to go over the policy limits of $1 million in this negotiation. Practically speaking, it becomes difficult for an insurance company to pay more than their policy benefits unless serious evidence of wrongdoing has been developed and senior decision makers have endorsed that type of negotiation. Maybe the boys would get money in court, but maybe not. It was always a crapshoot in these cases. So the Mediator knew when he woke up in the morning that this day was going to be about setting up a series of concessions that would take the parties from their extreme positions one step at a time.

———❧———

He wanted to get both sides to take the largest step right at the beginning. Because both parties had taken extreme positions on the issue of suicide, he asked them both to present their views of the case as if they were presenting the matter in court. He was hoping that the formality of each side's presentation would influence the other party, as they would envision the same presentation being told to the jury.

"I'd like to welcome everybody to my office," said the Mediator. "Since we've had plenty of time to speak before this meeting, and Ben, Gary, and their uncle Frank understand the process, I think it would be helpful if each side listens carefully as the attorneys present an abbreviated view of the case. Who would like to begin?"

The plaintiffs' lead attorney raised his hand slightly, and the Mediator nodded. "As you know," the attorney began, "we have prepared a video presentation that will demonstrate how we are going to present the evidence if the matter goes to trial. I'd like to begin by showing you that now."

"Why don't we let Ben and Gary sit this one out?" the Mediator suggested. The boys didn't need to hear their mother's death discussed in this manner, and their potentially emotional reaction would be damaging in other ways. Their attorney readily agreed, and an assistant ushered them into another office.

The attorney dimmed the lights and began the presentation. It was quite a production. A professional voiceover actor narrated the documentary footage, summarizing the dramatic, emotional highlights of the case. Convincing interviews with several forensic psychiatrists—whom the firm had hired to review the medical records and determine whether Maria's death fit into the definition of suicide as set forth in the policy—were quite persuasive in their unanimous belief that Maria's death was an accident and that Maria did not understand the consequences of her actions.

"Now," the attorney said, turning the lights back on, "I'd just like to finish up by summarizing what the psychiatrists said so that we're all clear on this. As you heard, they agreed on three main points. First, the hospital had already released Maria, indicating that they found her to have the requisite mental capacity to go home. Second, she went out on the ledge because, based on what the nurses were saying, she feared she was going to be taken to another hospital. And third, she reached for the nurse's hand but slipped; this is supported by the hospital psychiatrist's report that she wasn't intending to kill herself."

The defense quietly listened during the presentation. To the Mediator's eye they seemed stunned to see this kind of testimony. Clearly, they were moved by the emotional intensity of the video, though he knew they wouldn't admit it.

"Thank you," the Mediator said. He proceeded to summarize their case in a way that confirmed to them that he understood their position clearly. "With that said, I'd like to point out that point of view is everything in a trial. This case—like most cases—is like the famous Japanese movie *Rashomon:* in that film, each person who witnessed a murder told a very different story about what happened. Your understanding of what happened depends on your unique perspective on the situation." He looked at the people sitting at the table to make sure they were with him. "Okay," he said, "I think it's appropriate now to hear the insurance company's point of view."

The attorney for the insurance company was sympathetic but confident. "This is a terrible tragedy, and we're very sorry for the boys," she began. "But our job is relatively simple: to investigate what happened here and determine whether coverage applies. We believe it does not. Maria's policy has a two-year exclusion on suicide, and we believe—and our own forensic psychiatrist supports this belief—that she fully intended to kill herself." She paused and looked around the room.

"Let's look at the facts," she continued. "Maria walks into the ocean, leaving a note stating that she intends to meet her dead husband. And then she goes out on a ledge and jumps seven floors to her death." She paused. "It seems clear to us, and to our forensic experts, that her death was intentional."

"All right," said the Mediator, "I think you've both made your positions clear. Right now, I'd like to meet with each party separately, beginning with the defense." He was ready for the first move—and he hoped it would be a big one.

—◁◦▷—

"So what did you think of the plaintiffs' experts?" the Mediator asked the insurer's attorney.

"They were impressive," she replied, "but obviously they're hired guns."

"It's my understanding that if this case goes to trial, the burden shifts to the insurer to prove by a preponderance of evidence that Maria jumped off that ledge, right?"

"Yes, that's right," the attorney agreed.

"Do you have any concerns, based on what you've seen, that you could sustain your burden of proof?"

"Well," the lawyer said, straightening her jacket and fidgeting a bit, "anything's possible in court, but yeah, we think we can sustain it." She sounded nonchalant, but her body language told the Mediator that the powerful emotional content and expert witnesses in the video presentation had shaken her confidence. He decided to give that doubt room to grow.

"Look," he said, "that video made it pretty clear how they might spin their case in court. I think it's only fair for me to step outside so you and your client can talk about this privately. If you firmly believe you can win, then by all means go to court. But if there's concern in your mind, maybe we can talk."

When the Mediator returned to the room, something seemed to have shifted.

"Well?" he asked. "What do you think?"

"We still feel we have a good case," the lawyer said. "And we believe Maria intended to kill herself and knew what she was doing. But juries are unpredictable, it's an emotional case, and this law firm is out for blood. Nonetheless," she finished, glancing at her client, "we are not ready to pay the policy benefits."

The Mediator interpreted this statement to mean that the time was not right to pay the policy benefits, but that with a little more seasoning the insurance company might consider it.

"I understand. And I don't think we're ready to start the negotiation yet," observed the Mediator. "In my haste to shuffle the boys out of the joint session, I forgot to offer you an opportunity to hear more about how their lives are going, and I think that's an important piece of the puzzle. Let's meet back in the large conference room."

"Frank," the Mediator began, "maybe you can fill us in on what life's been like for Ben and Gary."

"It's been tough," said the boys' uncle. "They were both very close to their parents, and they were thriving at home before all this happened. We've seen them grow up, and they were always happy, outgoing—they both did great in school, lots of friends . . . now it's just video games. They don't talk too much. They seem sad. Gary is angry a lot. They already missed their dad, and then their mom . . ." He trailed off. "The way Maria died was horrible. How can you ever get over that?" He shook his head and looked down at his hands.

"We'll make it," he said. "We have to, I guess. But the boys are in trouble. Their grades have slipped, and Ben is starting to cause trouble in class. He was *never* like that before. They need help, someone to talk to. If we can help them get back on track, feeling good, God willing they'll go to college one day, somehow. But we're doing all we can financially just to keep them in clothes and food—and we have three children of our own. We love them, they're part of our family, and that's not going to change, no matter what happens. But it's hard for them. Given what happened to their mom, I worry for their future."

The insurer's counsel was trying hard not to appear devastated, but everyone in the room had been affected by Frank's story. "Thank you, Frank," said the Mediator. "I appreciate how tough it's been for you and the boys, and I want to thank you for coming here today." He turned to Frank's attorney.

"You have a pretty sympathetic family here—I think we can all agree to that. And we've seen your expert on the PowerPoint. But I'm wondering, and I think the defense is probably wondering, how the forensic evidence might play out in front of a jury."

"Well, I think I can get one of our forensic psychiatrists, Jim Forschner, on the phone right now if you think that would help."

"Good idea," said the Mediator. "We'll put him on speakerphone."

Dr. Forschner presented a formidable case against suicide. "Maria was stable for a long time," he said, "and she and her husband provided a loving home for their sons—even without the testimony of their friends to that effect, which I heard many times, their healthy social and academic lives will attest to that. She went through the trauma of her husband's sudden death, and that was tough. Clearly, something happened to cause her to jump in the ocean that day—it's not unusual to feel especially depressed on the anniversary of a loved one's death. But it was completely out of character from what I could see, and I've been at this job for thirty-five years now, in private practice and as a tenured professor. That one act just didn't seem to reflect her normal mental capacity." Everyone in the room was focused on the phone.

"She was still strong," Dr. Forschner continued. "She was working, taking care of her family; and she was resilient. All the diagnostic reports from her hospital stay showed she was clearheaded. If she wasn't, why was the hospital releasing her? They had no legal pressure to do so; in crass terms, they would have made more money from her case if they had simply transferred her from the general ward to the psych ward. But the hospital's psychiatrist, who worked with her from the time she was brought in, felt she was ready to go home, and he signed papers to the effect. I'm certainly willing to testify to a reasonable medical certainty on this matter in court, but I hope it doesn't have to go that far, for everyone's sake."

"Thank you, Dr. Forschner," said the Mediator. "That was very helpful."

When they ended the call, the Mediator looked around the room and said, "Why don't we all take a short break? When we come back, I'd like to meet privately with the insurance company and their attorney."

———∞∞∞———

The insurer and his attorney looked a bit more stressed this time around. The plaintiffs' evidence was starting to look like it might convince a jury, and Dr. Forschner would clearly make a good witness. And the plaintiffs had three more just like him in the wings.

"They certainly know how to package a presentation," the attorney said with a wry smile. "I think we're ready to deal. But $5 million is way out of line."

"I know they initially demanded $5 million," said the Mediator, "but judging from my further discussions with them I think they'll be flexible if you make a reasonable offer that includes a sizable portion of the $1 million policy limits."

"We're in something of a bind here," the claims manager said. "We don't want to risk giving away the entire policy benefits; that would leave us open to a charge of wrongly denying the claim, and then we'd be faced with a whole other lawsuit—" He stopped, after a look from his attorney.

"We recognize that there are some risks here based on what we heard from Dr. Forschner," the attorney said smoothly, "but we think that on balance we have a better shot at winning this case than they do. Bottom line, for us, is that she tried to drown herself and then jumped out of a seventh-floor window. We're not admitting anything here, but we're prepared to offer them $250,000."

"That's a substantial amount of money," the claims manager pointed out, "especially if they invest it wisely for the boys."

"Okay," said the Mediator. "I assume you have some flexibility."

"We do," said the claims manager, "but we're not paying the policy limits."

"This is a good start. Let me take it to them and see what they say."

—⁓—

"Please indulge my habit here," the Mediator said to the plaintiffs' attorney. "I'd like to do a short risk analysis and then we can jump into the negotiation."

"Fine," replied the attorney.

"Okay, then, how do you rate your chances of winning this case in court? More than 50-50?"

"Easily," said the attorney.

"You've certainly got sympathetic clients," said the Mediator, "but you're still going to have some difficulties, given the circumstances of her death. As the insurance company keeps saying, she jumped in the ocean and went out a window a few days later."

"No case is airtight," said the attorney, "and the family understands that they could lose. But our forensic evidence is much more compelling than theirs is, so I would give us a greater than 50 percent chance of winning. Perhaps as high as 70 percent."

"The insurance company is willing to offer $250,000," the Mediator told the plaintiffs. "I think there's some wiggle room, but they need to hear that you're within the policy range. What do you think of that?"

"Not much," said the attorney. "We're asking for many times more than that." The lawyer grew silent, contemplating his moves. "Maybe $5 million is out of the realm of possibility," he admitted, "but it's insulting to my clients to make an offer that doesn't even come up to policy limits. What do you think we should do here? It's important to us to present a strong face, but we understand the significance of settlement for these children. As good as we feel about the forensic testimony, we don't want the kids to experience another bad jury like they did in the medical malpractice case."

"I appreciate your sensitivity to the children's needs," the Mediator replied. "If you really want my thoughts, I think it would be important for you to let the insurance company know through your next offer that the children come first in this case—even before the jury. That would require a significant concession of at least $2 million."

"Look," said the lawyer, "we'll drop our demand to $3 million. Take that to them and see what they say."

Progress, thought the Mediator. And he walked back down the hall to relay the new demand.

—✺—

"Good news," said the Mediator. "They've reduced their demand to $3 million."

"Well, that's better, but it's not even close to what we're willing to pay," the insurer's lawyer replied.

"Let's put this in perspective," said the Mediator. "If this case goes to a jury trial, do you think your chances of winning are better than 50-50?"

"I'd say our chances are about 60-40," she replied quickly.

"Fine," said the Mediator. "Why don't you make an offer based on that analysis? That means you would offer $400,000, which is 40 percent of the contract benefit. If a jury finds in their favor, it'll award them at least $1 million, and there might also be punitive damages—and 40 percent of a few million dollars exceeds your policy limits."

The claims manager was getting agitated, but said nothing. "Do you think they'd accept $400,000?" asked the attorney, scrambling for a foothold.

"To be candid, I don't," the Mediator replied, "but I think it will move the ball up the court and cause them to reassess their position, particularly if it's clear to them that that sum represents a 60-40 analysis of liability."

—✺—

"They offered $400,000? That's not *nearly* enough to allow Frank and his wife to care for these boys until they're eighteen," said the plaintiffs' lawyer, "especially given their fragile psychological state. But we're interested in getting some closure here. Tell them that we'll consider reducing our demand if they simply pay the policy limits, like they should have done in the first place."

"I'll be glad to tell them that, but I think the explanation would have more teeth if it came with a modified demand," said the Mediator.

"We're serious about helping these kids. But we're also concerned about dropping too much and giving them the impression that we're anxious to settle. Tell them we'll counter at $2.4 million, but we want you to know that we have room."

By now, the defense was anxious but still not willing to give in. "Have they come down to below the policy limits yet so we can get this thing over with?" the attorney asked.

"Not yet, but they have dropped to $2.4 million, with an indication of flexibility if you offer the policy limits," the Mediator explained.

"That's crazy. If we were to offer the limits, it would send a signal that we were willing to pay *over* $1 million, and we're not prepared to send that signal. They need to get serious! We'll keep this going, but we want you to know that we're running out of room. My client will go up to $500,000 as long as you tell them that we expect them to come under the policy limits, or we could be finished for the day."

"I'll take it to them," said the Mediator, "but I don't think they'll go for it. Nevertheless, it will certainly send them a strong message."

"What's their problem understanding this?" said the plaintiffs' attorney, mildly frustrated. "They made a mistake in not paying off this policy in the first place. We're only asking for what we're due."

The Mediator knew from experience that when the plaintiffs' lawyer dropped his demand from $5 million to $3 million, it was a signal that he would eventually accept an offer closer to the contract limits. He also knew that the attorney knew that legally, once a negotiation with an insurer is forecast to go over the contract limits, it's difficult to get a claims department to agree, unless there was evidence of egregious behavior on the part of the insurer. Here, there was truly a genuine dispute as to whether the dead mother intended to commit suicide.

"Look, we've been playing verbal volleyball all day under the assumption that you could get a court to award damages that exceed the contract benefits," said the Mediator. "For you to do that, you would have to demonstrate that the decision to deny benefits was not only wrong but egregious. Don't you think a court will take a step back and look at the big picture here? After all, you still have to walk into court and explain why the woman was out on a ledge and ultimately fell to her death!"

"We understand that's a formidable task, which is why we will present forensic evidence," said the lawyer. "These boys clearly deserve all the money they can get from this tragedy. We simply don't want to leave anything on the table for these kids. The family understands that the case has some challenges. If you get us the policy limits, we will recommend it to our clients, but we're not sure how to present that to the insurance company without looking weak."

All the blustering and presentation of evidence they'd seen today was really toward one end: avoiding court. The Mediator knew that now it was just a matter of batting the ball back and forth over the net a few more times—and walking back and forth, carrying messages from office to office—until they arrived at that inevitable point.

The plaintiffs lowered their demand to $1.5 million, and the insurance company countered with an offer of $600,000.

The plaintiffs lowered their demand again, to $1.3 million, and the insurance company offered $650,000.

Finally, the plaintiffs said, "Tell them we'll go as low as $1 million, but that's it."

The insurance company responded, "We won't settle unless the number is under $1 million. We're not paying more than the original policy amount. Our offer is $675,000. That's it." Reading between the lines, the Mediator inferred that they might even pay $1 million, or come close.

Endgame, thought the Mediator.

—◦◦◦—

But the plaintiffs' lawyer had other ideas. "We won't accept that offer," he said. "We're out of here." The Mediator didn't buy it— they were clearly flagging. He decided it was time for another heartfelt talk.

"We're almost there," he said, "hang in with me. I know you recognize the importance of providing financial security for your clients. You've done an amazing job of backing up your case, and the insurance company knows it. Now you have a chance to get the family a chunk of money they were never going to get. It's pretty clear that the insurance company is done negotiating, but I think I may be able to get them to increase their offer a little more so these kids can be protected.

"I'd like to see how far they might go if they suspect there is an impasse. They might be more receptive to a suggestion from me at a higher number. I'll see if they will pay the policy limits, but I'm not optimistic. Assuming they are willing to move up a bit, I'd like you to talk about a number under $1 million," said the Mediator.

"Okay," said the lawyer, after consulting with Frank. They didn't want to look weak by coming off their policy benefits demand, but the lawyer realized he could use the office of the Mediator to find their exit strategy at a number that would take care of the children for a long time. "If you can get them to $750,000, I'll recommend the family consider it."

The Mediator went back down the hall—for the last time today, he was pretty sure.

—◦◦◦—

Back in the defense room, the claims manager and his attorney were looking tense.

"I realize you've made your last and best offer at $675,000," the Mediator explained to the claims manager, "but that won't settle the case. I've talked to the family at length, and I believe they would settle for a number under $1 million."

The insurance company lawyer sat up a little straighter. *She's called the company and knows she can't get them to go for paying the policy limits,* the Mediator realized. "If you can call the company and see if you can get $750,000, I think we can make a deal."

"Give me a few minutes. I'll make that call right now." The claims manager and the Mediator waited in companionable silence for her to return.

Ten minutes later she was back. "It's a go," she said smiling. "Make the offer."

———

The family accepted the $750,000 readily. It was a long way from $5 million, but they'd spent the day reframing their understanding of what might happen in court. They understood that the jury, despite the emotional sympathy and despite the testimony of experts, could just as easily find that Maria had intentionally committed suicide. In the end, they weren't greedy, and they were not prepared to gamble with Ben and Gary's future.

WHAT HAPPENED?

This negotiation showcases one of the most common dilemmas facing a mediator: having to reconcile the emotional and real necessity of providing financial security to people in need with the reality that there is a fixed amount of money available from the insurer. Although the children might have gained more through the court process, it was just as likely that they would receive nothing, which would have been yet another devastating blow. The key was to acknowledge that the negotiation was a zero-sum exchange and proceed accordingly.

The parties in a zero-sum exchange negotiation generally proceed from positions at extreme ends of the spectrum, with the goal of engaging in a series of concessions or moves that lead them into a mutually acceptable range. This type of negotiation is harmful to relationships, as it mainly focuses on the numbers. In this case, however, the relationship issues had to be addressed because they pertained to the future economic status of the children, who would be without parents for the rest of their lives.

In this case, the Mediator proceeded from the standpoint that the first set of moves would be the largest and take the least amount of time. He then engaged the parties in further moves designed to narrow the gap between each side. Ultimately in these exchanges, the gap is small enough that one side or the other is willing to make a final move, or the mediator makes a recommendation that bridges the gap—which is what happened here.

WHAT STRATEGIES CAN WE LEARN?

1. **Don't skip any moves.**

   The moves or concessions in a negotiation can be like those in a chess game: each move represents another step toward settlement, and each move—no matter how seemingly inconsequential—gets you closer to the endgame. When one side or the other wants to skip a move out of impatience or wants to stop playing because they don't like the game, you must let them know that they will be leaving money on the table by redefining the value of the negotiation. "Redefining the value of the negotiation" is a way of identifying differences that influence the other side to act cooperatively or competitively. By offering to skip a move, the party was revealing a position that was closer to their endgame. This effort at cooperation could be exploited by the other side.

2. **Remember that each move is symbolic.**

   Although a monetary amount is attached to each move, it's the *symbolism* of the amount—not necessarily the substantive amount—that drives the next move. The gap between the two parties' positions at any one point doesn't really tell you anything about what's really going on in the negotiation. You can learn more by looking at the nature of the concessions.

3. **Stress the probability of immediate financial security over the possibility of winning in court.**

   In negotiations, it's always a good idea to remember the truth of the old saying "A bird in the hand is worth two in the bush." In a case like this one, where you're dealing not only with money but with vulnerable human beings, this consideration can make a big difference in how long parties are willing to hold to extreme positions.

CHAPTER FOUR

A SWEET DEAL

Joe Pantoni and Fred Mastriani stared uncomfortably at one
another across the small conference room table. The old friends
and business acquaintances hadn't spoken to one another in three
years, except to exchange insults and threats, since Pantoni sued
Mastriani for more than half a million dollars and Mastriani
refused to pay. On the urging of their families and lawyers, they
had agreed to try mediation in order to keep their dispute from
becoming more public than it already was.

"Thank you for agreeing to meet with us today," Mastriani said
to the Mediator, nervously running a hand over his thinning hair.
"I think you'll agree that Joe's gotten us into a real mess here."

"*I* got us into it? Who tried to poison my client?"

The Mediator cut them off quickly before the personal attacks
got any worse. He wanted to encourage constructive discussion
today, not enmity. In fact, he had been asked to negotiate this dispute as a favor to the lawyers for both sides. The lawyers knew these
men well and were worried about them. Their close-knit Italian
American community shared many family, religious, and cultural
bonds; the ongoing battle between these two leaders had not only
split their immediate families but also caused countless other people to take sides, threatening relationships in a domino effect. The
lawyers were worried that if Joe and Fred couldn't resolve their differences soon, this dispute would tear up these men's families and
businesses and make them both pariahs instead of leaders.

In a somewhat rare show of unity, they had explained the case
to the Mediator over lunch a few weeks ago. Joe Pantoni owned
and managed Pantoni and Co., a confectionery manufacturing

business founded by his grandfather. Pantoni and Co. was very well established in the confectionery market and known for its fancy chocolate and candies. One of Pantoni's biggest sellers was after-dinner mints. Last year Pantoni did $5 million in sales of these mints alone.

Fred Mastriani also owned a family business. Mastriani Wrapping produced specialty wrapping and sold it throughout the country. Mastriani distinguished his company by using unique designs created by talented graphic artists. For ten years, Mastriani had sold specialty foil to Pantoni and Co. for one line of their mints.

Although Pantoni and Mastriani had a successful working relationship, they had known each other since childhood and were personally competitive. They traveled in the same social as well as business circles and were forever boasting to each other about their business as well as personal successes. Now, that competitive relationship, which used to be a friendly rivalry, had turned toward out-and-out combat.

—◦◦◦—

"I understand that your families have been friends for many years—going back to your grandfathers in Italy, I believe," the Mediator said. "I hope we can salvage that relationship for you today—"

"I can't see that happening," Mastriani muttered.

"I'm familiar with the outlines of your case," the Mediator continued, "but maybe you can paint in the details for me." He glanced at the two lawyers, who were sitting quietly. They had agreed to take a backseat during the negotiation and allow the Mediator to control the direction of the proceedings.

"It's a nightmare. I wouldn't even know where to begin," said Mastriani.

"I know exactly where it started," said Pantoni, launching into his story. "Three years ago my company landed a client we'd been courting for years, Hallmark Hotels. Hallmark asked us to provide them with exclusive logo-embossed chocolate mints to put on each guest pillow in their hotels across the country—that's $500,000 in annual sales for us. We were ecstatic. So, wanting to share the wealth, I turned to my good friend Fred, here," he said, giving

Mastriani a look filled with enmity, "and placed an order for specialty wrap with the Hallmark logo."

"Which we provided to specification and ahead of schedule," said Mastriani. "You had no complaints, as I recall."

"Just one, Fred," continued Pantoni. "Within thirty days, Hallmark returned almost all the mints. They smelled terrible—like a chemical spill. The Hallmark guests who had tasted them were complaining. Thank God no one got sick from the mints, but guests were disgusted by their smell and taste." He shook his head slowly. "Naturally, Hallmark demanded that we return the purchase price and also pay a penalty for their lost business and loss of goodwill."

"That sounds like your worst nightmare," the Mediator commiserated. "What did you do?"

"I asked my chief chemist to investigate immediately, of course. I thought there must be a problem with our manufacturing process. He did a thorough investigation, and found that the wrapping paper delivered by Mastriani was saturated with *toluene*. I couldn't believe it. It causes cancer. They put it in paint thinner!" He took a minute to make sure the Mediator had gotten the full impact and then went on with his story.

"Anyway, this toluene apparently leaked from the wrapping into the mints. I was fairly certain that Fred did this on purpose to destroy our connection with Hallmark."

"You're paranoid, you know that? I could sue you for that alone," sputtered Mastriani.

The Mediator guided the conversation back into a calmer channel. "I'm sure that was an upsetting discovery for both of you," he said.

"Upsetting's not the word," said Mastriani. "Impossible is more like it."

"May I finish my story, Fred?" said Pantoni. Mastriani said nothing.

"Thank you. Well, of course I refunded Hallmark's money, and I asked for another chance to provide the mints, with paper from a new manufacturer. And then I sued this son of a bitch for the price of the wrap and the $500,000 I should have gotten from Hallmark." He glared at Mastriani. "I'm sure Fred has his own version of events."

"Yes, the truthful version," Mastriani shot back. "As my grandfather always said, *Ogni medaglia ha il suo rovescio.*" In response to the Mediator's puzzled look, he translated: "There are two sides to every coin."

"Yeah," Joe fired back. "Well, here's what my grandfather used to say: *O mangiar questa minestra o saltar questa finestra.* Eat the soup or throw it out the window—take it or leave it!"

Fred looked at the Mediator with concern. "I was shocked, as you can imagine. I've been using the same paper for years, and I've *never* had a problem. Joe didn't even try to talk to me about this— he just filed a lawsuit against me. I couldn't believe he could turn on me so easily." Mastriani was breathing hard.

"My reputation as a businessman was on the line here. I understand Joe was upset, but he could have at least had the decency to come to me first. He betrayed my trust. My grandfather's name is on that company."

"My grandfather's name is on *my* company," said Joe under his breath.

"It sounds like you had a rough time, Fred," the Mediator said with some sympathy. "What was your next move?"

"I conducted my own investigation," replied Mastriani. "And what do you think I found? Nothing. No toluene in any of my wrapping. No toluene *in my entire factory.* Obviously, Pantoni and Co. must have caused the problem themselves, through improper storage or handling, and tried to blame it on me. I told Joe that there was no way I would ever pay him what he was asking for. And I won't."

"That's quite a story," said the Mediator. "Did you ever determine with certainty exactly what went wrong?"

The two men were silent, but both lawyers shook their heads.

"So you can't really determine the question of blame, and this fight has been going on for three years, without resolution? That must have taken a toll," the Mediator said, with some concern.

"Yeah," Mastriani admitted, "it's been rough, especially on our families. My wife is pretty upset about the whole thing. She and Joe's wife are good friends. I know Joe gives his wife hell when he finds out they've seen each other. We all used to get together, go on vacations together . . . Now we just avoid each other at business and social functions so we don't make a scene. Our children used to play with each other all the time, and now they don't."

"That's because you won't allow my boys to set foot in your house," said Pantoni. "I can't even go to Mass without having to see your face. The whole community knows about this," he said to the Mediator. "It's a shame."

"That's because you can't keep your mouth shut about it!" shouted Mastriani. "You have to see my face in church? Well, I have to go there and listen to you spouting off to someone about your precious lawsuit. I can't even imagine what you tell Father Michael in confession. Maybe I should ask *him* where the toluene came from."

"Gentlemen, gentlemen," said the Mediator, giving them the time-out sign with his hands. "I think I get the picture. I don't know who's at fault here—and at this point, I don't think it matters. I think when you finally do discover what actually happened to the candy, it might turn out to be a simple error that's no one's fault. We just don't know for sure. But it's pretty clear that each of you is so entrenched in your side of the story that you can't see what else might be going on. Right now, I'm going to ask your lawyers to take a few minutes and meet with you to discuss privately what direction you think this dispute should take. I'll join you separately in a few minutes."

Because Pantoni had initiated the suit, the Mediator met first with Pantoni and his lawyer. As he entered the room, Pantoni's lawyer was saying, "It's time, Joe. This just can't go on any longer." Pantoni was nodding, and looked tired. *Good work,* thought the Mediator. The lawyers were going to make his job a lot easier today.

"Forgive me for being so bold, Joe," the Mediator began, "but is it true that there's no proof of toluene in the wrappers?"

"Unfortunately, we've reached a dead end on this issue," said Pantoni's lawyer. "Joe knows how difficult it's going to be to prove the case in court, and he's not happy about it."

"You're damn right I'm not happy," grumbled Pantoni. "I *know* the toluene was in those wrappers, but they tell me the technology to prove it in court is too expensive. Fred's getting away with murder here!"

The Mediator went into what he thought of as "preacher" mode—all-purpose priest, pastor, rabbi, or teacher—an approach designed to appeal to the men's sense of family, community, and tradition. He leaned in a little closer and locked eyes with Pantoni. "Joe, you chose to bring this dispute into a system of justice that has some flaws. Maybe you're right. Maybe Fred's right. I don't know—and from what I can tell, you're not likely to be able to prove anything conclusively in court. I can tell you from long experience—and I think your lawyer will back me up here—that it's likely to get more brutal and bloody and end with two bodies on the floor and a lot of money down the drain. What I do know for sure is this: it's a real shame to see generations of friendship get flushed down the toilet.

"It saddens me to hear what has happened to your families," he continued. "Your children no longer play together, your wives can't enjoy each others' company without looking over their shoulders . . . and it sounds like there's way too much gossip in the community about you two. From what your lawyer has told me, the two of you are community leaders, and your community is being torn apart over this."

"Who are you, my priest?" Pantoni seemed taken aback by the Mediator's direct appeal.

"It seems to me that this dispute has dishonored both of your families, to some degree," the Mediator said, keeping the pressure on, "which is something I think your grandfather would have thought twice about. Our court system can't give that honor back to you—quite the contrary. In this case, it can only give you more headaches." He took a breath. "So what do you think about all this?"

"I appreciate your comments," Pantoni replied, "but this wouldn't have happened if Fred had handled it better from the beginning."

"You're still in blame mode, Joe," said the Mediator. "I can only help you out of this mess if you're willing to drop the blame, look forward, and work with me toward reconciliation. If you can do that, I guarantee you we'll get a settlement today that you'll find appealing. Are you willing to work with me?"

"You'll never convince me that Fred doesn't share some of the blame for this," Pantoni replied, in a last-ditch effort to preserve his side of the story, "but you're right—my grandfather would have had me in the woodshed for this. He was a real believer in preserving family harmony, family honor. I know I owe my business, my success, to his hard work. He and Fred's grandfather came over here together on the same boat . . . This is a real mess, isn't it?" Pantoni looked intently at the Mediator. "Okay. My lawyer told me to trust you, and that you were our best option. So, yes, I will work with you."

"Good," said the Mediator, smiling. "That's all I'm asking for. I'm going to meet with Fred and his attorney now, and see if I can get him on our team. Meanwhile, here's what I'd like you to do. Your lawyer tells me that you've made many charitable contributions over the years, so while I'm gone I want the two of you to come up with two or three deserving organizations that you think could use some money. Try to keep it close to home—charities that benefit your community or your church, whatever you feel strongly about."

"And then what?" asked Pantoni, his curiosity piqued.

"And then, if I can work it out, I'm going to ask you to make a generous donation in the name of Fred Mastriani."

Pantoni's eyes opened wide, and he rose up out of his chair, as his lawyer laid a restraining hand on the angry confectioner's arm. But, just as suddenly, he sat down and leaned back in his chair with a sigh. "Okay, it's time to end this thing. Whatever it takes, Padre," he said in a last attempt at sarcasm.

"Thanks, Joe. I'll be back in a few minutes."

<hr />

The Mediator entered the room where Mastriani was meeting privately with his lawyer, and found the two men in a heated debate.

"My reputation has been permanently destroyed by Joe and his outrageous lies!" said Mastriani. "He betrayed our friendship and my family's honor. If my grandfather was alive today he would *forbid* me from paying Joe even one penny."

"Honor?" said his attorney. "And exactly what are *you* doing to uphold the family honor? I can't believe we're still having this discussion. You know as well as I do that this case is destroying everything you've built up over the years. Frankly, I don't know if your marriage is going survive if this thing drags on much longer. And if we go to trial, even if we win, you might as well just put your house on the market and move to a town where no one knows you."

The Mediator broke into the discussion, trying to smooth some ruffled feathers and redirect the emotional tone. "Fred, you bring up a good point here. *Honor* is important in evaluating this case. From what I've heard, it seems that *both* your names have been dishonored. Would your grandfather really support that?"

"Maybe not," Mastriani admitted, "but—"

"I think maybe it's time to turn the disadvantage that has been created into an advantage," the Mediator said.

"I'm not sure what you mean by that," replied Mastriani, momentarily diverted from his one-track argument.

"Okay, imagine this: What would happen—to your family, your community, your business associates—if you and Joe were not only to solve this problem but to break bread together in public, say at a community or charity event?"

"It'll never happen," said Mastriani. His lawyer glared at him.

"Just imagine it," said the Mediator. "Take a minute."

Mastriani furrowed his brow, trying to imagine such a thing ever occurring.

"People would be blown away," said the Mediator. "And everyone in your orbit would feel relieved. Forgiveness is a powerful tool."

"Forgiveness, huh? This is business, not Sunday school." He looked at his lawyer. "I thought we were here to talk about the case. What's all this forgiveness bull?"

"Just listen to him, Fred. There's more than one path to settling this thing—and as I've told you many times, trial isn't the right one."

"Forgiveness would open the door to your families getting back together as well," the Mediator continued. "You want that, don't you?"

"Sure, I want that. But I don't owe Joe anything," said Mastriani.

"I'm not asking you to pay Joe a penny, Fred. I think we can come up with other ideas that could make this work," observed the Mediator.

"I'm listening."

"Why don't you and your lawyer talk about this a little more while I see if I can get something going with Joe," said the Mediator, happy with the way his little flock was slowly settling down and coming together.

—◦◦◦—

Returning to Pantoni's room, the first thing the Mediator saw was a list of charities on the whiteboard.

"I see you two have been busy," he said.

"Fred contributes to any number of Italian American charities. I think he'd find several on this list worthy," said Pantoni. Once he had made the decision to move on, he was ready to race toward closure.

"Excellent," said the Mediator. "What amount of money do you think is justified under the circumstances?"

"Well, I guess if we both absorbed half the cost of the loss, $250,000 would be in order," Pantoni replied.

"That's fine. I can ask him about it. But think about this: as a means of allowing him to save face, he might want to pay something less than 50 percent. Would you have any objection if I discuss this with him?"

"No objection, but I would like you to encourage him to go 50-50 here," Pantoni answered.

The Mediator was sure that with this plan Pantoni would feel vindicated, as Mastriani might make some concession. At the same time he could show his respect for his grandfather by compromising and making a gesture that would benefit the community as a whole.

—◦◦◦—

"Fred," said the Mediator, "Joe has agreed to make a $250,000 donation in your name to the charity of your choice. Would you be willing to make an equal contribution to the Italian charity of your choice in Pantoni's name in exchange for dismissal of the lawsuit?"

"Where did that come from?" asked Mastriani.

"It was Joe's idea," said the Mediator.

"Huh," Mastriani muttered.

"Fred," asked his attorney, "didn't you tell me you were planning to make a large contribution to a charity soon anyway?"

"Yeah."

"Fred," added the Mediator, "you can accomplish two things here: you can move on from the lawsuit and feel good that you've made a significant charitable contribution."

"Okay," Mastriani agreed after a little thought. "I guess it's worth it to me to let Pantoni have the credit for the contribution just to see our kids playing together again."

⎯⎯∽∿∽⎯⎯

The meeting ended the way it had begun, with both parties seated around the conference table. But this time the mood in the room was completely different. Joe and Fred had shaken hands on their deal, and Fred was already on the phone, telling his wife the good news. The Mediator felt particularly satisfied with the day's work: with the assistance of two grandfathers, he had helped reconnect a business tie, preserve family honor, and uphold community integrity. The Italian American Child Welfare Association had even gotten a sizable donation in the name of forgiveness.

WHAT HAPPENED?

The Mediator recognized that money was not the real issue in this case. What he had was two old friends, completely entangled in animosity but still wanting to find a way to reconnect with each other. Because they had blamed each other for a business mistake, they didn't know any other way out of this mess except to seek justice through the legal system. Unfortunately, "justice" in this case would only cost them both more money and aggravation. The challenge was to take both parties to a point where they would actively seek a way to reconnect.

The Mediator understood that although both men valued their businesses, stronger values motivated them: family, honor, church, and community. And neither man wanted to dishonor his grandfather's name. The Mediator chose to be authentic—to use a negotiation style that grew naturally out of his background and experience and to use resources that were familiar and natural. The parties saw him as credible not just because he was being honest with them, but because he was being true to himself: he was confident enough to mix it up when necessary to close the deal, and to get out of the way when he sensed that the parties were able to do it themselves. He also chose to be directive, adopting the role of priest, preaching to each side the benefits to their families if the case were resolved, and pulling out all the stops by recognizing the dishonor to the memory of their families by maintaining this dispute. In a sense, the Mediator was helping them rewrite their scripts so that each man could step out of the role of villain or victim and into the role of magnanimous benefactor.

In the end, Pantoni realized he could continue to push Mastriani and hold out for the money, or he could behave in a way his grandfather would have been proud of by trying to come up with some compromise that would end the dispute. Mastriani came to the same realization, and both men were grateful for an excuse to end the divisive dispute. Contributing the disputed money to a community charity allowed both men to be magnanimous and feel good about paying out something within the context of the dispute.

WHAT STRATEGIES CAN WE LEARN?

1. **Locate the leverage points in the deal.**

   Sometimes the obvious answers are right in front of you. If you are faced with an immovable object, such as a large "nonnegotiable" money demand, you have two choices: you can either hit it head-on, or you can survey the situation and search for an opening that would allow a shift to another angle of approach. In this case, it meant finding a creative way to split the difference without having the parties pay each other directly.

2. **Edit their script.**

   Parties often remain stuck in their positions because they are relating their narrative of what happened from a narrow viewpoint and in a negative or hopeless tone. As the mediator, you can take a larger view that looks not at one party or the other "winning" but at both parties working toward a mutual goal. One way to help them get to this goal is to edit their script—retell their story about the dispute as a positive, forward-looking construction that allows them to see their options in a new light.

CHAPTER FIVE

READING MINDS

The plaintiffs, Jean and Tom Forsythe, sat stick-straight with their lawyer and waited for the meeting to begin. The Mediator took in Tom's dark suit and Jean's nondescript but neat dress, put this together with their tight, closed expressions, and read them as a conservative, traditional, middle-class couple in their early sixties. *Maybe a little uptight,* he thought. He shifted his gaze to the defendants, Betty and Ramona, the mother-daughter owners of ABC Preschool. Both women sat with lips pressed tightly together and arms folded in front of their chests. *On the defensive already,* the Mediator decided.

The Mediator broke the silence. "I'd like to thank you all for being here today and being willing to work this out. Jean, Tom—I understand this case centers on your young granddaughter, Christy. Where is Christy today, by the way?"

"She's with my sister Sarah," replied Tom, "safe and sound." He directed those last three words to Betty and Ramona, who rolled their eyes.

"You obviously got Christy back," Ramona said. "Safe and sound. It all worked out. We don't understand why you want money from us."

"Because we suffered and you should pay," said Tom, looking her right in the eye.

"You've been suffering with Joanie for years," said Betty. "Who's paying you for *that?*"

"Let's leave this discussion for a moment," said the Mediator. He felt like a referee. "I'd like to ask each of your attorneys to briefly sum up your positions." *Maybe some legal talk will cool things down.*

"*Our* case is clear," said the plaintiffs' lawyer. "Tom and Jean specifically told Betty and Ramona that Christy was not to see her mother unsupervised, they negligently ignored that directive, and as a consequence the child's mother abducted her."

"They shouldn't be allowed to have young children in their care," said Jean in a clipped voice. "Their practices are slipshod."

"We care deeply for each and every child under our care," said Betty, "and you know that for a fact."

"We're quite confident that Betty and Ramona were not negligent," said the lawyer for the insurance company that covered the ABC Preschool. "And let's not forget that the child was returned unharmed."

"We've apologized over and over," said Betty in a tired voice. "It was a terrible mistake, but it will never—*ever*—happen again."

"That's right," said Ramona, looking at her mother. "I don't even know why we're here."

We're not getting anywhere with this legal stuff, thought the Mediator. The intense emotions told him there was more to the story than the negligence. "You know," he said, stopping the joint session, "instead of everybody shooting bullets at each other, I think it might be better if I met with each party alone. Everything we say is private and confidential—I won't disclose what you tell me to the other side without your permission." He hoped they would be a little more open if the other party wasn't there to snipe at them.

———⟞∞⟞———

Alone with Tom, Jean, and their lawyer, the Mediator said, "Tom, maybe you could recap what brings you here—for my benefit."

"All right," said Tom. "Here it is in a nutshell: these people allowed our drug-addicted daughter, Joanie, to abduct Christy from their preschool—against our strict instructions—causing us to go through hell. And they're going to pay for it."

"Could you back up a little? Tell me about your daughter."

"Joanie was a very nice little girl," said Jean in a level voice. "Very well behaved. A beautiful child, like Christy. She played tennis at our club, she was on the junior swim team. Everyone adored her. But when she turned thirteen she just went wild. I don't know what got into her. We did everything we could, but she defied our rules, ridiculed our values . . . She said she wanted a different kind of life than the one we had," she said flatly. "I guess she got what she wanted."

"What happened?" asked the Mediator.

"We just don't know," replied Tom, still mystified after all these years. "When she was fourteen, she just seemed to self-destruct. She dropped all her old friends and started hanging out with tough kids, kids who smoked and drank—in junior high! Her grades went from A's and B's to D's and F's. By the time she was sixteen, she was completely out of control. We even sent her to one of those boot camps, but she ran away and begged to go back to school. But in the space of a few months she dropped out of school, became addicted to heroin and cocaine, and got pregnant. Pregnant! She was just a baby herself." Tom was lost in the memory.

"It was obvious to anyone with eyes that Joanie couldn't care for herself, let alone a baby," Jean finished briskly, "so she and Christy moved back in with us."

"We had a honeymoon period of about three months," Tom continued. "Then she slipped back into her old patterns. She started using drugs again. She'd disappear for weeks at a time, sometimes living on the streets." The Mediator looked at Jean. She said nothing, but her eyes were troubled.

Tom said, "What did we do? Can you tell me? I have no idea." The Mediator could see that Tom had been down this road before. "We gave her everything. Everything. And she threw it all away . . . Well, finally, we just had to accept the fact that Joanie was not stable enough to care for Christy and might never be. So we applied for and got a court order allowing us to be Christy's guardians."

"Yes," said Jean, "and we put Christy in the ABC Preschool right away. We had heard *such* good things about them, and we wanted to give her a healthy, normal upbringing. Joanie came back to visit from time to time, but it was clear that she was on drugs. She looked wild, and she hadn't showered in a while. She kept talking about taking Christy and starting a new life, and that scared us. We never let her see Christy without our supervision. Then we got another court order to prevent Joanie from being alone with Christy anywhere."

"I brought that court order to Betty and Ramona personally," said Tom. "I told them *specifically* that Christy was never, under any circumstances, allowed to be alone with her mother."

"And what did they tell you?" asked the Mediator.

"They assured us that Christy would never be alone with Joanie," said Tom. "Then three months later Joanie showed up at the preschool and took off with Christy. Just like that!"

"Thank you," said the Mediator. "I can see that you've been through a lot with all this. Let me talk to Betty and Ramona and see what they have to say."

"I think I've got the general picture," said the Mediator to Ramona and Betty. "Can you tell me what happened the day Joanie came?"

"The administrator on duty that day was being pulled in twelve directions at once," Ramona replied. "If you've ever been in a school full of two- and three-year-olds, you know how easily that can happen," she said with a small smile. "Anyway, when Joanie showed up, the administrator just forgot about the court order and brought Christy out to see her mom. When she turned around, Joanie and Christy were gone."

"Ramona and I were distraught when we found out what happened," said Betty. "We called the police immediately, and they launched a search. They found Christy and Joanie three weeks later. So the story has a happy ending!"

"We were not negligent," Ramona said.

"It was a terrible mistake," said Betty. "We have informed all of our teachers and administrators about what to do if a similar situation arises in the future. Believe me, we are all well aware of the situation now. I just don't know what else we can do."

"Tom's okay, but Jean is cold as ice," said Ramona. "Can't she see how bad we feel about all this? It's not like we handed Christy over on purpose!"

"Honey," said Betty, "I think Tom and Jean feel guilty about the horrible way their own daughter ended up."

"Right, Mom," replied Ramona. "And they want to make this whole thing our fault so they don't have to feel even *more* guilty."

The Mediator went back to talk to the plaintiffs, wondering what he was going to do with all the animosity that was floating around.

———✥———

"Jean," said the Mediator, "I have children, and I understand how upset you must have been to discover that Christy was gone. But you got Christy back—the story did have a happy ending." As soon as the words were out of his mouth he regretted them.

"Happy ending?" Jean said, raising her voice for the first time. "This is what you call a happy ending? Wrap it up and put a bow on it? We were in hell for three weeks. We had no idea where they were, what had happened, if Christy was okay. And we had every right to be worried! They found that innocent child two thousand miles away, in a filthy apartment, surrounded by drug users and criminals. Her mother was too stoned to even respond when the police arrested her for kidnapping."

"I apologize for that remark," said the Mediator. "That was very insensitive of me." He could see that Jean was getting frustrated, and her brittle façade was starting to crack. But instead of giving her time to cool down, he decided to see if some of that real emotion lurking behind the sniping might help move things along.

"I think it would be helpful if we got back together for a joint session with Betty and Ramona. You obviously have a lot on your mind, and I think it's important for them to hear it."

———✥———

"I know you've heard each other's stories a number of times already," said the Mediator when both parties had assembled. "But I'd like to ask Jean to express—one more time—why they filed this suit. Jean?"

To almost everyone's surprise, as soon as she began speaking Jean burst into tears. "This has been terrible, a terrible ordeal. Do you know what it's like to have to choose between your daughter and your granddaughter? Joanie's life is vile. But she's still our baby. We love her. That doesn't change, no matter what you may think. I wish it did, believe me. I wish I didn't care. I think about her every minute of every day. I wonder where she is, if she's sick, if she's suffering. I worry that she'll die of an overdose, that she'll be murdered. I feel like I failed her, and I don't even know how. And now we have her beautiful baby, Christy, and we try to keep her safe—and then she disappears into that same hellish life her mother is living, and it's too much. It's too much!"

Tom, shocked by his wife's outburst, put his arm around her shaking shoulders. After a few minutes, she pulled herself together as much as possible and said evenly, "I have never faced such a painful dilemma, and I sincerely wish that no one else in this room ever has to go through anything similar."

Betty and Ramona were both in tears, and the lawyers both looked concerned. Jean's outburst seemed to have loosened something in Betty as well.

"I was terrified when I found out what had happened," said Betty quietly. "I thought it might be the end of my school, and that would be more than I could bear. Since my husband died, I spend all my time making sure things are running smoothly. It's my legacy to Ramona. When this awful thing happened, well, I felt out of control. It could all disappear in an instant. And if Christy had died, or never been found, I never would have forgiven myself."

"I was really worried about my mom," said Ramona, no longer edgy. "She was a basket case for three weeks. I kept trying to tell her it wasn't her fault, but she couldn't take it in. She just felt totally responsible. I was afraid that if Christy never came home, she might . . . I don't know. I was worried."

"Jean, Tom, we are so, so sorry for what happened to you," said Betty. "I know we bear some responsibility for your pain."

"Thank you," said Jean, with dignity. "I believe you understand now."

The Mediator looked around the room. Tom and Jean had lost their stiffness, and Betty and Ramona were somehow softer. "Betty, Ramona, I think we all understood Jean's deep anguish. And Tom and Jean, you may have learned something more about Betty and Ramona. It feels like the suspicious anger we began the day with has dissipated. Do you agree?"

They all nodded their agreement, still dabbing at their tears. "Now I'd like to go back to our private meetings and discuss our options."

———∾∾∾———

"Let's break it down," said the Mediator to Tom and Jean. "What are the things we can to do to solve this? I know you need to get paid," he said to the lawyer, who was working on a contingency fee. "Tom, Christy's just a toddler now, but you know how quickly the years can pass. I wonder if you would welcome a college fund for her?"

"Sure," said Tom. "We've already set aside money to pay for Joanie's recovery. We know she'll come around some day. So money for Christy's future would be welcome."

"Maybe there's something the school's insurance company can do for Christy—such as a structured settlement, which is a form of long-term annuity. What do you think?" he said to the attorney.

"Sure, it just depends on how much they're willing to offer."

"Tom, Jean, I think that in order to get them to do something above and beyond like this, you'll need to display some recognition that they are not bad people. Accidents happen. If they're willing to own up to their responsibility in Christy's abduction, may I tell them that you understand how things could have gone so wrong?"

"Yes," said Jean. "We trusted them, and so the shock was that much greater. But it's time to go on with our lives."

"Let's discuss our options," the Mediator said to Betty, Ramona, and the lawyer from their insurance company. "There will be some money paid here, but I want you to know that Jean and Tom have acknowledged that you are not bad people, that they were very upset because they had trust and confidence in your staff. Having spent time with you today, they now recognize that there was no ill will here, and they'd like to bury the hatchet."

Turning to the lawyer, he said, "Thank you for being here today. Since Christy's still young, it's not a huge damage case, but maybe you could put some money away in a structured annuity fund for her college education. You'll definitely get more bang for your buck that way."

"Actually, I was thinking along those lines myself. We've already done the math. If we invest something in the area of $50,000 now, when she turns eighteen she can get $25,000 a year for four years.

"Sounds doable," said the Mediator. "And if you can add something for the lawyer, he can get paid now and we can settle."

"Test the waters and see what they say," said the lawyer, and the two women agreed.

"Great!" said the Mediator. "Just one more thing. Betty, when I go to present this settlement may I remind them that you once again apologize for what they've been through?" *That's why these people needed a mediator,* the Mediator mused. *It's just too uncomfortable for them to talk directly to each other.* His goal today, however, was not to create healing but to get the deal done and make everyone feel better without putting them in an uncomfortable position. Perhaps through this apology the healing process might get started.

"Yes, of course," said Betty, "please do that for us."

—✺—

"Tom and Jean," said the Mediator, "good news—Betty and Ramona have asked me to convey their apology. And the insurance company would like to do something for Christy. They agree that some kind of college fund through a structured settlement is a good idea."

"We told you we like the idea," said the lawyer, "but what kind of numbers do they have in mind?"

"I'm not sure of the exact numbers," answered the Mediator, fudging a bit—he didn't want to make it too easy for the lawyer— "but in my mind it's $20,000 or $25,000. And we'll get something for you, too."

"You know we're really glad to get this for Christy. That's all we really wanted. But of course the fee payment is a great bonus."

"Okay, let me run this by them."

—✺—

After more discussion, the parties came up with a plan that pleased everyone. The insurance company put $50,000 into a structured annuity that would net Christy $100,000 when she was ready to go to college. And they added $15,000 in lawyer's fees.

Jean and Tom felt satisfied with this arrangement. Their primary concern was Christy's well-being, and this trust fund would directly enhance her future. They also wanted to get back to their lives and to caring for Christy, and this settlement would allow them to move on as quickly as possible. Betty and Ramona were relieved as well. They too could get on with their lives and make sure every child who came into their care stayed there, safe and sound.

WHAT HAPPENED?

The complexities presented by this case were at two ends of the spectrum of value. On the tangible end, the Mediator had to help bring financial closure to a situation in which monetary damages were difficult to assess. On the intangible end of the spectrum, the Mediator recognized the need to restore to the parties a sense of their own value. Although there were certainly individual problems to solve in terms of damages, he felt that the real work here would be on the emotional level. On the basis of that assessment, he decided to use the "transformative" approach, which aims at creating deeper changes in the parties' attitudes toward one another and the problem at hand, changes that may affect how they react to other issues they face in life.

In this approach, you as mediator strive to generate empowerment and recognition. Empowerment gives the individuals the strength to handle their own problems and come to their own conclusions. Recognition means that you acknowledge their problems and let them know that you understand their unique situation. In this case, the Mediator made sure to recognize the importance of the high level of anxiety the parties experienced— the grandparents for Christy's safety, the day-care providers for the child's safety and also for the future of their school—during the three weeks following the abduction; he then facilitated the discussion to release the emotional roadblocks to meaningful problem solving. Once that was accomplished, the parties began to truly empathize with one another, appreciating each other's pain and letting go of hurt. The Mediator was able to use that empathy as a means for creating opportunities to settle.

That done, the Mediator went back to problem solving—he still had to manage the lawyers. Tom and Jean's lawyer, who was working on a contingency fee, would want some reasonable monetary amount to go to Christy and would need to be paid for his work on the case. That part became fairly easy once the transformation occurred, because the parties weren't focused as much on the financial side of the case anymore. The Mediator drew from his experience and suggested a structured settlement that would help pay for Christy's college education. That met the insurer's goals and also addressed Tom and Jean's long-term needs for their granddaughter. At the same time, the Mediator got the insurer to pay the lawyer what amounted to a fair fee on top of the annuity.

WHAT STRATEGIES CAN WE LEARN?

1. **Be prepared for a case to require you to switch between two different approaches.**

   Improvisational negotiation means being prepared to respond to the situation in the moment. Some cases call for switch-hitting: you may need to use both the problem-solving and transformative approaches in the course of one negotiation. Sticking with just one approach sometimes leads only to an extended dialogue with no hope of reaching closure. If you can alternate between approaches as necessary, you can address *all* the issues. You will also help the parties remember that the name of the game is closure, and that closure can be accomplished only through understanding and negotiation.

2. **Use the transformative approach to encourage empathy and reduce the emphasis on financial retribution.**

   Create a safe environment where each party can begin to empathize with their former enemy. By helping them struggle together to understand each other, you can begin to restore the sense of strength that they lost as a result of the initial conflict, and set the stage for compassion and growth. Once this occurs, the question of monetary compensation will take care of itself. This approach, commonly known as the transformative approach to mediation, is used primarily when you determine that an emotional barrier—anger, resentment, or some other form of internal strife—is blocking the parties from moving forward. Look for clues in word choices, body language, and facial expressions that signal intense emotional turmoil.

3. **"Read minds" by observing body language and listening closely.**

   When you are able to intuit motivations and predict actions, it may look like mind reading. But it's not magic. You can learn a lot about how each party sees the dispute by paying attention to body language and listening closely not only to their words but also to the emotional tone behind their words. If you give them the opportunity, most people involved in a dispute will gladly talk about themselves, which gives you a chance to ask more questions and gain more information about their perspective. Once you see things from their point of view, you can stay one step ahead of them by anticipating how they might react and managing the negotiation accordingly.

4. **Phrase your questions the way a jazz musician phrases music: offer opportunities for creative response from others in the room.**

   Jazz musicians invite one another into a musical conversation by listening and responding. One plays a key phrase of a song, with the assumption that the other musician is ready to respond with an answering phrase. Each invites the other to elaborate in his or her response, as opposed to leaving the other musician closed down and with nothing to play. Improvisational negotiation involves more than just the mediator: it also requires the participation of other parties. When you send signals—through words and action—that you would like the other party to open up or hold back or speed up, and so on, you are depending on the other person to understand, respond, and take the negotiation to the next level. As a mediator, you need to invite parties to play their own melodies by using open-ended phrases, such as "Tell me more" or "What do you think about that?" In this way you encourage rather than shut down conversation and information.

CHAPTER SIX

ROCK STAR

"Barry couldn't make it today," said Mick, rubbing his fashionable stubble nervously and looking uncomfortable.

The Mediator glanced over at the plaintiff, Jack. If Mick looked uncomfortable, Jack looked miserable. Apparently Barry, the focus of the dispute, hadn't even bothered to come.

"Mick, you're Barry's manager, is that right?" asked the Mediator.

"Yeah," Mick replied, "and I also manage the band—Ironangel." The Mediator was intrigued. In just a few years, Ironangel had shot to the top of the charts and become rock legends. Their leader, Barry van Diemen, had been compared to everyone from Mick Jagger to Kurt Cobain, but he was in his own league: a rock god. Now Jack Capellini, a minor rock legend by association—he had played under contract with Barry for three years—was threatening Barry with a lawsuit.

"Look, Jack," said Mick, leaning closer to the wiry guitar player, "after three years on the road together, you and I know each other pretty well. But I'm Barry's personal manager, not yours. This is business, you know?"

Jack ran a hand nervously down one arm, tracing the complicated Japanese tattoos that covered him from fingertip to shoulder, interrupted superficially by his black muscle shirt. Everything about Jack fairly screamed "rock star," but the Mediator could see that this young man, coming up hard on thirty, was fighting to hold back tears. The Mediator thought he'd give Jack a chance to collect himself before he spoke, so he turned to Barry's manager.

"Mick," said the Mediator, "why don't you sum up Barry's side of the story for us?"

"Sure," Mick began, clearly uncomfortable to be cast in the role of bad guy, at least in Jack's eyes. "Basically, Ironangel is Barry—he writes all the songs and sings lead. The rest of the band have been with him since the beginning, and they're his oldest friends: Jared plays lead guitar, Dooley plays bass, and Rick's the drummer. Four's good for a small club, but when they tour and record they need more sound to fill those stadiums, so we hire other musicians—organ, electric violin, whatever, as many as we need. Jack signed a three-year contract to play second lead guitar. He toured with us and played on a couple of our albums. He got a regular paycheck, just like the other contract musicians. After three years, Barry started getting into ambient music, house, electronic stuff—he didn't need another lead guitar. Jack's contract was up, so we let him go. That's the whole story. Sorry, dude," he said, trying hard to be sympathetic.

Mick looked to the Mediator for direction, and they exchanged glances. In preliminary discussions before today's meeting, the Mediator had discovered that Jack and Mick had a good relationship—the hard feelings were between Jack and Barry. Mick told the Mediator that his main concern was to keep his client's life as trouble free as possible so that he could concentrate on his music. When Mick said he was willing to do whatever he could to settle things quickly, the Mediator asked him if he'd be willing to act as a "sponge," soaking up some of Jack's animosity toward Barry. "That should speed things up," he explained. Now he silently signaled Mick to get ready.

"Jack?" said the Mediator. "What's your side of the story?"

"Um," he looked at his lawyer for reassurance. "Look, can I start at the beginning?"

"Start wherever you need to," said the Mediator.

"Okay, well . . . I picked up my dad's guitar when I was six, and I've been playing ever since. Me and my two best friends started a band in junior high, and we played all through high school—dances, parties. It sounds lame, but we were hot! I loved it. Forget college. Forget the straight life—all I ever wanted to do was play music.

"After high school, the band split up. My friends went to college, but I just joined another band and worked hard on my playing. I got a fake ID and played bars and clubs, wherever I could. I started getting known around town, sat in with a lot of bands, got some studio work, but nothing steady.

"Then one night, the owner of the bar I was playing at turned me on to Barry. He was just getting started with Ironangel, but I'd seen him play a few times over the last couple of years, and I knew any band he had would be amazing. Barry said the band already had a guitar player, but they needed another one so they could go a few more places musically. Hey, when they asked me to sign a three-year contract I jumped at the chance. I figured if nothing else, we'd make good music.

"But I had no idea. The band took off, like, *overnight*." The Mediator nodded his head as he listened to Jack's story. Ironangel was known—revered, in some cases—around the world, and had sold millions of records. Stories of Barry's exploits and girlfriends regularly made the tabloids. And for three great years, Jack had been along for the ride.

"I knew my gig with Ironangel might be temporary, but that didn't matter. I was making great music, living out my dream. Who doesn't want to be a rock star? *And I was one.* I played in huge venues here, in Europe, in Japan . . . I played on two albums—*Hot Metal Paradise* is a classic—it went platinum in a week. That was awesome. Then they let me go."

"That must have been pretty tough on you," the Mediator said.

"Yeah, well, I knew it was coming," Jack shrugged. "I had my three years with Ironangel. People knew who I was now, so I figured I was in a position to play with almost any group in the world. Which I did, and which I am. But music is not the most lucrative profession, despite what you might think. My friends started telling me that I was entitled to royalties on *Hot Metal Paradise*—they saw my name listed as cowriter on a lot of cuts. I started feeling kind of bad about the whole thing, and asked Mick about it. He said he'd pass it by Barry, but Barry never got back to me." He looked pointedly at Mick. "My lawyer said I should file suit to get my money—people do it all the time; it's no big deal. So we did that.

"But what Barry did next was really harsh," he said, openly glaring at Mick, who looked miserable but listened without defending himself or his client. "He turned around and sued *me,* asking for an injunction that would remove my name from any historical reference that showed I had been a part of the band. Like I never existed, like I never spent three years with Ironangel. I mean, how is that even possible?" He paused. "I loved being in that band," he said. "I couldn't believe it. What the hell?" Jack shook his long hair over one shoulder with an angry twitch, suddenly back in the moment.

"My lawyer told me I couldn't use the band's name until this case was over, but it's dragging on and on. Now I can't get gigs. People think there's something wrong with me. I don't exactly live a rock star life, but I'm really starting to need that money now. This whole thing has gotten way out of control."

"Jack," said the Mediator, "how much do the royalties amount to that you say Ironangel owes you?"

"I don't really know," replied Jack, looking at his lawyer.

"Less than a couple hundred thousand dollars," the attorney said vaguely. "We know it's not a huge amount, but it's enough to justify bringing this action."

"I'm confused," said the Mediator. "If you wrote those songs, it seems to me that you'd expect to get the royalties—and you'd know how much you were owed."

Jack shifted uncomfortably in his chair. "Well, the royalties are a little murky. I didn't actually *write* those songs. A recording session with Barry is pretty free-form—all the musicians add a little something to the mix, and Barry's the kind of guy who puts the musicians' names on the writing credit."

"Barry's a creative genius with a generous heart," Mick added, "but he's not much of a businessman. I put out fires for him every day, but I have to let a few burn."

"So there's nothing in writing naming you as the composer of these songs?" asked the Mediator.

"No, but my lawyer here thought I might have a case, so . . ." He looked at his lawyer. "And that's when Barry got upset and wouldn't let me say I'd been in the band."

"Come on, Jack," said Mick, "none of the musicians ever expected to get any royalties. Do you really want to look like you're trying to take credit for the music of Barry van Diemen?"

Maybe the amount of money is no longer the critical thing here, thought the Mediator. "Jack, I don't know how much money you're going to realize out of this, especially after the lawyers get done going to court and spending all of it. Can you help me understand what's significant about this whole thing in addition to the money?"

"I don't know," Jack mumbled, thinking out loud. "I need to work more. And to do that I need to be able to say that I was in Ironangel."

"Okay," said the Mediator. "That makes a lot of sense. But what's the bottom line on what you hope to get out of this negotiation? Why are we here?"

"Money would be good," said Jack, glancing at his lawyer, "but it's more than that. Bottom line? I would like to keep the credit for having written those songs with Barry. To make sure people understand that I had that connection with a legend, with that amazing music, that I was part of all that. And I want to keep working, keep my reputation, and be able to say that I played with Ironangel when they were at the top of their game. I haven't spoken to Barry in over a year. It really hurts that he didn't even bother to get out of bed and come here today."

"Have you tried talking to Barry since all these suits have been filed?" the Mediator asked.

"No," admitted Jack. "My lawyer called his lawyer—and Mick."

It was clear to the Mediator that Jack was a friendly, talented, but uncomplicated guy who was completely out of his depth in the legal world. He was pretty sure that if he could just get Jack and Barry talking, they could work it out without lawyers. "Mick," said the Mediator, "do you think we can get Barry on the phone right now?"

"Probably," said Mick. "He said he'd be available if we needed him."

The Mediator looked at Jack. "Do you think maybe if you talked to Barry the two of you could straighten this thing out?"

"I don't know. I guess. Maybe."

"Do you want to try?"

"Sure, why not? Nothing to lose now, right? Man," he added, "I feel like I'm going to throw up."

Barry's manager could see Jack's distress, and his heart went out to him. "I really hope you guys can work something out so you don't have to fight it out in court. Barry's really burning out on that; it seems like everybody's suing him for something now that he's got money."

"Maybe you and Jack can try to come up with a compromise proposal before we make the call," suggested the Mediator.

"Excellent," said Jack, relieved to have a plan. The Mediator listened as the two men began discussing options.

"Barry's not really such a bad guy," said Mick. "He's just tired of all the hassles. Maybe you should just drop the royalty talk. He might be willing to meet you halfway if he could see you weren't really out to get a piece of him."

"What if I tell Barry that I'll consider taking half the money I was asking for if I can tell people that I was in the band?"

"Don't give it up so quickly, Jack," said his lawyer. "You're worth more than that."

After they kicked around a few more ideas, without getting anywhere, the Mediator decided to coach Jack through the negotiation. "Jack, maybe you can tell him that the money is important to you, but not as important as being able to say that you were in the band for three years. That's the truth. Then you can leave the door open to let *him* come up with a proposal."

"I like it," said the lawyer. "You do deserve some compensation for your time and skills, Jack. And this leaves some room for negotiation."

"Sounds good to me," said Mick. "Let's do it."

Then they called Barry to see what he would say.

———✺———

"Barry," Mick began abruptly, "I'm here with Jack, at the guy's office—the mediator? He thinks you and Jack just need to hash this out together. You up for that? Yeah. Good. Okay. Jack and I have been talking about how we could make this thing go away, and here's the deal. He's willing to come down on the royalties if you'll just agree that he can say he was a member of Ironangel for three years. I'm putting you on speakerphone now. Jack's right here."

"Hey, Barry," said Jack awkwardly. "It's good to talk to you, dude. We don't need no stinkin' lawyers, right?" The Mediator thought it was a good sign that Jack was attempting a joke, even an old one. "So, here it is. I don't want to steal your name. I'm just trying to get some gigs here. It really hurts me that you're trying to prevent me from even saying I played with the band. I don't want to sue you, man. I hate that crap. And I'd be poison if I did that—who'd hire me? I loved playing with Ironangel, but it's over. I get it. I don't care about the money. I just want to get on with my music and not have everyone think I'm a liar or an ass. So that's it."

Barry listened without saying anything until Jack was finished. "Jack," said Barry, "it's good to talk to you. Really." To the Mediator's ear, he sounded very, very tired. "You know how crazy my life's gotten in the last few years. Everybody's suing me for something. The friggin' paparazzi are everywhere. I can't even get a minute to write. Look, I like you. You were the only guy in the band I could count on to show up on time, right?" Mick and Jack both laughed. "So if you just want to tell people you worked in the band, that's fine with me." He paused. "Listen, next time I'm in town I'll give you a call and we can jam on a few things I've been fooling around with. Your lawyer and Mick can talk about the money—we'll work something out." He paused and then said, "You played awesome guitar for Ironangel, Jack. I'll tell anybody who asks me. You deserve a great career."

Jack grinned. "Dude, you don't know what you just did for me. If you ever need *anything*, I'm there." And after a little more mutual admiration and a shoutout to Mick, Barry hung up.

"Yes!" Jack shouted, shooting out of his seat and thrusting his fist in the air. He and Mick embraced.

The Mediator was enjoying this healing moment in rock history, but he knew there were a few more things to clear up. "Let's wrap up the royalty situation before we go," he said.

"Good idea," said Jack's lawyer, looking relieved to be back on firmer ground. "You know Jack's got his name on a lot of those songs as cowriter," he began.

"Yeah, along with the rest of the band and whoever else was playing that day," said Mick.

"Jack," said Mick, looking the guitar player in the eye, "how about if we offer to buy out your royalties for, say, $50,000?"

Jack was still flying high from his conversation with Barry, but his lawyer was right there. "Make it $75,000 for *Hot Metal Paradise,* and a reasonable portion of the returns from the second album, let's say $25,000. And we want it in writing that Jack is allowed to say he played with Ironangel."

"Done," said Mick.

WHAT HAPPENED?

Mediation is very stylistic, and it would be a mistake to say that there is only one way of handling any particular case or that certain mediators offer the correct approach at any given time. In this case, the Mediator chose a style that reflected a facilitative approach. This is a less directive approach that allows the parties to come up with their own ideas about settlement rather than having the mediator impose a proposal on them. This requires the mediator to help the parties understand the issues and explore a variety of approaches that could result in closure. Sometimes this approach calls for a narrow view of the legal issues, and other times it requires a broad view of the personal motivation of the parties. In this case, after the Mediator had heard Jack's story, it seemed clear that the whole case was based on a misunderstanding, and a broad view of the situation was warranted.

By the time he got to mediation, even Jack was unclear about why he was suing Barry. When his attachment to the band was allowed to come to the surface, he became clearer about what he really needed: to move on with his career and be able to tell the world he was a member of one of the greatest rock bands of our time. Although Jack had been relying on the royalties from the album, they were secondary to his need to feel better and to have a future in music. He and Barry had never really talked about what was going on, and Barry was so busy being a rock star and defending himself from attack that he never took time to consider Jack's situation or way of thinking. The Mediator knew that Barry was basically a sensitive, introverted guy, and he suspected that Barry might actually be *afraid* to attend the mediation because he just couldn't handle one more assault. The Mediator thought that just getting the two of them together to talk things out might do the trick, and it did.

WHAT STRATEGIES CAN WE LEARN?

1. **Create a pressure-release valve.**
   The tension that naturally flows from a highly charged dispute needs an outlet. You can create a pressure-release valve by setting up an agreeable key player to act as a

"sponge," absorbing some of the intense feelings for a key player on the other side. Coach the sponge in the importance of listening without responding, but assure him or her that immediately after the discussion, the focus will be on solving the problems at hand.

2. Discuss common concerns.

Redefine the issues of the dispute by discussing all the things the parties have in common. Such a discussion can lead to a softening of positions and a desire to accommodate the underlying agenda that is driving the dispute. Review the parties' long-range goals and emphasize that their goals are not actually in conflict.

3. Construct and recommend a practical solution.

If the parties are proposing options that satisfy their needs but fail to consider the other side, come up with a scenario that could help both achieve their goals. They are looking to you as a coach for guidance and direction, particularly when they are deadlocked. If they are not warm to your suggestions, ask them to repackage their proposal in a way that addresses the other side's concerns.

CHAPTER SEVEN

GRATITUDE IS THE ATTITUDE

"You're offering Ken $25,000 as compensation for the death of his father at the hands of your insured?" Ken's lawyer appeared to be insulted on behalf of his young client, who sat silently next to him.

Ken had pressed for a much higher amount, a sum that wouldn't have been out of line in most cases. But this case was different, and privately the lawyer understood why the company's offer was so low. There were special circumstances, an unusual relationship between the father and son. In spite of this (or perhaps because of it), the amount of money offered by the insurance company had become the real sticking point in this case and brought them to mediation.

"Look, we know that any time you lose a parent it's just awful," the insurance company's lawyer explained patiently. The insurance company's claims manager nodded sympathetically. The kid was only eighteen. They all felt bad. "No amount of money will really compensate your client, but in this case asking for $500,000 is just, well, ridiculous. As you know, in our system we ask the jury to look at what amount of 'love, comfort, and care' the plaintiff lost. Ken and his dad, Tom, were estranged for years—most of the boy's life. They didn't see each other, didn't speak to each other . . . our investigators have told us that Tom spent most of his time in bars and on the street, drunk." He shot Ken a sympathetic glance. The Mediator sensed that the lawyer felt some sympathy for the plaintiff, but he had a job to do.

"In fact, it was drinking that led to Tom's death." There was a brief silence—they all knew the story.

It had been two o'clock in the morning when Ken's father, Tom, finished his nightly tour of the local pubs. He was only forty-two, but his years of alcoholism had made him old before his time and had long ago cost him his job and his family. His driver's license was long gone too, so as usual he was weaving unsteadily home on foot. As he stepped off the curb, perhaps thinking he had the green light, a motorist turned right into his path. For once in his life he was lucky: Tom died instantly. Ken, his sole survivor, filed suit for wrongful death.

"According to the legal instruction the jury will be receiving," the lawyer continued, "we don't think they'll give Ken much money. What did he really lose? We sympathize, but we don't get where the damage would be. I'm afraid Ken just doesn't have much of a case."

The Mediator saw that the insurance company was taking a hard line in this joint meeting, but it seemed to make sense given the estrangement between father and son. Meaningful consensus seemed very far away, and he was thinking hard, trying to determine the best way to steer the proceedings. He had noticed that the whole time the lawyers were speaking, Ken was gripping the arms of his chair as if letting go would launch him into space. Maybe there was something he needed to explore with this determined young man.

"I think we all understand your position," the Mediator said to the defense lawyer. "I'd like to talk to both parties privately to discuss where this negotiation goes from here. With your permission, I'd like to start with Ken and his attorney."

—◦◦◦—

"What's up, Ken?" the Mediator said. "I could see that you were about to burst during that meeting."

Ken was agitated and on the verge of tears. "I really wish someone would have let me talk in there," he said hotly. "You have no idea what I lost when my dad died, no idea at all. I haven't even told my lawyer. The insurance company made it pretty clear that they think he was a useless human being and I'm better off without him. They see him as a drunk and a deadbeat, and I get that.

He was. I hated him for years, the way he just abandoned me and my mom, and watched her struggle, and he never even picked up the phone to call me, but—" Ken's fury was about to spill over into sobbing. He was a big kid, over six feet, on his way to college and career, but the sad little boy he'd been when Tom left the family all those years ago was doing the talking now.

"Here," he said suddenly, thrusting a well-worn envelope at the Mediator. "Read this. Then you'll see."

"What's this?" The Mediator looked at the lawyer, who looked equally surprised and somewhat concerned.

"My dad wrote me this letter a month before he died," said Ken. "Just read it."

Tom had written a heart-wrenching letter to his son, brief but searingly honest and filled with remorse. Apparently, after more than a decade of spiraling downward, he had finally hit bottom and was starting to look for a way back up to the light. He was pleading forgiveness for a life full of pain—not his own, but the pain he had caused his son. He wrote about the few good times they had shared, and how he carried those memories close to his heart. He wrote about an epiphany, an urgent desire to break free of his addiction and get back to some kind of normal life, about the social worker who was sticking by him even though he wasn't perfect and sometimes slid back, and about his hope that someday Ken would forgive him, his hope that they could somehow repair their damaged relationship and really be father and son.

The Mediator finished reading the letter and pushed it silently across the table to Ken's lawyer. By the time they had finished reading it they were both choked up. The Mediator thought, *I really made a mistake by not letting this kid talk at the joint meeting.*

"Why didn't you show me this before?" his lawyer asked Ken gently.

"I don't know," Ken replied, wiping his eyes. "I didn't show it to anyone. It was private. I just hid it away until I could figure out what I wanted to tell him. But I didn't even get a chance to write him back."

Ken's lawyer said simply, "The insurance company needs to know about this."

"I agree," said the Mediator, "and I think we should have Ken express how deep the loss is to him. I suspect the insurance company will reassess its position once they see the letter. But let me talk to them first."

———

Rather than just carry messages back and forth between the parties, the Mediator wanted to make sure that his thinking was transparent to the insurance company. "We've all been missing something," the Mediator explained to the defense party. "There may have been more loss of love, comfort, and care than any of us have seen so far. Ken has something he wants to express to you. Would you mind meeting with him?"

"Sure," the defense lawyer replied, "if you think it will help."

"Great. Just give me a minute to get set up."

———

The Mediator felt that the intimacy of the letter would go over best in a setting that was warmer and less legalistic than the conference room, so he arranged to hold the joint meeting in an office that was set up like a living room, with comfortable couches and chairs. When they were all settled, the Mediator turned to Ken.

"You told me in the other room that you had some things to share with the claims manager about your relationship with your dad."

Ken was trying to hold it together, but he broke down in tears immediately. "We were finally getting back on track," he began. "My dad reached out to me, I was reaching out to him. He sent me this amazing letter . . ." Ken was completely choked up.

"Would you mind showing him the letter, Ken?" prompted the Mediator.

Ken handed the letter to the claims manager, who read it and handed it to his lawyer. To the Mediator's great relief, the claims manager responded with grace.

"Ken," he began, "I want to thank you for sharing this letter with us. It's a very private thing, and I know that bringing it here took a lot of courage. I can't even begin to imagine how much it must have meant to you to get this from your dad." The Mediator saw that the claims manager was deeply affected; clearly, the letter had touched something in his own life. "Can you tell me more about your dad?" he asked. "What was he like when you were little?"

"I have some good memories of him, from before he became a raging alcoholic," said Ken, surprised and pleased at the claims manager's reaction. Haltingly, he shared long-untold stories of a fun-loving young dad who carried him piggyback, took him to ball games, and brought him gifts when he returned from trips away from him. It was obvious that Tom had been a good father, at least for a few years. Even though Ken and his dad had been estranged for more than half his life, Ken's mother had encouraged him to keep those good recollections in his heart. Part of him had hated his dad for leaving, but another part held on to the hope that someday Tom would come back. And just when it looked like there was a chance that Ken's dream might come true, Tom was killed. They all felt Ken's deep loss and sadness.

"Maybe we could do something to recognize your dad," said the claims manager, and the lawyers nodded in agreement. They came up with several alternatives, which the insurer was willing to finance—but the donation to Alcoholics Anonymous hit a nerve for Ken.

"I've been to AA meetings for children of alcoholics," Ken said with some excitement. "I can't think of a better gift than that type of donation."

This offer went a long way to assuaging Ken's feelings, and the young man had become much calmer. "Can I say one more thing?" he asked the Mediator.

"Go ahead, Ken."

He seemed uncomfortable with all eyes on him, but he forged ahead anyway. "I just want to say that I'm really glad I brought my dad's letter today. It's awesome that you're willing to do all this for him. Thanks."

It is always a nice surprise when the parties turn out to be interested in going beyond money to real human understanding. But the Mediator knew it was time to bring practical matters back to the table. A simple acknowledgment of Ken's loss and a modest donation to Alcoholics Anonymous weren't going to be enough here; the case had already been filed in court. He spoke up, deciding it was time to inject some reality into the warm, fuzzy atmosphere that had been created.

"I think it would be helpful if I met privately with the defense team in order to discuss the issue of fair compensation in this case," said the Mediator.

———✺———

Meeting separately with the claims manager and defense attorney, the Mediator said, "I can't thank you enough for your gesture of goodwill in offering to make the donation to Alcoholics Anonymous. Obviously, it allowed Ken to feel comfortable that you understood the depth of his feelings toward his father. However, we're here because our system of justice deals with compensation, and you know Ken's lawyer will be looking for you to put more money on the table.

"Now that you know there may have been more to the issue than we first assumed, let's discuss how you can compensate for that."

The claims manager said, "Given the circumstances, we would be receptive to increasing our offer. It would help us if we had a better sense of what Ken's lawyer is seeking. Can you please get a demand out of him?"

"I'll see what I can do," the Mediator replied, and went into the other room to meet with the plaintiff.

Addressing Ken and his lawyer, the Mediator observed, "It appears we have made some tremendous progress here. The insurance company does recognize that there is more to the damages here than they originally thought. At the same time, they are aware of the difficulty in the relationship between Ken and his father and are not prepared to go overboard on the compensation. They said if you would make a reasonable demand in view of the obvious challenges in your case, they would make a sizable move."

"That's encouraging," said the lawyer. "We've been talking about this when you were out of the room, and we feel that a revised demand for $375,000 is fair—it wasn't a great relationship, granted, but it was beginning to move forward. The accident ended any chance Ken and Tom had to repair things."

The Mediator saw that this could be a turning point, and he jumped on it. "I think your demand will create some momentum in this negotiation and will be well received by the insurance company," he said, clearly pleased. "Let me pass that on to them and get you an offer. I'll be right back."

The Mediator then met separately with the claims manager and his lawyer, explaining the offer and giving the defense an opportunity to put a good foot forward.

"As you can see, they came down to $375,000, which is a dramatic reduction from their original demand of $500,000. You can demonstrate your commitment to settlement by making a six-figure offer."

"Well, given the new information we've heard here today, we're prepared to offer Ken $150,000," said the claims manager.

Now that the logjam of emotions and misunderstandings had been dissolved, things were moving quickly. The Mediator shuttled back and forth between conference rooms, the plaintiff's attorney countered with a demand for $300,000, and the case settled for $250,000.

What had appeared to be an insurmountable obstacle—the money—turned out to be the least of Ken's concerns. The acknowledgment of his efforts to redefine his relationship with his father could be quantified after all, and the insurance company could and did help the case turn the corner: by showing some understanding, by listening to the story, and by demonstrating appreciation for the son's concern.

WHAT HAPPENED?

Deal making in the rough-and-tumble world of litigation does not always go down as it did in this case, but people who demonstrate their gratitude toward others before, during, and after a mediation session generally end up with a better deal. Although this might not square with traditional negotiation tactics, it is a fundamental truth that I've observed after having mediated thousands of cases. Conversely, I have observed that parties feel indignant when others don't listen or show at least a little appreciation. This usually results in some type of barrier that prevents a case from settling.

When these barriers come up, it is generally because one side has such an extraordinarily high opinion of their own abilities and viewpoint that they fail to pay attention to the signals coming from the other side. When put in the position of receiving a confession from their opponent during negotiations, they falter badly. The only response they have is "No," because either they don't know how to show gratitude or they feel that doing so would be a sign of weakness. Some people simply don't know how to react. What they don't understand is that gratitude allows individuals to achieve success by creating more value in every situation and relationship. Expressions of gratitude directed to an opponent create value by challenging a person to reciprocate with another concession.

In this case, once gratitude was expressed by all the parties, both sides were able to see the case for what it was objectively worth and to reach agreement fairly quickly.

WHAT STRATEGIES CAN WE LEARN?

1. **Look for clues in body language.**

   Keep your antennae up while lawyers are describing the case to see how the parties react. If you observe someone sitting uncomfortably, crossing arms, fidgeting, or turning red in the face, it's a good sign that a nerve has been touched. When that occurs, make sure you have a chance to confront the party privately so that you can find out where the minefields are in that person's mind.

2. **Listen for the abstract needs of the parties.**

   What's tangible and measurable is often not the driving force behind the negotiation. Identifying an intangible need, such as recognition or understanding, will unlock the negotiation process.

3. **Steer the conversation back to the substance of the dispute.**

   Once you've scratched the surface and dealt explicitly with the abstract needs of the parties, you've dealt with the intermediate step that is critical before negotiation, namely, allowing parties to express themselves. It is now critical to focus the discussion on the substance of the dispute, which is usually defined as "fair compensation."

After all, that is what our civil justice system provides, and why the lawyers brought the case to mediation. The parties will be ready to assess the money issues realistically once the emotional barriers have been cleared away.

4. **Encourage the parties to move forward with the process because it will lead to closure.**

Tell the parties in an emotionally charged case that it's important to acknowledge the deep loss or anger they suffer, but also remind them that the process of negotiation is a key step toward closure and that it is your job to move that process forward.

CHAPTER EIGHT

MEMORIES

Ray, the general manager of Vista State Park, straightened the papers in front of him. As he looked down the long conference table to where the plaintiffs sat, he was confident that his offer would be accepted. Who could turn down that much money?

"According to our research," he began, "$800,000 is adequate compensation for your loss, and that's what we're offering."

Martha and Jim Amato, the plaintiffs, were stunned. Martha felt sick to her stomach, as if she had been punched. The pain of her boys' deaths had seemed impossible to bear, but the insensitivity of this negotiation was brutal. Three years earlier, near the end of a long summer vacation, Johnny, eight, and Scott, ten, had been riding their bikes in the state park near their home—just as they had nearly every day since June. But on this day, a Parks Service gardener who had been drinking on the job got in his state-owned truck and drove straight across the bike path, crashing into the boys and killing them instantly.

Martha and Jim were devastated: everything they valued had been taken from them in an instant. After the funerals, filled with anger and grief, they filed a suit against the state for the deaths. But instead of there being a speedy resolution that would let them get on with their lives, the negotiations surrounding the case had dragged on for three years with no settlement; neither side wanted to make the parents relive their children's death in open court. Finally, on the eve of trial, the parties decided to make one last effort: mediation.

It was early in the Mediator's career. He'd recently left a judgeship, where he was known for his decisive handling of cases. He was confident that his experience on the bench would serve him well as a mediator, and so far it had. He knew that both sides were optimistic that his expertise would soon help resolve this ordeal, and he intended to do everything he could to settle the case quickly.

On the appointed day, both parties—Martha and Jim and their attorney, and Ray and the state's attorney—were gathered around the long table in the largest of several conference rooms at the Mediator's office. But what had begun in hope now seemed doomed to failure. Furious and in tears, Martha railed at Ray. "No amount of money will bring back our boys. We know that." She locked eyes with her husband, whose grief had imposed a deep silence. "But to put this kind of price tag on the lives of our children is a slap in the face." She turned to her lawyer and declared, "If that's all they want to offer, we'll see them in court."

"Martha, I know how you feel, but let's give this a little more time." The lawyer spoke soothingly, but inside he was seething. This mediation was falling apart almost before it had begun.

Martha and Jim relented, and the negotiation dragged on for another hour, as both sides grew more and more tense. Finally, feeling that the emotional tension in the room was not helping the process, the Mediator decided it might be helpful to separate the parties into two smaller private rooms where he could talk to them privately about the issues.

In his long judicial career, the Mediator had been through these kinds of negotiations in court countless times, and he had always been successful in moving cases along to speedy and satisfying settlements. He felt that if they could each talk about their money issues privately, he could help them find a number that would work for everyone.

—————

When the Mediator entered the plaintiffs' conference room, Martha was fuming at her lawyer, her hands balled into tight fists. "These people are idiots! Our children are priceless. Can't they see how insulting their offer is? They think that throwing money at us will make everything just go away? Fine. If they insist on treating Johnny and Scott like commodities, tell them we won't take a penny less than $1.2 million."

Listening to Martha and seeing the determination in her face, the Mediator felt his optimism drop another notch. Clearly she was not going to be willing to compromise. He turned to Jim, the calmer of the two, thinking he might be clearheaded enough to talk more about the money. But even the stoic Jim had finally found his voice. Glaring at the Mediator, he said, "We've had enough. We're not making any further concessions in the name of our children! Tell them we'll see them in court."

Jim's attorney tried to calm him down. "Jim," he began in a quiet voice, "the two of you have a gut-wrenching story to tell, but I just can't guarantee you that the jury will give us a better result than the state is offering right now. You both need to think this through carefully. I'm going to leave you two alone to talk privately before we decide to adjourn this meeting."

Reluctantly, they agreed to take twenty minutes and think things over. After their lawyer and the Mediator left the room, they just looked at each other helplessly. They really didn't see any way out of going to trial.

———※———

Twenty minutes later, the Mediator rejoined Martha, Jim, and their attorney in the private office and learned that their feelings hadn't changed. But the Mediator had adjudicated many tough cases, and continued to feel that he could turn this one around. He'd had an amazing settlement record when he was on the bench. Enough listening: it was time for him to take a stand. "I'm pretty sure I can get the state to consider splitting the difference," he said confidently. "What do you say to that option?"

Flatly, Jim said, "Forget it."

"We're done with that," Martha said. "The jury will understand our pain, even if the state doesn't," she added. "Justice will not be served until the state is made to pay. It has to hurt them as much as they hurt us." She was gripping the edge of the table, her knuckles white.

In desperation, the Mediator threw out another time-proven suggestion. "How about this?" he said brightly. "I've done this in other cases, and it's worked well. We'll flip a coin, and who ever wins the flip will get their final settlement number." He looked at

Martha and Jim expectantly. They were speechless, stunned by what they perceived as his complete lack of sensitivity. Flip a coin? This was not their idea of what mediation was about. In unison, they stood up and began to put their coats on. Without even a glance at her attorney, Martha announced, "This mediation is over."

The Mediator couldn't believe what had just happened. What else could he do? He had tried his best, but apparently some cases just didn't want to settle easily. "Okay," he said after a long, uncomfortable silence. "Let's reconvene with the state, just to confirm that this case is going to go to court."

—◦◦◦—

Back in the large conference room, Martha let her frustration with the mediation spill out. She spoke directly to Ray, who had slumped back in his chair in exhaustion and frustration. "You people just don't get it," she said, holding back her tears. "They were our *children*. They had *names*. They were living, breathing boys. Their lives were short, but they were priceless. They should be remembered."

Silence hung in the room. Martha's frustration and despair were palpable. Without a word, Martha and Jim rose from their seats. Their lawyer, seeing it was over, began putting his files back into his briefcase. On the other side of the table, Ray's attorney was also putting his files in order. What more was there to say? The Mediator was miserable. Nothing in his judicial career had prepared him for this feeling of failure. What was worse, he didn't understand how the negotiations had gone so wrong.

But as everyone stood, preparing to leave after a very long day, Ray remained seated, Martha's final words echoing in his mind: "They were our *children*. They had *names*. They were living, breathing boys. Their lives were short, but they were priceless. They should be remembered." She must have said that a thousand times, but *they just hadn't heard her*.

"Wait!" he blurted. Everyone turned to look at him. Quickly, he turned to his attorney and whispered, "Look, I think we've been approaching this in completely the wrong way. This case isn't just about how much we owe: *it's about their kids*."

Ray looked Martha and Jim in the eye. "I'm so sorry," he said. "Your kids do deserve to be remembered. We've had our eye on the money for so long, planning our court case, that we lost sight of Johnny and Scott and *their* value—as human beings."

With that, Martha began sobbing. Jim, too, was fighting back tears. Someone was finally paying attention in the right way. *Finally,* Martha thought. She'd gotten them to think of her sons as people, not as accident statistics that were going to cost them money. For the first time in a long time, she felt listened to.

"Let me tell you about my kids," Jim began suddenly, digging in his wallet and pulling out photos. "Johnny was an incredible soccer player, a goalie. We spent every weekend at the park watching his games. I miss his friends." Jim stopped, lost.

Martha continued softly. "He and Scott fought sometimes, but they were really close. Scott couldn't have been more different from his brother. He was so funny, a real comedian. And he loved to perform. The teachers didn't always like it, but they always forgave him for his pranks." The group listened as Jim and Martha colored in the outlines of their sons' brief lives.

"Our kids were everything to us," Jim explained, almost pleading. "Our family has been broken—forever. We can't just erase their memories. Money won't take their place. We still have boxes filled with the letters and cards that we received after your driver killed them. They are missed. That will never go away."

The room was quiet, the presence and loss of Scott and Johnny suddenly evident. The Mediator felt a bit lost when he realized there had been a breakthrough that had nothing to do with money or moving things along in a timely manner or anything he had done. Thinking of his family, he realized that there were subtleties in mediation that the courts didn't have time for. Some of his tried-and-true techniques just weren't going to work in this context. He swallowed his pride and realized that he had a lot to learn. Right now, he needed to change his approach.

So, when the moment seemed right, he began again, on a completely different track. Looking at Ray, he said, "Perhaps there's something the state could do to memorialize these children."

Ray looked up. The general manager had kids too, a fact he had been trying to bury in order to get this negotiation accomplished in a "businesslike" way. Suddenly, he had a new idea.

"We've had to rebuild that bike trail to repair the damage the truck caused. How about naming it after the children? We can put a memorial marker at the site of the accident," he suggested.

Now the state's attorney was energized. "That's a great idea! We could consider setting up a scholarship fund in their name. I know none of this will bring Scott and Johnny back, but we would like to honor their lives. Everyone who rides on that trail will know their names."

Martha and Jim softened as the rage they had carried around for three years began to dissipate. It became clear that a trial would not be necessary, and they soon hammered out an agreement that satisfied all the parties. In addition to the bike trail and scholarship fund, the state added another $50,000 to their original offer, and the case settled for $850,000.

By the end of the following year, the state had constructed a new bicycle trail named after the children, and marked it with a plaque. The Scott and Johnny Amato Scholarship Fund was endowed by the state to help send children in need to summer camp. Now everyone who rode that trail would remember Johnny and Scott: their lives added value to the entire community.

WHAT HAPPENED?

Understanding underlying motives can be a key that unlocks what looks like an unsuccessful negotiation. In this case, it was the sudden recognition that the case wasn't solely about money but also about responding to the parents' need to feel that their children's lives were being valued. As long as the Mediator believed the problem was all about finding the right number, he was missing an intermediate step in the process: understanding and listening to the parties. Inevitably, the case stalled. When there was a general recognition of both the monetary issues and the very real concerns of the family, the dispute progressed toward a resolution that satisfied both sides.

This approach to negotiation underscores the idea that value is not always monetary. It cost the state relatively little to name the trail after the children and erect a plaque, but that gesture was worth hundreds of thousands of dollars to the parents and settled the case.

The Mediator took a wrong turn at the very beginning. He was accustomed to dealing with courtroom situations, where the key players—attorneys and judge—tend to use a narrow approach that is limited to finding the magic number that will close the case and clear the docket as quickly as possible. He was also uncomfortable with the level of emotion involved in the case. He understood the defendant's monetary offer and was concentrating on crunching the numbers. But he was not allowing himself to get *in synch* with what were broader, more personal concerns of the plaintiffs. He realized that there was some sort of emotional barrier, but he couldn't identify it.

The Mediator's narrow focus caused him to miss the fact that money was not the only issue on the table. The parents gave a number of clues that the issue was not simply financial: Martha's statements that "No amount of money will bring our boys back" and "Our children were priceless" should have made their feelings clear. Had the Mediator been open to just listening to the parents talk about their children in the beginning, he might have been able to unlock the case and settle it much sooner.

What Strategies Can We Learn?

1. Discover what people really value.

Figuring out what each side values most gives you the tools to close the deal. Always remember that you can add value in many ways, only one of which is in currency. Respect, honor, compensation in kind, even a simple apology may have more value for people than money.

2. Be willing to vary your approach.

Just because your approach works for you in most cases, don't count on it working in every case. Be true to yourself, but assume the role that's needed in the moment: the coach who gives direction, the bartender who listens and elicits information, the litigator who asks probing questions, the decisive judge who lays down the law. Sometimes just hanging back and allowing the lawyers and the parties themselves to get the work done is a good skill!

3. **Overcome barriers by listening to people and letting them know you hear them.**

    In virtually every negotiation there is some type of barrier that can prevent the parties from negotiating realistically. Whatever the barrier—it might be psychological, or it could involve a party's strategic attempt to use information to their advantage—you will need to identify it before negotiating. Pay attention to verbal clues and body language. One way of eliminating the barrier in a highly charged emotional case is to help parties perceive each other more fully and accurately than if left to themselves. You can do this by demonstrating that you hear their plight and acknowledge them.

4. **Get in synch.**

    Each case has a rhythm of its own, a tempo that emerges during the session that will tell you when it's time to listen and when it's time to act. Actions that don't follow that rhythm will be counterproductive. To succeed, you'll need to feel the tempo of the mediation, getting in synch with the parties and their counsel by listening and following their cues. It's almost like a drummer who maintains the beat of a jazz trio. The drummer listens for the clues from the lead player and learns quickly to adapt a beat to the music. You do the same by stepping into the shoes of each party and looking at the dispute through their eyes. To do this, be conscious of your preconceived notions about the outcome and let them go. The parties will get a sense that you understand them and are pulling for them to achieve their desired outcome. In this way you build a reservoir of trust you can draw from later.

CHAPTER NINE

WORKING AT THE CAR WASH

Sal straightened his already straight tie, smoothed his Italian suit, folded his hands on the table, and gazed out the window. Tall and thin, his black hair going gray at the temples, he was making a real effort not to look at Armin and Nadia, the worried middle-aged couple who sat across from him.

Armin and Nadia gave up trying to catch Sal's eye, and huddled with their attorney, speaking in low voices.

Sal's lawyer, all business, made a show of looking through his papers.

As the Mediator walked into the room, he felt the tension slap him in the face. This promised to be interesting and not quite what he'd expected. He had learned the basics of the case a few days earlier, when the attorneys submitted their briefs. On the surface, it seemed to be a dispute about money: the couple had defaulted on a loan Sal had extended, and Sal was threatening to take their business. But the palpable tension in the room, and the body language of the parties—all immigrants to the United States from Lebanon, with long, complicated ties to one another—told him that perhaps money was not the real issue here. It was a sense of respect, pride, and friendship that would be won or lost in the negotiations.

"I'd like to thank you all for coming today," the Mediator began. All eyes, suddenly, were on him. "I know this is a litigated case, and we have some legal issues to discuss, but I'd like to begin by hearing a little about what brings you here. Sal? Maybe you can start."

But instead of telling his story, Sal shot out of his seat and began yelling at Armin and Nadia. "I absolutely demand you turn the car wash over to me! I gave you a loan. You didn't pay me back. What am I supposed to do?" His face flushed with anger. The phrase "purple with rage" flew into the Mediator's mind. The perfectly groomed Sal had gone from zero to sixty in seconds.

"Listen," Armin interrupted, almost in tears. "We're just as upset as you! It's our life at stake! We have no intention of hurting you!"

"I don't believe you!" Sal shouted back, pounding his fist on the table. Both lawyers looked startled.

"Whoa, whoa, let's dial this back," said the Mediator, wishing he had a whistle. It had been a long time since he had had to act as referee. "We're here to listen to each other," he said quietly but firmly. "So I'm going to have to make a rule of no interruptions. From now on, only one person at a time talks and everyone else listens. Understood?"

By this time Sal was sitting down again, looking somewhat abashed. Armin was trying to pull himself back together, and Nadia just looked miserable. "Sal," said the Mediator, "I'm going to give you a chance to regroup. Armin, maybe you and Nadia would like to tell us your side of the story."

"Yes, yes," said Armin, nodding energetically. "I would like to start from the beginning."

"Please," smiled the Mediator. "How did all this start?"

"Four years ago," said Armin, "Nadia and I came here from Lebanon. We have a lot of family and friends here, like Sal," he explained, without irony. "We worked hard, and last year we decided it was time to start our own business. We got a government loan and opened our car wash.

"But it costs so much more for everything in this country, maybe we weren't ready, I don't know," he said, shaking his head. "The government loan wasn't going to be enough to keep the business going. So what could we do? Of course, we turned to our family, our friends."

"Sal has been our family friend for years; for generations our families have done business together," Nadia explained earnestly. "I thought, let's ask Sal for a loan. He has lived in this country many years, and owns three very successful restaurants." She gave Sal a sad look, but he just sat up straighter.

"May I say something?" Sal asked, once again dignified.

"Certainly," said the Mediator. He was relieved: both parties seemed to want him to understand what had happened. At the very least they had backed off from their initial confrontation.

"It was my pleasure to help them," said Sal. "I was helped by a relative when I first came to this country, and I always hoped to be able to pass that assistance on to someone else one day. I love Armin and Nadia. But I told them: we are friends, but this loan is a business contract. I loaned them $125,000 and told them that I expected to be paid back within one year, and they agreed."

When Sal finished speaking, the Mediator reflected sympathetically, "It's always a difficult situation when we mix friendship with business." Armin, Nadia, and Sal all nodded their agreement in unison, and Armin continued his story.

"Yes, well, we were both very grateful," he said, "and we invested Sal's money in our car wash. The business did well, but even after some months it was still not earning a profit. It was very discouraging, but we did not want to give up. We laid off one of our employees to save money, and we worked longer hours. We didn't spend a penny that didn't need to be spent." He glared at Sal.

"So then it was twelve months," he went on, "and Sal wanted his money, of course. We understood that. He's a businessman, and he made a loan. I explained that the business was still in the red and that we couldn't pay back all the money, but we would be glad to give him a partial payment, which he accepted."

"May I speak?" asked Sal.

"It's okay," said Armin to the Mediator.

"Yes, I accepted the partial payment, and Armin assured me I would receive the remainder shortly. But then another six months went by, and nothing. I'm a reasonable man, and they took advantage of my good nature and our family history. They gave me nothing!" His voice was rising, but he was still self-contained. "Then, one night, they walked into one of my restaurants for dinner. They were spending money on dinner, but they didn't have enough to pay me back? Of course, I told them to get out. I was furious. I told them that I didn't want to see them or talk to them again until they paid me what they owed me."

"How did you feel when Sal told you to leave?" the Mediator asked the couple. He was on dangerous ground here. He wanted both parties to hear and understand how each other felt, but he didn't want to risk another confrontation. But if one did flare up, perhaps it just meant that more angry energy needed to be released before these parties would really be able to talk about their situation. He didn't know too much about Lebanese culture, but he suspected that an angry and emotional argument, which might signal violence in the more buttoned-up culture he operated in, was the natural, accepted, and mutually understood method of communication in many parts of the world. He decided to let them have their comfort zone—within limits.

"We were in shock," Nadia replied. "We had no idea he was so angry. The last time we saw Sal we were on very good terms. I still don't understand what happened."

"You don't understand what happened?" Sal cut in. "We had an agreement and you took advantage of our relationship to break it. I was so angry that I called my lawyer, and he said I had the right to sue." He turned to the Mediator. "I agreed, and we filed suit immediately. I want the money they owe me, and I demand they transfer ownership of the car wash to me." Now Sal was looking angrily at Armin and Nadia.

"I see," said the Mediator. "Armin, can you tell me what happened on your end?"

"When we heard that he was suing us, we didn't know what to do. If he took the car wash, we would have nothing! We're doing the best we can. We don't want to lose our business. We felt like he had stabbed us in the heart. We were so glad when our lawyer told us we could go to mediation—to talk to Sal, to explain, just to talk to him, that's all we want. We just want to tell Sal how we feel, and try to work it out. I told Nadia, once we sit down together, Sal will remember how close we used to be, and maybe he will understand. But maybe I was wrong."

With that, Sal shoved his chair away from the table and began pacing around the room, clearly at the end of his rope. "*I* don't owe *you* anything!" he screamed, looming over Armin and shaking his fist.

Armin, in real emotional pain, suddenly began shouting at Sal in Arabic.

This was getting out of hand, and the Mediator rose out of his seat. But before he could get a word out, Armin stopped speaking and Sal stopped pacing and sat down. The Mediator didn't know what Armin had said, but he thought perhaps hearing words spoken in his native tongue had gotten through to businessman Sal on a visceral level. Even he had been affected by the raw emotion that Armin could express only in the one language the old friends still had in common. Whatever had been said, the atmosphere in the room had changed completely.

"I'm so sorry," said Sal, breathing hard and trying to comb his hair with his fingers. "I lost control, and for that I am sorry. I seem to have forgotten that friends are still friends, despite business dealings."

Armin and Nadia exchanged glances, and Armin said quietly, "Thank you, Sal. I accept your apology. We are so sorry we were not able to pay you back sooner. All we want is to be out of debt and have you back as our friend."

The Mediator decided it was time to step in. "You've made some progress here today," he said with approval, "and we're moving in the right direction. I think this would be a good time for all of us to take a short break, if that's all right with everyone." Both parties and their lawyers agreed, relieved to be able leave the pressure cooker for a few minutes. "After the break," the Mediator continued, "I'd like to speak to each side privately—with your lawyers, of course. As you know, this is a litigated case, and there's a trial pending. If we can resolve the legal issues quickly, we can get back to the issue of your friendship."

<hr />

After a short break, the Mediator sat down to speak privately with the couple and their attorney. They were calm now, and had already began to think about how they could solve their problem.

"Maybe there's some way you could shift your resources around so that Sal gets his money and you don't have to lose your business," said the Mediator.

"Yes," said the lawyer. "I was talking to Armin and Nadia about that just before you came in. They think that, with the recent upswing in the real estate market, they may be able to take out a second mortgage on their home. They have a very strong relationship with their bank, so establishing a line a credit is a very good possibility."

"Yes," Armin said hopefully, "we'll do whatever we can."

"That's a good idea," said the Mediator. "Let me talk to Sal and his lawyer and see how they would feel about that. Meanwhile, maybe the three of you can come up with some concrete ideas."

—◦◦◦—

But Sal's lawyer wasn't thrilled. He'd been using his time to get Sal worked up about foreclosing on the car wash, and he was single-mindedly sticking to that plan. "Wait a minute," the lawyer said, when the Mediator explained that Armin and Nadia might be able to find a way to raise the money and save the relationship. "From a legal point of view, *we've got them.* You might want a friendship, Sal, but you hired me to get you your money, and I'm telling you that you don't have to compromise!"

"Sal," the Mediator said calmly, "your lawyer is correct. From a legal standpoint you do seem to have a good case. But to go through the legal system and foreclosure and all that goes with it will take time—and it'll cost you a bundle in legal fees," he added, looking at Sal directly. "Honestly, I think there may be some ideas from the other room that will get you your money faster and save you having to go through this legal process."

Before Sal or his lawyer could cut in, the Mediator pressed on. "Listen, it's clear that this relationship is important to you. I know you want to work it out, or you wouldn't be here—you'd have left after the first five minutes." Sal sat impassively, listening but saying nothing. *Time to get tough,* thought the Mediator. "For Armin and Nadia, saving your relationship is their top priority. Do you want to invest in that relationship, or in burying them? You could just as easily ruin them financially. You have a choice here." As he spoke, the Mediator leaned in toward Sal closer and closer, with his lawyer in the background observing the conversation.

"What are their ideas?" said Sal finally, locking eyes with the Mediator. He was completely ignoring his lawyer, who was giving him frantic signals.

Good. Sal's ready to negotiate now, thought the Mediator, taking note of the shift. "I think it makes sense for you to hear Armin and

Nadia's ideas directly from them. I'd like to call for a meeting between the parties—without lawyers, if that's all right with you," he said, acknowledging Sal's attorney at last.

The lawyer shrugged, resigned. "Fine," he said. "Why not?"

When the Mediator got Armin, Nadia, and Sal in a room together, emotions rose to the surface quickly. But this time the mood was not one of rancor but of reconciliation.

"Sal," said Armin with prompting, "we want to take care of our debt." Nadia nodded intently, holding back tears. "Our lawyer tells us that your lawyer is threatening to take the car wash, but I can't believe you would really do that. You know that would ruin us. We came to this country to have a better life, like you. We know you wouldn't do this."

Sal responded in Arabic, and the three of them spoke in their native language for a while, no longer yelling. Nadia had stopped crying, and all three of them had their brows furrowed and clearly were trying to work something out. Once again, the Mediator had no idea exactly what they were saying, but their body language was universal: they were making progress.

"It sounds like you've found something that might make sense," he said when their conversation seemed to have ended. "Can you tell me what it is—in English?"

"Of course," said Sal, smiling. Relieved to be back in the role of helpful friend, he was transformed from uptight businessman to warm restaurateur. "They have worked out a way to pay me back; they'll take care of it. Our lawyers can handle the details. I've invited them to dinner at my restaurant, and they can keep the car wash. What do I want with a car wash anyway?"

At that they all laughed, and then they embraced. And just as suddenly as it had begun, it was over, and they began sharing old family stories.

"I'll leave you alone to reconnect," said the Mediator, and he went back to meet with the lawyers, who still had the issue of the money to deal with.

—∞—

"Congratulations," he said. "You guys did a great job. The case is now settled. Now can you tell me what happened?"

"Well," said the couple's lawyer, "they think they can pay back some of the money immediately. They've come up with several different options to obtain the funds. For the balance," he said to Sal's lawyer, "they're willing to commit to getting it to you in sixty days. Legally, of course, it will take much longer. Why don't you give them an opp—"

"Hey hey hey," interrupted Sal's lawyer. "They've had plenty of opportunity. If they can do it in sixty days, we'll agree. But no longer than that."

"Okay," said the lawyer. "They have already received preliminary approval for a Small Business Administration loan. I'll let them know you're open, but that it can't go longer than sixty days." Finally, they agreed to pay Sal $62,500 immediately—as soon as they secured the line of credit—and the remainder in sixty days. In return, Armin and Nadia could keep the car wash. Sal even said that the two could come into his restaurant any time for a free meal. Sal's lawyer seemed to have resigned himself to a reduced expectation on his legal fees. And the Mediator felt as if he'd taken a whirlwind trip to another world.

But he was still puzzled. As Armin and Nadia were leaving, the Mediator asked, "I don't speak Arabic, and I have no idea what the two of you were talking about, but I know you must have said something to Sal that caused the whole case to turn around. What was it?"

"Oh," Armin replied, smiling, "I reminded him that forty years ago in Beirut, when Sal was just a kid and his family was struggling, my father gave Sal a job at his dry cleaning plant. From the money he earned at that job, he was able to help out his family and save enough to start his own first small business."

WHAT HAPPENED?

It may seem that the Mediator did very little here, but look again. This case shows how a receptive mediator can set the stage and transform an inherently hostile and angry situation into one of mutual cooperation. Here, a long-term friendship was on the verge of destruction over a matter that was easily fixed. The Mediator's role was to manage the tension that existed between the desire to win at all costs and the intangible human concerns that formed the underlying foundation of the conflict.

Clearly, the he said–she said was getting in the way of resolution. In order to uncover the real concerns and remove the emotional barriers, the Mediator chose to disengage the problem-solving process and ask a series of open-ended questions that put the blame on no one, but merely sought to elicit information. From there, the balance of the process was a matter of listening and setting up the parties to communicate with each other.

The Mediator had a choice: he could allow the parties to tell their short version or their long version of the events. He decided to open up the floor to the long version, which could potentially have escalated the emotional tension. But because the Mediator served as a receptive audience, the tension was eventually transformed into constructive problem solving.

The Mediator influenced the parties first by establishing control and trust and then by drawing out information about each party in a constructive way. He established trust by following his instincts, which directed him to give the parties an environment that permitted their cultural background to rise to the surface. From their perspective, getting angry at each other and speaking loudly in their native tongue were useful and normal. The Mediator could have closed the door on their communications when they yelled at each other, but instead, he allowed things to sizzle up. He used empathy to encourage them to talk, and later allowed them to talk to each other for the first time in a long time, without their counsel present. This was also a dangerous move, particularly in a litigated case, as it's critical to recognize the importance of the attorney-client relationship, which is put in an awkward position when the attorneys are not present to protect their clients. This should only be done after appropriate consultation and with approval of counsel. The Mediator used this strategy only when he realized that they were committed to solving the dispute and wanted a chance to salvage their relationship.

The case also presented the issue of managing cross-cultural relationships. The parties were from Lebanon and had a strong connection to each other, yet they were battling in an American justice system that didn't recognize their complex relationship or allow them to speak their minds. The Mediator realized that this cultural connection could serve as a conduit into facilitating their communication. Recognizing that for them, anger and hostility might be more volatile and short lived than it would be for people raised in this country, the Mediator allowed the parties to be the center of attention and fully acknowledged their points of view. This created an emotional link between the Mediator and the parties to the dispute, and allowed them to develop trust in the mediation process. When the Mediator discovered that they really did like each other, which was not apparent at the outset, it was a matter of coming up with a simple solution to the money problem and empowering the parties to reconnect.

WHAT STRATEGIES CAN WE LEARN?

1. **Clear the air by encouraging cooperation and drawing parties into their stories.**

   When problem solving begins too early in a negotiation, parties are forced into taking positions that may soon result in an impasse. You can avoid this by priming the pump with thoughts of cooperation. Begin by painting a general picture of the success you envision for them, and draw the parties out so that they can tell their stories in a narrative fashion. Often, simply telling the story clears the air somewhat, and you can circle back to solving specific problems after it becomes clear that the climate has cooled down and both parties are ready to listen.

2. **Deconstruct the conflict by asking open-ended questions.**

   When the parties spend their time looking inward, focusing on their subjective concerns, they tend to get stuck in blaming each other. You can chip away at the uncertainties that form the basis of the dispute by doing something as simple as asking open-ended questions that provide forward-looking direction. This technique, in which you combine the skills of a cross-examiner with the tenderness of a psychotherapist, allows the parties to look at the case from a more objective vantage point. Problem solving begins when they look forward and begin to work together toward the same goal.

3. Listen for what's not being said.

Listening for the meaning behind the words is a vital tool for any mediator. You can uncover the true direction of the case by watching for clues in body language, in positive or negative responses, and in other unconscious giveaways. Conflicts are stressful, and under stress people go on automatic pilot. They quickly explain or defend themselves, using words that do not necessarily express what they really mean. Even as they are defending their positions, they are often anxious to reveal their secret objectives. It's easy to mistake their words as representative of their true wishes. But hidden behind words spoken quickly under stress is a wealth of information. Once uncovered, the information reveals motivation that you can use to craft a turning point in the negotiation.

4. Expose the parties to the underlying emotions of their perceived opponents.

You can help parties perceive each other more accurately by choosing to expose them to the emotional reaction of their adversary. This is a strategy that can easily backfire. But it can work if you prepare the ground well, making sure the parties understand that hearing and empathizing with each other's position, even if they don't fully agree, will help them bring about what they all want: closure. In a case where business or personal relationships are truly at stake, this technique can often unlock firmly closed doors.

CHAPTER TEN

TRANSFORMING THE JOURNEY OF REVENGE

"We feel terrible about what happened to Rudy," said the lawyer representing Dr. Sakura's malpractice insurer. "Dr. Sakura knows he made a mistake, and he's willing to pay for it. But Rudy's demand of $2 million is just too much."

From across the table, Rudy stared in bitter disbelief. "My life will never be the same," he said slowly. "And you think I'm asking too much? I'm not asking *enough!*"

"You know that the most the law allows is $250,000 for pain and suffering damages," said the Mediator quietly, taking his eyes off the pulsating vein on Rudy's forehead and looking at Rudy's lawyer. If the case went to trial, Rudy could receive a judgment for as much as the jury wanted to award, but, under the law, the judge would have to reduce it to $250,000. And, as Rudy's lawyer was well aware, the jury might decide to award Rudy *less* than $250,000—perhaps as little as $25,000—depending on what Rudy was able to prove for pain and suffering.

"I know that," the lawyer replied. "But as you can see, Rudy feels very passionate about what happened to him." In premediation briefings, Rudy's attorney had asked the Mediator to help him convince Rudy about the realities of the judicial system. Now he shot the Mediator a meaningful look.

Everyone the table agreed that what had happened to Rudy was pretty bad. Rudy, fifty-five, had started out with the best of intentions. A scientist, he read several newspapers and various medical journals regularly, and he knew that prostate cancer was one of the leading causes of death for men his age and older; at least one acquaintance had had a close call. He felt healthy and was pretty sure that nothing was wrong with him, but he believed in taking preventative health measures whenever possible, and his doctor agreed it was time for a blood test. This test was inconclusive, so he had a biopsy taken of his prostate.

Three weeks later, Rudy heard from Dr. Sakura, the young doctor who had performed the biopsy: the results were positive. He had prostate cancer. The doctor gave him three options: he would wait, checking periodically to see if the tumor had grown, he could have radiotherapy to try to shrink the tumor, or he could have surgery. This would solve the problem, the doctor advised, but there could be some associated side effects. Rudy was terrified. He did not want to have this cancer growing inside him one minute longer than necessary. He discussed his options with his wife, and they both agreed that he should have the surgery, a prostatectomy, as soon as possible. Despite the possibility of side effects, he was ready.

Rudy had the operation less than two months later and, as he had been warned, there were side effects. The surgery left Rudy with mild urinary incontinence, and he was unable to achieve an erection. Rudy was unhappy about the results, but he was philosophical—the surgery had been necessary to save his life. He planned to have a second surgery to insert an artificial sphincter into his penis to help him achieve an erection.

But three weeks after Rudy had the prostatectomy, Dr. Sakura called to say that he had made a mistake: he had read Rudy's X ray backwards, and the surgery had been performed on the wrong side. He would need a second surgery. Rudy was consumed by rage. The side effects were taking a toll, and he was already facing surgery for the implant. And now they were telling him he had to have another operation. He was so angry that he could not talk about it with anyone—not his doctor, not even his wife.

Rudy stayed angry and grew more bitter. He had the second surgery and the follow-up surgery. The side effects subsided, and he was able to get an erection again, but he was still livid about the mistake. He had endured another month of agony: two surgeries and more pain. He prided himself on being a professional, and he could not understand how anyone—especially a doctor, another scientist—could have been so careless and done something so damaging to him. His anger spilled over into everything he did. He could not concentrate at work, and he pushed his friends and family away when they tried to talk to him about it.

The one thing Rudy could focus on was revenge. He sued Dr. Sakura for $2 million—an amount that exceeded the highest amount of damages that had ever been awarded in a similar case and that recent tort reform legislation had made virtually impossible to award. He didn't care if he was being unrealistic. He was determined to get every last penny he could from them. He was prepared to fight a long battle in court if necessary.

Dr. Sakura, it's fair to say, was shaken. He had been practicing for only a few years, and nothing remotely like this had ever happened to him before. He openly conceded that he had been at fault in Rudy's case. He had made a mistake, and he was prepared to pay Rudy for it. However, he—and his insurer—thought that the amount of money Rudy was demanding was outrageously high. There was no way he was going to pay Rudy anywhere near what he was asking. The doctor didn't want to go to court, but he would if necessary: his lawyer had assured him that Rudy would not get an award in court as high as he wanted.

Meeting separately with Dr. Sakura and his counsel, the Mediator quickly recognized that Rudy's expectations were beyond the reach of the doctor.

"Obviously," the Mediator explained to Dr. Sakura, "Rudy is not taking into consideration the limitations on damages he can expect to receive in court. He's speaking from anger. I think if you can offer him something reasonable it will allow me to open up the dialogue about the realities of our court system."

"On behalf of Dr. Sakura, we are prepared to offer $75,000 to settle this case, but we will not go higher," the insurance company's lawyer said.

"Do I have your permission to offer that amount to Rudy? I need to warn you that if that is indeed your final offer, it doesn't leave us any room to negotiate."

"We don't want to upset him any more than he already is. Tell him we're sorry this has happened and offer him $50,000. Let's see what he says," said the insurance company's lawyer.

Before Rudy's attorney could respond to the Mediator's information, Rudy exploded. "You've got to be kidding," he yelled. "I can't believe you think that amount could possibly compensate for the pain and humiliation I've suffered." Rudy got up and paced around the room. He was so upset he could not stay in his seat.

The Mediator decided it was time to step in. He remembered Confucius's advice: "Before embarking on a journey of revenge, first dig two graves." The way this negotiation was headed, bodies would soon be flying everywhere. A little reframing of the situation was in order.

"Rudy," he began, "I think I understand where you're coming from, and I can certainly understand your anger. You took your doctor's advice to have surgery in good faith, you had a good attitude about the painful recovery and the side effects, and then you were kicked in the head with this need to have the whole thing happen *again*. You feel that you've been treated badly, and I can sympathize. You have suffered, much of it for no good reason, and you want to be compensated. It's natural to seek revenge, and a malpractice case is a common route—I should know; I see a lot of this in my work," he smiled, trying to ease the tension a bit. "In fact," he continued, "my wife's uncle recently took a similar situation all the way to a jury."

"Oh yeah?" said Rudy, on alert. "What happened?"

"The jury found for medical negligence, but they also found that the negligence didn't cause permanent injury, so he got zip. Essentially, he spent thousands in attorney fees on a case of revenge, and got nothing. He's pretty bitter about it."

"Well that really sucks," Rudy said. And then he suddenly began to unload everything he had been holding inside for months. "Do you know how it feels to know that you might never be able to have sexual intercourse again? What it's like to have to wear diapers because you can't control your bladder? To undergo weeks of painful recovery *and then have to do it all over again*? Just because some young doctor put the X ray on the light box *backwards*?" Rudy was shaking, and the Mediator was pale.

"I've been in and out of the hospital for months now. It's humiliating. I was in the middle of two research papers, and I've had to put all that aside. I'm in danger of losing my funding over this. My wife wasn't happy about the diapers and the sexual aspect, but I think it's my anger and frustration over this that's really getting to her. This nightmare has almost destroyed my career *and* my marriage. I just want what's coming to me, and I want that doctor to hurt as much as I did. I want him to understand how what he does can affect people." Then, just as suddenly as he had begun, he was finished.

The power of Rudy's emotional outburst reverberated in the room. Rudy was pale and shaking; even his lawyer was silent, clearly shocked by his client's rage. Then the Mediator said, "Rudy, I think we can all appreciate what you've been through, and I think it might be a good idea to take a break now." He asked Rudy and his lawyer to take a short break and regroup. "I'll be back in fifteen minutes to talk about next steps with both of you," he said.

———

Moving back to the room where Dr. Sakura and his insurance company's lawyer were waiting, the Mediator summarized Rudy's intense emotional outburst.

"I feel awful about what happened to Rudy," said Dr. Sakura, visibly upset. "I don't know how I made such a simple error. I guess I was just tired."

"We sympathize with Rudy," his insurance lawyer added, "but at the same time, we don't want to capitulate to his demands. Did they respond to our $50,000 offer?"

"I think the problem is that when Rudy heard that number he bounced off the walls and hasn't yet recovered. So, no, they haven't responded," observed the Mediator.

"What can we do? We obviously cannot negotiate against ourselves," said the lawyer.

"I'm banking on the fact that Rudy finally had a chance to let off some steam and that when I get back in the room, reasonable minds will prevail. At this point I recommend you do nothing and offer no more money. I'll tell you when I need you to make another move," said the Mediator.

—◦◦◦—

The first thing the Mediator noticed about Rudy was that the angry vein on his forehead had subsided. Rudy was clearly feeling better.

"Rudy," said the Mediator, "something seems to have shifted for you."

"Yeah, maybe so," said Rudy. "I thought I'd never get the anger out of my system, but my whole body feels lighter." He glanced at his lawyer, and it was clear they had been talking. "I know that I'll need to compromise in order to get this over with. I just want to get it resolved and get on with my life."

"That's good to hear," said the Mediator. "As you know, Dr. Sakura has made you an offer of $50,000. What are your thoughts?"

"We're willing to discuss realistic options," said Rudy before his lawyer could speak. "But not that one. Tell them I'm willing to take the maximum under the law, which is $250,000."

—◦◦◦—

Dr. Sakura and his lawyer were both encouraged and discouraged by Rudy's latest demand, but they agreed to think it over. At least progress had been made.

"We do appreciate Rudy's coming down out of the stratosphere," said the lawyer. "Unfortunately, he doesn't leave us much choice but to try the case, since we couldn't do any worse in court."

"I recognize that," said the Mediator. "Do you think he could get $250,000 if it went to court?"

"Anything is possible," replied the lawyer, "but our research and experience show that he'll probably get something in the $100,000 range. Go ahead and offer him the $75,000—but we're running out of room here," said the lawyer.

Before they had finished their meeting, however, the Mediator got word that Rudy wanted to see him.

—◦◦◦—

Rudy's lawyer said, "Rudy wants to end this thing now," he said. "We're ready to cut to the chase and give them our last offer that we feel we could take in good conscience to settle the case, but we really need your help."

"What have you got in mind?" asked the Mediator.

"Rudy is willing to take half of the limit he could receive in court, or $125,000. He understands the huge emotional investment involved in going to court, not to mention the costs in bringing in experts to prove our case. We think this is more than reasonable."

"What's interesting is that Dr. Sakura's insurer is willing to offer $75,000, so you're not that far apart," said the Mediator.

"You know that won't do it!" snapped the lawyer. "We're just not sure where to go from here. You know what we want. Do whatever you think is necessary to get it. Rudy has had enough of this situation."

"If you really need $125,000, then I would suggest that you counter with a higher number, perhaps $175,000, to see if you can get them to gravitate toward the middle," suggested the Mediator.

The lawyer exchanged a glance with his client and replied, "That's fine with us. Go ahead and do it."

—◦◦◦—

"I've got some good news," said the Mediator, addressing Dr. Sakura and his team. "Rudy is finally coming around and is willing to counter your $75,000 offer at $175,000."

"If I'm doing the math correctly, it looks like this case has settlement value slightly over six figures," observed Dr. Sakura's lawyer.

"You may be right. I realize you didn't want to pay more than $75,000, but considering the downside if this case goes any further, would you consider meeting in the middle at $125,000 if I could assure you of closure?" asked the Mediator.

"We wouldn't be happy about that number, and I would consider it only if you told me the case were over. I will not allow you to offer it, however," said the lawyer. This response told the Mediator that the lawyer didn't want to be put in a position of offering all of the party's money without the assurance of a deal, because he knew that that figure would then serve as a floor for future negotiations. If he wasn't assured of closure, he would likely authorize the Mediator to offer a smaller sum, with the idea that he could move up to $125,000 if he felt it would get the case done.

Sensing that the deal was in his hip pocket, the Mediator perked up. But before he could respond, Dr. Sakura chimed in.

Dr. Sakura looked glum. "Listen," he said, "I respect your expertise here, and I really do want to get this over with, but I've never been in this position, and I feel like I'm rushing into things. I'd like to get a second opinion before I consent to this thing."

"That's fine," said the Mediator. "Is that something you can do now? Is there someone you can call?"

"Yes, I'd like to call my colleague," said Dr. Sakura. "Give us about half an hour."

Returning to the room half an hour later, Dr. Sakura surprised everyone. "I have it on good authority that $125,000 is way too much to offer in a case like this," he announced.

The Mediator was puzzled. "Really? Who told you that?"

"You know I've never been in this situation before, but I realized I was in way over my head—I had no realistic way to make this decision. So I called my mentor, Dr. Whitcomb. He told me to get a second legal opinion, and gave me the number of a lawyer he knows who specializes in these cases. So I called him, and he told me that there's no way Rudy could get that much in court and that I should play hardball."

"That's interesting," said the Mediator, making a successful effort not to show his annoyance. "Can you tell me the name of the lawyer who advised you?"

"Sure," said Dr. Sakura. "Greg Gunderson. Maybe you've heard of him." The Mediator started breathing again.

"Greg and I have been involved in many cases together," he said. "He knows how I work. I think he recognizes that I wouldn't support this type of settlement if it wasn't fair to everyone involved. Would you mind if I called him to chat for a moment? If Greg is willing to back me up at $125,000, are you willing to consent?"

"Yeah, okay, sure." Dr. Sakura was knocked off balance by the Mediator's unexpected one-two punch of ego and leverage, and he began to apologize. "I've never been sued before; I don't know what to do. Maybe I'm just getting too much advice."

But the Mediator was already getting Gunderson on the phone.

"Greg," said the Mediator. "How are you? I understand you gave some advice to one of the parties in a negotiation I'm handling—Dr. Sakura."

"Hey, I didn't know this was your case," said the lawyer. "What's the story?"

The Mediator sketched in the relevant details and said, "I know Rudy's not going to get $2 million out of this, but if it goes to a jury he's going to get something. And the doc here is going through agony being sued for malpractice. I know he just wants to get this tied up so he can go back to saving people's lives. The insurance carrier is willing to put $125,000 on it, and I highly recommend you back him up here."

"Hey," said Gunderson, "you and I have done a lot of good deals together, and I trust your instincts. If this is your recommendation, I'll recommend he takes it. Put him on the phone, and I'll tell him myself."

No graves to dig, the Mediator chuckled to himself, *just two live bodies who can get on with their lives.*

WHAT HAPPENED?

In this conflict, Rudy's anger was extremely strong and controlling. It was clear that Rudy desperately needed an atmosphere that would allow him to express his rage before he could get realistic about the settlement. The Mediator chose not to put Rudy in the same room as Dr. Sakura, sensing that the downside if Rudy went over the top outweighed any potential benefit. Letting people express anger to each other is not always the best approach to making a deal. Your task as mediator is to identify what would optimize the chances for settlement and simultaneously to address the concerns of the parties. Once Rudy expressed his rage to the Mediator about what happened to him, he was able to be more flexible and to reach a reasonable compromise settlement with the defendant.

But it turned out that simply venting wasn't the end of the story in this case. The Mediator had to go beyond the table to find the decision makers—an outside doctor and an outside lawyer were vetoing the deal. The Mediator was able to leverage his relationship with the outside lawyer to make the deal happen, a tricky move that required the outside lawyer to have trust and confidence in the Mediator.

In order to persuade Rudy to become more realistic and discuss a settlement within the limits set by the legislature, the Mediator shared the experience of his wife's uncle, a story that Rudy could buy into. If you can establish common ground between you and the parties, they can often achieve peace of mind, which leads them toward agreement. By making this connection, you reduce the fear and suspicion the person has about you and your role and increase your ability to be directive with your upcoming recommendation about not going to court.

What Strategies Can We Learn?

1. **Use reframing as a tool to disperse attitudes of anger and revenge.**

   People who are angry and seeking revenge tend to see their story in stark black-and-white terms—a perspective that does not lead to good decision making. To help parties let go of this mind-set, reframe their story for them by summarizing its essence in simple terms, acknowledging their goals and desires for the outcome of the case. By doing this you demonstrate your understanding and acceptance of them and encourage their trust in you. Once they see that you are not the enemy, you are in a position to help bring them into a zone of agreement.

2. **"Sell" your personal philosophy and make recommendations based on that.**

   In order for the parties to accept your recommendations, you first need to get them to buy in to your philosophy— whatever that might be. For example, in this case the Mediator told the story of his wife's uncle in order to sell the idea that it can be dangerous to go to court. Sharing a story like this helps you make a personal connection. Once the parties accept your philosophy—"I could lose this case in court; maybe I should just work on settling now"—they achieve a certain peace of mind that eventually leads to agreement.

3. Leverage your relationships.

Deal making may not always happen in the caucus room, but
can sometimes go as far as the back room. Because you
have now gotten them to buy in to your philosophy, the
parties will be amenable to your suggestions. If you have a
contact that might be an influence in the final decision
making, you can offer to leverage your relationship with
that contact to help the parties achieve agreement. Only
do this if you have the agreement of both parties.

CHAPTER ELEVEN

A "HATS-ON" APPROACH

The Mediator was out of his element. It had been warm when he left home, but here in eastern Canada it was beginning to get cold. *I forgot to bring a hat!* he said to himself, immediately recognizing the irony: this whole case was going to be about head coverings.

———

The dispute centered on a two-story building located in the heart of an Orthodox Jewish neighborhood in a Toronto suburb. The building was owned by Mr. Gold, a wealthy philanthropist who was well known and respected in the local Jewish community. For many years, Mr. Gold had leased the building to an Orthodox Jewish school. When the school administrator, Rabbi Frank, asked Mr. Gold to consider selling the building to the school, Mr. Gold replied that he would do so, for $2 million—but they would have to raise the funds within thirty days. When the school was unable to raise the funds in the time frame allotted, the deal fell through.

Word traveled quickly in the community that Mr. Gold was willing to sell the building, and he soon made another deal. After some dickering, he agreed to sell the building for $1.8 million to the Fine Group, an investment group of secular Jews. Rabbi Frank was very angry. What would happen to his school? It was a central part of the community. He was not about to sit idle while their school building was sold to someone else, let alone a secular group. He decided to contest the contract in court.

This move provoked a dispute that threatened to split two very public groups in the Jewish community, the Orthodox and secular

Jews, and Mr. Gold would be regarded as the wedge that drove these groups apart. This was especially troubling to him, because he did not want to see his name and reputation dragged through the mud. Although the secular group wasn't troubled by the prospect of a court case, Mr. Gold and Rabbi Frank opted for negotiation. In fact, Rabbi Frank had originally asked to have this dispute moved from outside the secular system to the traditional Jewish religious or civil court of law, the Bet Din. But when both Mr. Gold and the secular group objected, it was agreed that the case would be decided by a mediator—but not a local mediator, who all the parties felt might be biased. And he had to be Jewish. What the parties didn't realize was that the mediator doesn't make a decision, but rather helps facilitate communication, put deals together, and reduce conflict. The parties would soon learn this when they met their mediator.

The Mediator fit the criteria: he was not Canadian, and he had been *bar mitzvah*. And because of that, he knew that a big part of his strategy would involve the question of whether or not to walk into the mediation room wearing a *kippah*. The wrong decision could end the negotiation before it had even begun.

The head covering in question is variously known as a *kippah* (Hebrew) and a *yarmulka* (Yiddish). By whatever name, the purpose of the skullcap is to reinforce the idea of God as higher authority, and wearing it shows respect for God and God's laws. In his daily life, the Mediator, like most secular Jews, never wore a kippah. In fact, he didn't even own one. On his annual visits to temple on high holidays, he took one from the box of cheap black-and-white satin skullcaps and returned it on his way out.

After he had agreed to participate in the case, he wondered what the parties were expecting of him—not only in his grasp of the facts but also in terms of his potential biases. Mediators are often called *neutrals*—and neutrality seemed especially crucial in this case. If he wore a kippah to show respect to the sensibilities of the Orthodox Jews, the secular group might lose faith in his impartiality. If he chose *not* to wear a kippah, the secular Jews probably wouldn't give it a second thought, but the religious Jews might take it as a sign that he was sympathetic to their opponents' cause. Regardless of his decision, there would be an impact.

In the end, he decided to enter the room wearing the kippah. He believed that this small piece of cloth would serve to open opportunities on the Orthodox side of the table and was not very likely to evoke suspicion on the secular side. But now he was faced with another question: What kind of kippah should he wear? Orthodox Jews often wore colorful knitted kippah, held on with pins. Scholarly Jews might wear large black felt or satin skullcaps. Ultra-Orthodox Chasidic Jews might even wear fur hats on the Sabbath. There was a different kippah for every sect and personality. In the end the Mediator decided to stay nonaligned, and borrowed a simple black satin kippah from the rabbi at his temple. But when he walked the chilly streets of eastern Canada on the way to the negotiation, he thought that the warm fur hat might have been the right choice!

—◦◦◦—

"As far as we're concerned," said the lawyer for Mr. Fine's secular group, "we're ready to take this case to court right now. It's clearly a contract dispute as to who had the rightful opportunity to buy the building. The Fine Group signed a bona fide purchase agreement for $1.8 million, and we're confident of victory at trial." Mr. Fine, sitting quietly and calmly, looked almost bored. The Mediator had to agree with the attorney—there was no legal reason for Fine's group to negotiate. The Mediator was conscious of the slight but unaccustomed weight of the kippah as he looked at the other participants: secular group—no kippahs; Rabbi Frank—black velvet kippah with silver embroidery; Mr. Gold—simple satin kippah, similar to the Mediator's. The Mediator hoped he'd made the right decision.

In contrast to the cool Mr. Fine, the more emotional Rabbi Frank—who desperately wanted to keep his school—was ready to come out fighting. "I could not agree less," he said. "Not only do we have Canadian law on our side, we also have moral law, biblical law, and the backing of the entire Jewish community." He glared at Mr. Gold. Caught in the middle, the wealthy man said nothing. His attorney, sitting to his left, seemed more like an appendage than a colleague.

The Mediator, who had gotten a crash course in Canadian law from his colleague in Toronto (whose office he had borrowed for the meeting), thought the law rested pretty firmly with the secular group, as it would in the United States. The real problem was going to be keeping peace in the community.

"As you know, I'm new to your community," said the Mediator. "I'd like to begin by meeting with each party separately, to get a good idea of where each of you stands in this matter. If it's all right with everyone, I'd like to begin with Mr. Gold—after all, it's his building that's the focus of our discussion."

—◦◦◦—

Mr. Gold seemed pleased to be first, and he shook the Mediator's hand as they sat down together in a smaller private room. "I'd like to get this matter settled as quickly as possible," he said. "All I've ever wanted to do was sell the building; I didn't think a simple business deal was going to turn into a debate on my moral rectitude!" His attorney sat quietly and said nothing, clearly only there for effect.

The Mediator could see that Mr. Gold was used to making his own deals, so he got right to the point. "If I can get one of these parties to buy the property, will that make you happy?"

"Absolutely," said Mr. Gold.

"Great," said the Mediator. "What number do you feel comfortable with?"

"I'd like to get $1.8 million for it," he replied immediately. "That's the price I agreed on with Fine. Why should I come down from that?"

"Very good," said the Mediator. "Let me see what I can do."

They shook hands again. As the Mediator opened the door to leave the private office, Mr. Gold said, "Look, I'm not interested in playing hardball here. I have to live in this community after all of this is over. Whatever you do, I would appreciate it if you'd just make sure I come out of this with my good name intact."

—◦◦◦—

Next, the Mediator met with Mr. Fine, who had been waiting patiently for his turn.

"Mr. Fine," said the Mediator, "I appreciate your being here today. I know when you made your offer on the building that you didn't realize you would be getting into such an entanglement."

"That's quite an understatement," Mr. Fine responded with a tight smile. "Rabbi Frank and his school can certainly find another building to rent."

"Yes," said the Mediator, "I'm sure they could. But I'd like you to think about how it would look to the community if you displaced them. They are a devout Orthodox group, and I understand they have been in that building for decades. From what I understand, and from what Rabbi Frank said earlier, they will not go happily or quietly."

"This building is a good investment," insisted Mr. Fine. "You can see for yourself that the neighborhood is undergoing a renaissance. Why should we let that go just because the school couldn't get a building committee together?"

"Maybe there's a way to achieve both of your goals," mused the Mediator, thinking out loud. "Would you mind if I spoke to Rabbi Frank for a moment?"

"Not if it will get this mess settled," said Mr. Fine.

———

The Mediator knew that Rabbi Frank would be the key player: he didn't own the building, but he held all the cards. If he felt that his school was being displaced unfairly, he would not hesitate to bring it to the community, tying up the sale in litigation and dragging Mr. Gold's name through the mud. It was at this moment that the Mediator most depended on the symbolic power of the kippah to help him.

The two men shook hands and sat down. "Rabbi Frank," said the Mediator, "if you don't mind, I'd like to tell you what I believe you'd like to gain from this negotiation."

"Certainly," said the rabbi, a bit bemused but curious.

"I believe your main goal is not so much to buy the building as it is to be assured of permanency and respect. You want your school to remain in its traditional surroundings and continue to be an integral and valued part of your community, and you don't want to be chased out because of a business deal gone wrong."

"That's right," agreed the rabbi.

"If we can get Mr. Gold and Mr. Fine to work out a solution that will allow that to happen, would you be open to hearing it?"

"I would," said the rabbi. "But we would also like to know that, if we were able to raise the money, we might someday be able to buy the building for ourselves and thus assure the future education of our students' children and their children."

"I think I know a way that can be arranged," said the Mediator.

———

In a final meeting with Mr. Fine, the Mediator decided the timing was ripe to make a specific proposal that addressed what he considered the overall goals of each side.

"Mr. Fine," said the Mediator, "this has obviously been a long day, and we are now coming to the end. Each side has given me many ideas that might solve this case, and I have taken them all into consideration. I would like now to ask you to consider the following proposal. If you endorse it, I would make the same proposal to the rabbi. I'm sure Mr. Gold will go along with it, since he would be getting exactly what he is looking for."

"I'm all ears," said Mr. Fine, "but I still have my doubts, since Rabbi Frank has been so stubborn throughout this mess. Maybe you will surprise me, young man!"

"All right, here's the proposal: you pay Mr. Gold $1.8 million for the property, as already agreed. Rabbi Frank and his school become your tenants on a long-term lease, perhaps ten years, at a modest discount. We can work out the details in a few minutes. The school will have an option to buy the property from you in five years at fair market value, which would be determined by a neutral appraiser recommended by the local appraisal society."

Mr. Fine looked interested and concerned at the same time.

"I appreciate your fine work," said Mr. Fine, "and the proposal seems to make sense to me. However, given the attitude of the rabbi, I'm afraid that if I let you tell him that I would do that deal, he would ask for more."

"Your point is well taken," acknowledged the Mediator. "If you are telling me now that you would endorse this proposal, I can phrase it to the rabbi in a way that doesn't commit you and actually protects you in the event of future negotiations."

"As long as you can make sure that I'm not put in a vulnerable position, I'm going to trust that you know what you're doing. You have my endorsement," Mr. Fine acknowledged.

"Great! I'm going to speak to the rabbi privately. With luck, I'll be back in a few minutes," the Mediator said enthusiastically.

"Rabbi Frank, thank you for your patience today. I realize it's been a long day, and we're still not there yet. As I told you this morning, flexibility and patience are the currency of this process. We're now at the point where I think I have something that will pay off for you," said the Mediator.

"You sound very confident. I like that," said an optimistic Rabbi Frank.

"What I'm about to propose is something I am concurrently proposing to the Fine Group. I have already given them the details and have asked them to think about it for a few minutes and let me know if it is acceptable. I told them, and I'm telling you, that it's not negotiable. I simply want each side to either accept it or reject it. I can tell you that I wouldn't make this proposal unless I was fairly confident that it made sense for both sides based on the information each of you shared with me during the day."

The rabbi was curious. He had never been presented with such a black-and-white option before. After all, everything seemed to be negotiable.

"Are you saying that you are not looking for a counteroffer to your proposal?" he said in disbelief.

"That's exactly right," the Mediator replied. "This is a final option, and I don't make it lightly. I think we have gotten to know each other well enough today that I hope you trust I wouldn't lead you astray. I recognize it's a bit unconventional to ask you to accept or reject, but I'm confident that you will find it appealing."

Despite misgivings about the approach, the rabbi was indeed comfortable with the Mediator and began to see him as a trusted adviser. He was willing to hear the proposal.

—◁◦◦▷—

"I think we all did a very good day's work here," said the Mediator.

The gathered parties, all tensions dissipated, agreed. The Mediator had brokered a deal that promised something for everyone. The Fine Group would buy the building from Mr. Gold, for the agreed price. They would then lease the property to Rabbi Frank's school group for ten years, at a discount. After five years, the school would have an option to buy the building from the Fine Group at fair market value. So the Fine Group got their equity buildup for the next five years, Rabbi Frank's school got discounted rent and an option to buy, and Mr. Gold got to sell the property and keep his reputation.

"I believe this calls for a celebration," said the Mediator, producing some paper cups and a bottle of kosher wine he had bought just for the occasion. And they raised their cups in a toast.

—◁◦◦▷—

After it was all over, the Mediator wondered if the kippah had really made a difference. He asked his Canadian colleague to approach the parties about their reaction, partly out of curiosity and just in case he ever had to make a similar decision.

"Interestingly," his friend reported back, "Rabbi Frank told me that he felt it showed a connection and a sensitivity to their way of life. He said that he knew immediately that you were not an observant Jew"—here the Mediator winced—"but that wearing the kippah showed that you had *kavod*, or honor, for them."

"The secular group, on the other hand, initially had reservations about you. They were suspicious—whose side were you on? But as the negotiations progressed, they saw that the kippah allowed you to indirectly communicate with Rabbi Frank in a way that they could not. Since their ultimate goal for the meeting was to resolve the dispute, they thought that your 'connection' with the Orthodox Jews, whatever it was, would help them get there faster."

WHAT HAPPENED?

Preparation—especially when it is applied with a view to the dispute as a whole—is one key to success. Here the Mediator's success in reaching agreement between the parties had as much to do with his knowledge of the interplay between various Jewish groups, and the expectations they would have of him and the negotiation, as it did with the facts of the case. Similarly, wearing the kippah during the negotiation allowed the Mediator to use the symbol of the skullcap to break down barriers and make personal connections. It was the one way the Mediator could speak the language of all the parties and get in synch with their objectives.

Mediators must abstract what is common to all parties, ignoring for the time being the differences among them. In this case, as in most cases, the Mediator was looking for common goals that would make the discussion possible. He realized quickly that even though the negotiation had begun somewhat combatively, the parties were not really in conflict: Mr. Gold wanted to sell, the Fine Group wanted to buy and then lease the building, and Rabbi Frank wanted to stay put and consider buying down the line. Once he determined this, creating a deal that would work for everyone was not difficult.

The real challenge was coming up with a process to close the deal. The parties were typical negotiators, coming from a culture where horse trading was widely accepted. Once the Mediator was able to come up with a solution that no longer required any horse trading, he had to convince the parties to trust his instincts and allow him to serve not only as an adviser but also in a sense as the rabbi to the entire group—the person they were looking to for spiritual and practical guidance. Having achieved this trust, he was able to make a proposal that required no further concessions.

WHAT STRATEGIES CAN WE LEARN?

1. Use the symbolic process to your advantage.

In communication, words aren't everything. Some messages are conveyed through certain symbols, and in order to get our message across we sometimes need to make a conscious effort to connect with these symbols. Wearing the skullcap was a symbol that sent a nonverbal message that the Mediator understood the language the parties were speaking—he understood where they were coming from. This opened the door for them to trust the Mediator and permitted the parties to reveal their goals without compromising their position.

2. **Make a settlement recommendation only when you sense all parties are receptive to change.**

Timing is everything. The key to making a settlement recommendation is to create an environment in which all the parties are truly receptive to change. This requires using your instinct to determine when it is more likely than not that the parties will say yes to your suggestions. This instinct is built on the signals you have received from the parties after you have floated ideas and watched their response, as well as on the information you have learned about their ultimate goals in the negotiation.

3. **Create a sense of urgency about closure.**

Once you have determined the point of no return in the process and you are certain that the conditions are right for closure, it's time to drive the parties to the end of the deal. To do this, make a recommendation that essentially packages the dispute in a manner that doesn't require any further negotiation.

PART TWO

"SHOW ME THE MONEY (OR SOMETHING OF EQUAL VALUE)!"

Creative Solutions

CHAPTER TWELVE

LIAR, LIAR!

She's the perfect sexual harassment plaintiff, the Mediator thought as Andrea sat down at the conference table with her attorney. Dressed demurely in a navy blue suit and white blouse, her dark curly hair framing her face, she looked the part of the conservative young businesswoman. It was easy to imagine that she had been victimized by her boss, Sam, who was already sweating and looking uncomfortable, grateful for the oversized boardroom chairs that contained his bulk.

"Sam Dement is the kind of guy who just won't take no for an answer," Andrea's lawyer began, staring pointedly at Sam. The disheveled defendant nervously combed through his beard with his fingers and looked miserably down at the table.

"It's not hard to see how it happened," he continued. "A one-man office with one part-time receptionist—no one was there to stop him, and she couldn't afford to lose the job, even a low-paying one like that. He practically held her captive! We believe that $750,000 is just compensation for the humiliation he forced on her." The Mediator decided to break into this impassioned plea. Andrea's lawyer was clearly ready for court, a fact that was not lost on Sam and his attorney.

"Andrea," the Mediator began, "can you tell me your side of the story?"

"Well," she replied, smoothing her skirt, "every time I came to work he asked me for a date. At first I tried to be polite. I told him I had a boyfriend. After a while I just told him he wasn't my type and I wasn't interested, but he just wouldn't listen. I couldn't believe it—I mean, he's been married for twenty years. He's got two kids. Honestly, I thought the whole thing was disgusting. Then one afternoon when I was making coffee in the office kitchen he went completely over the edge." She stopped, seemingly on the edge of tears. "He wanted to, you know, pleasure himself while I watched. I told him this job didn't pay me enough to stand for this, and I quit."

The Mediator had already been briefed on the story, but Andrea's vivid rendition had left an indelible image in his mind.

"Sam Dement must be made to take responsibility for his obnoxious actions," Andrea's lawyer said. "He's got a lot to lose if this case goes to trial," he continued. "He claims we're asking for a lot of money in damages, but I would ask him to carefully consider exactly how much it's worth to him to preserve what's left of his reputation."

Andrea sat quietly during this speech, and Sam seemed shell-shocked. He was in deep trouble. Not only did he risk losing his family over this, but his job was also in jeopardy. Sam, the failure in his successful family, had his job only through the grace of his younger brother, who ran the family business and had given Sam a small branch office to manage at the behest of their mother. But even his mother would not be able to keep his brother from firing Sam if scandal threatened the good name of the business. That's why Sam had asked for mediation in the first place.

Sam's attorney broke the silence and addressed the Mediator: "I wonder if Sam and I could meet with you privately before we go any further?"

—◈—

In sexual harassment cases, passions are high, and deception or stretching the truth is a given: clients can lie to lawyers, and lawyers can then unintentionally lie to opposing counsel. One side blames the other, who vehemently denies that anything ever happened. Lawyers often end up accepting their client's point of view and can easily end up lying to themselves. In court, where the search for truth is the focal point, this web of lies can be very hard to untangle. In a mediation, however, determination of right and wrong is beside the point: the parties are looking for a deal, not absolution. But nothing had prepared the Mediator for the particular spin on he said–she said that he was about to encounter in the case of Andrea and Sam.

"I'd like Sam to explain his side of the story," the lawyer began once they had closed the door on the small office.

"Okay," he began slowly, "I know I shouldn't have crossed the line and touched Andrea."

"No one's accusing you of having sex with Andrea," the Mediator replied, somewhat puzzled.

"I know," said Sam, "but that's what happened. There was a touching period, lots of it in fact. Basically, she's lying about everything." He paused. "Because I still owe her $2,000 from our arrangement."

The Mediator was stunned. *Arrangement?* What was going on here?

"See, I've been having sex with Andrea for more than two years—practically the entire time she's been working for me. No one could live on her salary; she works three days a week and makes, what, ten bucks an hour? Get real." In a weird way, he seemed to be enjoying himself even though he was still sweating bullets.

"You've seen Andrea, and you've seen me. Do you think she'd sleep with me out of love? She charged me for her sexual services, and I was happy to pay her for them. But it got a little out of hand. For a long time I was paying her in cash. Then I guess I got careless and started writing her personal checks. Then my wife wanted to redecorate the house, my oldest boy is starting college in an Ivy League school—the money was just pouring out of me, and I couldn't afford Andrea anymore. In the end, I owed her a couple thousand dollars. When I couldn't come up with the cash, she got mad and went to the EEOC—the Equal Employment Opportunity Commission, can you believe it?—and said I was harassing her. From there she hooked up with this lawyer, and here we are." Sam sat with his arms folded across his chest, emboldened by the truth.

"And you're telling me this—why? You know this admission might expose you to even more liability . . ." The Mediator was at a loss, looking back and forth between Sam and his attorney.

"Because I'm tired of this life. Believe it or not, I'm sorry about using Andrea that way, I'm sorry about betraying my marriage. If this case goes to court and my wife finds out about what really happened, I'll lose everything that matters to me. I just want to put this behind me and start fresh. But I don't want to pay what Andrea's asking for; that's extortion as far as I'm concerned."

"You know that consent could be considered a complete defense to a sexual harassment case," Sam's lawyer chimed in.

"Yeah," said the Mediator, "but the jury will know that you're not supposed to dip your pen in the company inkwell. There's a good chance that Sam's behavior will not sit well with the jury."

"Sure," the lawyer agreed. "But as you can see, Sam is anxious to make sure his family doesn't find out. We're ready to resolve this now, provided the terms are fair. But you need to give the plaintiff and her lawyer the message that we know this was a consensual relationship."

"All right," said the Mediator, "but we're still stuck in a he said–she said situation unless you can actually prove that you paid Andrea for services rendered."

Sam and his lawyer exchanged glances. "Would you mind stepping out for a minute?" the lawyer asked the Mediator. "I need to talk to my client in private."

Out in the hall, the Mediator listened to the hum of their raised voices. He often let parties have their own space to figure things out, and these two really had something to talk about. Soon, the door opened.

"Come back in," said the lawyer. "We have something to share with you, but we don't know how to use it. We can prove that Sam actually paid Andrea for sex, but you need to keep it confidential for now." Now they both looked nervous. This must be pretty hot if they weren't even sure they wanted to share it with the Mediator.

The lawyer continued. "You said that unless we can prove payment it's going to be a tough case, right? Well, here's the proof."

At that, Sam lifted his bulging briefcase from the floor, laid it on the table, and pulled out five cancelled checks totaling approximately $7,000, drawn on his personal account and made payable to Andrea. "These checks are what I paid Andrea for sex over two months. Believe me, this amount exceeds her monthly salary by more than a few thousand dollars!" Sam was embarrassed yet relieved at this opportunity to share his moment of truth with someone who would listen.

The Mediator felt in his gut that Sam was not lying and that Andrea's lawyer was probably completely in the dark. Still, he was thinking that it wasn't important to be judgmental about the truth. He recognized that the prize in this case was not necessarily the truth, but getting the parties to reach an agreement.

"I'd like to talk to Andrea's attorney privately," he said. "May I have your permission to use this information about the checks and the consensual relationship if I deem it necessary?" he said.

"Look, this is our case," replied Sam's lawyer. "We have to trust you as the mediator, but you can understand that we feel pretty exposed right now. We just want you to guide us—do what you feel will best move us forward." He thought for a minute and said, "Okay, go ahead. We'll wait here."

Now the Mediator was faced with a choice: he could create some drama by confronting Andrea with Sam's story. She'd been pretty calm up to this point, but he had little doubt that her response to Sam's charges would be to deny them, and probably angrily. The better choice, he thought, would be to deal with it in a more businesslike way by talking to her attorney in private and gently prodding him about his client's relationship with the boss. The attorney seemed to be the driving force in this case anyway. For the most part, Andrea just seemed to be along for the ride.

He returned to the office where Andrea and her lawyer were waiting. "Can we step outside for a minute?" he said to the lawyer. "I'd like to ask you a question."

"Well?" said the lawyer, closing the door. "What's going on?"

"I'm wondering how much Andrea has really told you about what went on in that office," the Mediator began.

"You know what happened," the lawyer replied impatiently. "What's your agenda here? Do you think you know something I don't know?"

"I'd just like you to talk to your client one more time about the extent of her personal and physical relationship with Mr. Dement," he said gently, but firmly.

"What do you mean 'physical' relationship? We're not alleging that here," the lawyer replied.

"I realize that, but there are some things I learned from Sam that might be useful to you in evaluating the case, and I'm not at liberty to disclose them at this time. I just thought it would be in your best interest to question your client one more time before we jump into this negotiation."

"Fine," the lawyer replied, "but I can't see where you're going with this." He went back into the office and closed the door firmly behind him.

He returned quickly. "Andrea denies that she and Sam ever had any type of physical relationship. Do we have a response to our $750,000 demand to settle?"

The Mediator saw that Andrea's attorney was going to need some tough love in order to consider another side of the story. He would need to evaluate Sam's credibility before he could reevaluate his own case. And because Sam's story was so over the top, the Mediator doubted the lawyer would believe it secondhand.

"I have an idea. Please go back in and wait with Andrea for a few minutes," said the Mediator, heading back down the hall.

———

"Sam," he said, "I'd like to ask your lawyer to allow you to meet with Andrea's lawyer alone."

"What do you mean alone?" the lawyer shot back. "I'm his representative."

"Look," the Mediator explained calmly, "Andrea's lawyer will need to evaluate Sam's credibility if he's going to recommend that his client reduce her expectations on this case. So that he'll have no excuse to question Sam's credibility, I'd like to put Sam in a room with him so that the unfiltered truth will come out. He'll see that there was no chance for Sam to prepare any answers, and he can draw his own conclusions. Naturally, I'll remain in the room as the referee so he won't jump all over Sam, but I would like to give him this opportunity to question your client."

Slowly, the lawyer said, "Okay. I've never done anything like this before. I guess I'm going to have to trust your instincts here."

"Great," said the Mediator. He trotted back down the hall to speak to Andrea's lawyer.

—◦◦◦—

"Andrea," the Mediator said as he walked into the plaintiff's office, "your lawyer and I need to do some work together, but you don't need to be involved. This might be a good chance for you to take a break—stretch your legs, get some coffee." She looked to her lawyer confirmation. He was puzzled by the Mediator's request, but just said,

"Go ahead. I'll call you back in when we're ready."

As soon as Andrea left, he said, "What's going on here?"

"There's a little more information we need to exchange before we can continue this negotiation," replied the Mediator. "I'd like you to meet with Mr. Dement.

"I think we may make better progress if you have the chance to question Sam privately about his relationship with Andrea. By the way, Sam is willing to talk to you alone—without his attorney—so you can evaluate his story. I'll be the referee, but there will be a few ground rules." The attorney looked excited but dubious.

"First," the Mediator continued, "you've got to ask him some open-ended questions so he has a chance to tell you what's on his mind. Second, I can stop the questioning at any time. And third, I request that there be no argument or debate about his story. The whole purpose is for you to evaluate his credibility, because I feel that his story is in sharp contrast to what your client has told you."

"I look forward to it," said the lawyer.

—◦◦◦—

Sam sat in his chair, nervous and sweating. Andrea's lawyer was in gear, and he began cross-examining Sam as if they were in the courtroom. "Mr. Dement," he began formally, "I understand you have some things to tell me about your relationship with Andrea."

"Yes," he replied quietly. "She's lying. She knows I owe her some money but nothing near what you have been asking for."

The lawyer looked a bit confused. "What are you talking about?"

"Ask Andrea," Sam shot back, his voice suddenly much stronger. "She knows exactly how much I owe her. We've been sleeping together for a couple of years, and she's been charging me for sex. When I ran out of cash, she decided to bring a claim."

"Hold on a minute," said the lawyer with some heat. "My client never had any contact with you, and you know it. You disgust me."

Sam flushed deep red and sat forward in his chair. "Counselor, the Mediator thought it would be helpful for me to explain my side of the story to you. Believe me, I understand that what I did was wrong. But if you want to insult me like that, we don't have to talk."

"Why don't you let Sam explain a bit more," the Mediator said in a calm tone. "I think you may begin to see a different picture here."

"Okay, I'll listen. But I'm very leery of what he has to say," replied the lawyer, unwilling to back down too much. "Go on, Mr. Dement."

Sam sat with his arms folded across his chest and told his story. "When Andrea was first hired, I was lonely. She and I were the only two people in the office, so it was kind of an intimate situation. My relationship with my wife was on the rocks, and from time to time Andrea and I would talk about it. She seemed to understand. Then, not too long after she was hired, she started seducing me." Andrea's lawyer was shaking his head, completely unbelieving.

"Look, I know it sounds crazy, but that's what happened," Sam insisted. "Anyway, after the first time, I wanted more. She told me she would continue only if I paid her for it, which I gladly did.

"We began to have sex every time she came to work. It was sort of a joke because she charged various amounts for different sex acts, kind of like a menu of services. I paid her in cash, and things were just fine. Then I started to run out of cash, so I wrote her a few checks out of a separate account I maintained. When that account disappeared, she got mad, and we got into a fight."

The lawyer was taking copious notes, obviously in shock but unwilling to admit that Sam's story might have validity. "Where did you allegedly have these affairs?"

"Well, there weren't a lot of choices. Sometimes we'd do it in the computer room, and other times we just locked the front door and did it in the reception area. She was very creative as long as she knew she was getting paid." Now Sam was really enjoying himself.

These details finally seemed to have an effect. Andrea's lawyer was clearly shocked and dismayed, and he excused himself to confer with Andrea.

———— ❧ ————

Not surprisingly, Andrea issued a series of denials, which her lawyer dutifully brought back to the table. "Andrea says that the $7,000 represented bonuses and raises that Sam promised her," he reported. But he couldn't help but recognize as truth Sam's calm responses to his questions. Despite the show of denials, the Mediator could see that both parties were now eager to move toward settlement.

Finally, Andrea's lawyer, still trying to save face, dropped his demand dramatically to $350,000. Sam's lawyer, knowing they had the evidence, countered with an offer of $40,000. In the end, Andrea accepted $125,000—a nice increase for her over the $2,000 Sam owed her. It wasn't exactly a win for Sam, mused the Mediator, but it was a price Sam seemed more than willing to pay to keep the case from exploding in open court and to keep his marriage and family intact.

WHAT HAPPENED?

Once the Mediator had heard Sam's version of the story, he knew he had to create a safe space in which Andrea's lawyer, predisposed to believe Andrea, could really hear and accept what Sam had to say. Knowing that Andrea's lawyer appeared ready and willing to take this case to trial, the Mediator decided that the best way to get him to appreciate the new information was to create a rhythm similar to the one the lawyer created in the plenary meeting at the beginning of the session. In other words, he wanted to organize a trial-like atmosphere in which the lawyer would discover for himself whether the evidence supported his case. This was done through a structured deposition-like meeting, without Sam's lawyer.

The Mediator's shuffling the deck by removing Sam's lawyer and having Sam meet with the plaintiff's lawyer privately was an unusual approach that disarmed the lawyer and caused him to conduct a very realistic evaluation. The Mediator decided to approach the situation using a technique in which the issues were viewed in a very narrow manner. Rather than open a Pandora's box and question Andrea directly about her relationship with Sam, he focused on the credibility of Sam's story. At the same time, the Mediator chose to adopt a facilitative role by asking questions and setting the stage for Andrea's lawyer to come to his own evaluation of the evidence, as opposed to telling Andrea's lawyer how the Mediator felt about the evidence. Although it is often useful in a particular case for you to opine about certain evidence, in this situation the Mediator was convinced that a direct demonstration from the party who was telling the story (Sam), without any lawyer preparation, would be more reliable than giving his own opinion.

Courtroom proceedings are very structured: the parties have to follow a strict set of rules, and things can drag on for a long time. But in a mediation room, you create the structure and the rules. In this case, the Mediator re-created the legal mind-set without all the rules by letting Andrea's lawyer cross-examine Sam. Bringing them face-to-face in this familiar way allowed the plaintiff's lawyer to be educated and to test the reliability of information that normally would have come to him secondhand from the Mediator. The Mediator kept it safe by pulling the lawyer out before he had the chance to get upset, allowing the information to sink in, and giving the lawyer the privacy to talk things over with his client and reach his own conclusions.

WHAT STRATEGIES CAN WE LEARN?

1. **Check the reliability of your information.**

   It's always a good idea to double-check that the information you've received about a case is true, but is especially crucial in a sexual harassment case. When someone reports a new bit of information (such as Sam's reporting the consensual relationship with Andrea), asking how the person intends to demonstrate the fact in court can often provide surprising results. Other times, people offer inferences—statements about matters that are not directly known, based on what has been observed. Listening for inferences from either side allows you at least to mentally check the reliability of the statement and direct the parties to a better understanding of the evidence.

2. **Use the environment to effect change.**

   Putting different people together at various times during the mediation can be helpful, but it can also be dangerous. Notice how the Mediator set up the meeting between Sam and Andrea's lawyer and set forth some ground rules before the meeting to ensure its success. Be a people mover, but make sure it won't backfire on you.

3. **Help clients and lawyers perceive each other more fully and accurately than if left to themselves.**

   By reviewing the potential evidence of each side privately, you gain valuable insight into the lens through which the parties and the lawyers are viewing the situation. As mediator, you have the clearest lens because you have a bird's-eye view of the entire scope of the case rather than the narrow focus each side brings to the table. You can refocus each side's lens by clarifying information that would have the biggest influence on how each side views the dispute.

CHAPTER THIRTEEN

THE HANDICAP

Elizabeth sat up straight and smoothed her impeccably styled hair. She was always gracious, even under fire, although the Mediator sensed some fragility. Carmen, her attorney, provided all the backbone they needed, smiling the smile that had scared less experienced lawyers into settling quickly. But she was well matched by the defense lawyer, George, who stared back unblinking, straightening his tie and squaring his shoulders under his perfectly pressed Brooks Brothers suit. As a partner in what was arguably the state's top corporate law firm, he had faced Carmen down before.

A very interesting group, thought the Mediator. *It's going to be a long, slow dance.*

Until her abrupt termination several months earlier, Elizabeth had been one of several highly paid investment counselors who were responsible for one of the largest nonprofits in the United States. She had served the organization well for many years, but the unexpected stock market meltdown caught her by surprise. When the organization began losing tens of millions of dollars per month, it opted to terminate Elizabeth, claiming that her advice had put them in a tailspin. At age sixty, with only a few more years left before retirement, Elizabeth had been dealt a devastating blow to her confidence and dignity. She was convinced that the company had sought to save itself at her expense: using the investment losses as a pretext for hiring younger investment counselors whom they could pay much less. She was suing for wrongful termination based on age discrimination, but she didn't know if she'd make it to the end of the case.

For Elizabeth, a woman who had defined herself by her job and took pride in being in control, the court battle was worse than the actual termination. Recently, her psychiatrist had diagnosed her as suffering from clinical depression and prescribed medication, and her relationship with her husband of thirty years was deteriorating. Her nerves were shattered every time she was confronted during the litigation about her experiences at the job. She was always very proper in her business and personal dealings, and the mere thought of her former colleagues giving depositions in which she was the focal point was embarrassing to her. She still had friends at her former employer's office, and despised the thought of having to bring them into her controversy. She certainly had no wish to see any of them in court. Meanwhile, the amount of energy she spent answering written questions posed by the lawyers and researching the minutiae in her old files began to take their toll. Each day the dispute continued was another day taken away from her life. The only exit strategy available to Elizabeth was mediation, and the nonprofit had readily agreed to participate.

Meeting together in the large conference room caused Elizabeth to panic a bit, but the Mediator calmed her down and assured her that this was much more polite than a courtroom meeting. He let her know that she would hear some things from counsel for the nonprofit that she might disagree with, but that it was in her best interest to not say anything and let her attorney present her case.

"Let's get started," said the Mediator. Elizabeth's counsel gave a short but thorough statement about how she would try this case if it ever went to court, and why it appeared to her that the firing of Elizabeth was actually a pretext so that they could hire younger investment counselors at less money.

When she was finished, the Mediator said, "Thank you. It is my understanding that the defense has a presentation at this time. Please proceed, counsel."

"Thank you," said the counsel for the nonprofit. "We appreciate everyone attending this mediation and we're confident we will be able to work together to help settle Elizabeth's case. However, in evaluating the case, we have come to a different conclusion about the reason for her termination, which we would like to explain."

Counsel then provided notebooks with specific data demonstrating the large financial losses the corporation was experiencing on a monthly basis under Elizabeth's guidance. By the time they had concluded their presentation, the Mediator could see that the positions of the parties were miles apart. In response, he called a time-out and split the parties up into separate rooms.

—◦◦◦—

He met first with Carmen and Elizabeth, and inquired, "Have you had a chance to evaluate the numbers on the financial loss the corporation just provided?"

"Yes we have," said Carmen immediately. "While the corporation did lose substantial monies, what they forgot to tell you is that Elizabeth was following the investment strategy set out by the board of directors. They are not willing to take responsibility for their own decisions."

"So you're saying that Elizabeth took instructions from the board on how to invest the funds?"

"Of course," she responded. "That's the elephant in the room, and they know it."

"Could that be viewed as a double-edged sword in this case?" queried the Mediator. "By that I mean, is it possible that taking such a position could result in an implied admission that Elizabeth was simply a pawn and getting paid a substantial salary to do nothing but follow directions without any independent thinking and judgment?"

The lawyer pondered this for a moment. "I see what you are saying. Elizabeth was hired not only to listen to the board's instruction but to advise the board on its investment strategy." She paused. "We recognize that this case is not a slam dunk."

The Mediator then turned to Elizabeth. "Elizabeth, were you given much independence in your investment strategy?"

"Well, my department was given some broad directives. But on a day-to-day basis we were permitted to move money into several different funds without obtaining approval. And, yes, they did rely on my advice. But I can't help it that the market tanked. This is a cyclical thing, and I tried to tell them to be patient."

It was beginning to become clear that responsibilities might go both ways in this case, and the Mediator decided to ask Carmen the ultimate question: "How much is your client asking in damages?"

"Elizabeth is seeking $1.5 million," she replied, staring the Mediator down. The negotiation had started with a bang.

"Carmen," said the Mediator, somewhat aghast at her astronomical request, "I think we all know that the organization isn't going to go for that. Exactly what are you thinking here?"

"Look," said Carmen. "We are prepared to be reasonable, but they need to be sent a strong message about what it means to terminate a sixty-year-old woman and about the difficulty she will have in gaining future employment. We also want to test their mettle to see if they are here to do business."

"Candidly, Carmen, my sense is that demanding a number over a million dollars might cause the corporation to gasp and lose confidence in the negotiation. I will do it if you want me to, but I need to know how flexible you'll be," said the Mediator.

"Elizabeth and I understand the importance of being flexible. Obviously, if they make a serious move we'll be prepared to come below a million dollars."

The Mediator acknowledged their demand and made his way into the room with the nonprofit management.

—⫘—

Carmen will be coming down slowly, thought the Mediator. *But at least she expressed a strong desire to negotiate.* Dutifully, he took her request to George, which was predictably rejected.

"You have got to be kidding. There is no way we will pay anything *near* $1.5 million. You can tell them that if they don't get realistic, we're going to have to shut this session down now," said an exasperated George.

The Mediator encouraged George to stay with the program, as there was plenty of room in the initial demand.

But after several hours and some small moves by the corporation, the demand was $800,000 and the offer only $50,000.

In private session with the Mediator, and frustrated at the slow pace of the negotiation, George said, "There was no age discrimination here. Elizabeth let the organization down—she cost us millions. You tell them we're willing to offer $150,000. That's one year's salary, a more than generous amount of severance pay."

—∽∽∽—

"He offered $150,000?" Carmen said in mock astonishment, when the Mediator reported George's offer. "Tell him we're willing to drop our demand to $500,000." The Mediator looked at Elizabeth. She was still poised but was clearly starting to fray just a bit around the edges. She remained quiet but hung on Carmen's every word, her body language and deference to her lawyer sending a clear message that she wanted closure and would be willing to settle for something below the $500,000.

"Should we bring Solomon into the room at this point?" the Mediator asked with a smile.

The women looked at him in puzzlement for a moment and then Carmen laughed. "Are you asking if $325,000 would settle the case? We'll consider it, but it's quite a bit under what this case is worth. We're still looking for a higher number."

"Okay. Let me talk to George and see what we can come up with." For the first time in many hours, the Mediator began to see the light at the end of the case. Carmen had provided him with key information about the range of possibilities on the plaintiff's side. Although the parties appeared to be locked up in dramatically different positions, his knowing that Elizabeth would settle for something in the range of $325,000 was enough for him to decide to try to settle this case relatively quickly by using the "handicap" approach, which had worked for him many times before.

—∽∽∽—

"George, we're going to handicap this negotiation like a horse race," the Mediator grinned. "We look at the best odds that an outcome would occur under different scenarios." He began writing on a whiteboard as the lawyer and his client watched intently.

"For example," he said, "if you offer $450,000, there's a 90 percent chance the plaintiff will accept it. What I'm doing here," he said, still writing, "is listing a range of damages. Then I'll handicap each number within the range according to how likely it is to be accepted by the plaintiff." When he was done, the board looked like this:

$450,000 = 90%
$400,000 = 75%
$375,000 = 65%
$350,000 = 60%
$325,000 = 50%
$300,000 = 40%
$250,000 = 35%
$200,000 = 20%

When he had finished, the Mediator said, "I'm going to use my influence to make a joint recommendation using whatever numbers you tell me to use." This was a bold and seemingly biased move by the Mediator, but very deliberate: he knew that the midpoint was a number he could likely sell and that George and his client would want him to urge a number that had a good chance of success.

"All right," said George. "Give us a moment to mull those numbers over."

Although this approach seems eminently fair, it's relatively calculating, because the Mediator knew that George had to select the number that gave them the highest chance of success yet was still within their acceptable range, which happened to be $300,000 to $350,000.

"We can go as high as $300,000," George finally responded. This answer told the Mediator exactly how much the organization was willing to settle for.

"All right, George," the Mediator replied, "let's see what I can do with that."

———

Armed with this information, the Mediator went back into Elizabeth's room and spoke to her and her lawyer about the numbers. Instead of telling them that the organization would pay

$300,000, he used the handicap technique again. When he was done writing, the board looked like this:

$200,000 = 80%

$225,000 = 70%

$250,000 = 65%

$275,000 = 60%

$300,000 = 50%

$325,000 = 40%

$350,000 = 30%

When he was finished, he said, "You tell me which number you want, and I'll use my official capacity to make a recommendation to George. I won't tell him that this is the number you chose; I'll phrase it as though the suggestion is coming from me." Elizabeth and Carmen nodded. "But I need to warn you," he continued deliberately, speaking directly to Elizabeth, "that if the number you pick is too high, it's quite possible that George will reject it, and the case will go to court."

Elizabeth did not want to go to court, so she had one clear choice: $300,000. That number yielded the highest possible likelihood of acceptance within the range her attorney thought was fair as well as in terms of the handicap put on the board. "I would be willing to go to $300,000, but not a penny under that number," said Elizabeth. "I just want to get on with my life, and that will certainly help me do it." At this point the Mediator knew that the deal was virtually done.

Ordinarily, Elizabeth's lawyer would charge a 40 percent contingent fee of the total outcome. But because this case was being mediated and would be settled *before* litigation commenced, Carmen was still handling the case on an hourly basis, resulting in approximately $20,000 in legal fees. Elizabeth would get to keep $280,000—substantially more than if they had settled after the case was filed. Elizabeth understood that she would have to win at least $500,000 after the case was filed in order to put the same money in her pocket, so the decision to settle was something of a no-brainer for her.

And so it was: within another hour they had worked out the details of settlement. Everyone shook hands, and Elizabeth went home to start the next phase of her career with a very comfortable cushion of safety.

WHAT HAPPENED?

There is a certain predictability to negotiations over money when parties are finally in a monetary range that each side views as somewhat reasonable. The negotiation is predictable because there is a relationship between the steps in the process, just as in a dance. (In fact, mediators often call this process "the dance.") As each side makes concessions, the parties gradually draw closer. Typically the negotiation will gravitate toward the midpoint between two reasonable offers. Once the parties either come down or move up from what each side might have viewed as insulting initial offers, it is up to you as the mediator to create the pressure that forces them toward the middle of the zone.

In this case, once the parties were locked up between one year's severance pay at $150,000 and a demand of $500,000, the Mediator's experience told him that the gravitational pull of the negotiation should settle the case in the area of $300,000. Then it was a matter of keeping the music playing long enough for the parties to dance around to the midpoint. The Mediator could also have chosen to keep playing the messenger, asking the parties to continue making incremental concessions with the hope that they would eventually meet somewhere in the middle. His awareness of Elizabeth's discomfort led him to choose the handicap technique, because it is a particularly effective approach for people who dislike the negotiation process and are anxious to conclude the mediation. It provides a way of accelerating the tempo of the dance without penalizing either side, and gives the Mediator the type of intelligence that allows him to be both creative and practical.

WHAT STRATEGIES CAN WE LEARN?

1. **Identify the parties' financial objectives and bottom line.**
   Once the negotiation has reached a point where two reasonable offers have been made, it is helpful to learn what the

parties view as an endgame without actually asking them the question, "What is your bottom line?" Most people are unwilling to disclose their bottom line directly, but are not afraid to give you signals as to what their financial goals might be, as they recognize that you will help them reach those goals if the other side is receptive.

2. **Provide a spectrum of possible damages to each party, with the likelihood of settlement shown as a percentage.**
   People tend to respond positively to graphics. Creating a continuum of possibilities on the board gives the parties a comprehensive picture of how the case might conclude, without their having to make any commitments. Watch the parties closely for a response to each step on the continuum in order to determine their willingness to make commitments.

3. **Offer to make a recommendation at whatever number each party believes will result in success.**
   The parties look to you for direction and leadership. This means making suggestions that could lead to settlement. By offering to make a recommendation using whatever number the party chooses, you empower the parties and also help them feel that you understand their plight.

CHAPTER FOURTEEN

LEGALLY BLIND

Jamie sat behind the wheel of his classic red Mustang convertible, driving to his first day of classes at community college. Even though the chill of fall was in the air, he kept the top down—what was a convertible for, if not to drive with the top down? As Jamie approached the college, traveling southbound, he decided to drive straight through the main intersection and park in a lot at the far end of campus, near his first class. It was early morning, and no one was around; it seemed he had the street all to himself. He smiled. He had a great car, it was a beautiful day, he was young and eager, and life could not be better.

But he didn't reckon on Vivian, sitting low behind the wheel of her four-door Oldsmobile sedan, heading northbound on the same street. Vivian had always enjoyed driving. She was in her eighties now, and didn't take long trips anymore; but she was fiercely proud that, unlike so many of her friends, she could still get to the grocery store and medical appointments under her own power. She was moving up the block at the speed limit when she suddenly realized that she needed to take a left at the intersection.

Vivian made a sudden left turn—right in front of Jamie, who had no time to get out of her way. The awful noise of screeching brakes, metal crushing metal, and breaking glass brought every-one in the neighborhood out to see what had happened. As blood mixed with gasoline in the street, police cars and ambulances screamed onto the scene. It was a terrible sight. Jamie's Mustang was totaled, and Jamie was unconscious. He wouldn't make that first day of school for a long time.

The emergency medical team used the jaws of life to cut Jamie out of his car; they rushed him to the hospital, where he remained in a coma for approximately six weeks. He finally regained consciousness, but his catastrophic injuries had left him paralyzed from the waist down. Fortunately, at eighteen, Jamie was young, strong, and determined. But it would take more than a year of grueling therapy to get back on his feet, and he was still left with some residual problems. Vivian was badly shaken, and her car was crushed, but she sustained no serious injuries.

Clearly, someone was at fault. But who? Vivian was sure that Jamie had been speeding, which he vehemently denied. Jamie was sure that Vivian was too old be driving. Like most people in their position, they decided to let their insurance companies straighten out the mess. Vivian's company was sure they could win—after all, they had Vivian's word that Jamie had been speeding. And Vivian, a dignified woman who was still quite sharp, seemed to be a highly credible witness.

Yet after five years of litigation, the case remained in dispute, and both parties began their preparations for trial. Jamie was suing for the limits of Vivian's policy: $2 million. This was big enough money that her insurance company, concerned about a runaway verdict, suddenly hired a different law firm, one noted for its expertise in high-exposure matters. On the eve of trial, however, the judge encouraged the attorneys to give mediation a try in one last effort to settle out of court.

Jamie's lawyer, Michael, paced the carpet in the Mediator's office, where the parties had gathered to discuss the case. He was clearly agitated. This mediation had been going on for hours. Jamie sat quietly, resigned. Michael had warned him that this would probably be a very long day.

"My client had the right of way," Jamie's lawyer said to the Mediator, his voice rising. "This is undisputed. I can't *believe* the insurance company is holding back on settlement because they think Jamie was speeding. The evidence simply doesn't support their theory!"

Vivian's new attorney, Dave, was a seasoned and sophisticated trial lawyer. He sat back and watched his opponent, opting for caution in his approach. He'd been brought into this case at the last minute and hadn't had the time and luxury to nail down all the details, which was quite contrary to the way he usually handled cases of this magnitude. Nevertheless, he was fairly relaxed about his chances of success. After five years of litigation, he assumed that the previous attorneys had gathered the relevant facts and that the case was prepackaged for him simply to be tried.

"We do believe the jury will find Vivian at fault," he responded. "But since Jamie was speeding, we view Vivian's fault at maybe 10 to 20 percent, with Jamie shouldering the lion's share of blame."

The Mediator wanted to understand how the insurance company reached this conclusion. "Do you have any expert opinions to support this apportionment of fault?"

"Absolutely," the defense lawyer said. "Our experts have made an animated re-creation of the scene that will demonstrate to the jury that this accident would not have occurred if Jamie had been traveling at a reasonable speed for the area."

This guy's ready to go, thought the Mediator. *Still . . .* "I'm curious, Dave. What's the basis of the expert's analysis? Exactly what was the data he relied on to reach his conclusions about Jamie's speed?"

The defense lawyer, a consummate professional, responded without missing a beat. "That's a good question. I'm glad you asked. We inspected the skid marks on the street, which, as you know, can tell an expert a great deal about rate of travel. Our primary source of information, of course, was our client, Vivian. Based on her description, as well as the review of skid marks on the street, we estimate Jamie's speed at about 70 miles per hour in a 35 mile-per-hour zone. Vivian makes a fantastic appearance, and we have no doubt that she will be absolutely credible in front of the jury." He looked the Mediator straight in the eye and said, "We are very confident in our analysis of this issue." Jamie and his attorney exchanged glances. They'd heard all this before.

But the Mediator still had questions. He knew that drivers aren't always paying the best attention to what's going on around them. Unfortunately, he couldn't question Vivian about her experience: she was not required to be at the mediation because her insurance company was handling the case for her and making all the decisions on the settlement.

"Tell me," he pressed, "how certain are you that Vivian could make an accurate estimate of speed when she was in the process of turning left at the intersection?"

Dave didn't even have to look down at his files. "Our experts have reviewed her deposition testimony and have advised us that her estimates will withstand cross-examination. If we were not confident, we would have settled this case a long time ago. We are ready for trial."

Then the Mediator was struck by a thought: this guy was new to the case. Had he even *met* Vivian? He decided to approach the subject carefully. "What's your assessment of your client?"

The defense lawyer coughed briefly. "Well, I haven't yet spoken to her personally, but the insurance company tells me she is *outstanding*. The proverbial little old lady from Pasadena. Everybody's grandmother, a volunteer at the senior center, and a former schoolteacher to boot. A perfect witness for us against a speeding college kid." Jamie scowled at that comment, but remained silent.

The Mediator wanted to be sure he understood the situation. "So you haven't actually met her, but your carrier has informed you that your key witness is terrific. Don't you think it might be useful to make a personal assessment before taking this case to court?" As soon as the words were out of his mouth, he regretted saying them.

Dave flushed, clearly insulted. "Of course I will meet with her before the trial," he snapped. "Are you suggesting that I'm not doing my job properly?"

"Not at all," the Mediator replied, shaking his head by way of apology. "I certainly didn't mean to imply that. But, just from what I've heard in this room, it seems like the insurance company has reached some drastic conclusions on a potentially catastrophic case without consulting you—their primary trial lawyer. I just thought that they might want a second opinion from you before telling the plaintiff that he is 80 to 90 percent responsible for his own medical problems." At this, he shared a brief glance with Jamie.

The room was silent for a moment. "Look," said the Mediator, "it's been a long morning. Let's break for lunch and try again when we've all gotten our blood sugar up to a healthy level."

—◦◦◦—

When they reconvened after lunch, the Mediator decided it would be more productive to put the parties into separate rooms and talk to them privately. He hoped there was something that one of the attorneys might feel more comfortable talking about when his opponent wasn't present. He asked Dave to be patient for just a while longer while he met with Jamie and Michael.

The Mediator entered the small office where Jamie and his lawyer were now installed. "Here's the situation," he began. "The defense is taking a hard line on the speed issue. Is there *anything* else you can tell me that might allow them to reassess the situation?"

This was the moment Michael had been waiting for. Without saying a word, he pulled out a file he had obtained from a medical facility concerning Vivian's physical condition. *What's going on here?* the Mediator wondered. Vivian's physical condition had never been an issue in the case.

But when the Mediator began reading the file, his perception of the case changed completely. The file revealed that Vivian had been treated for quite a few years at the university eye clinic; her own doctor deemed her legally blind. Unfortunately, Vivian had been unwilling to give up the freedom her car afforded her—she was a self-sufficient woman who dreaded having to rely on others. At that time the Department of Motor Vehicles went ten years without renewing licenses for good drivers, so Vivian still had her license. At the time of the accident, however, Vivian should not have been driving.

The Mediator was stunned. "How did you find out about this?" he asked.

Jamie's lawyer smiled broadly. "We noticed that Vivian had trouble reading certain documents we showed her at her deposition, and we had a hunch that she might have eye problems. Our investigator determined that she was getting treatment for cataracts and other conditions, so we issued a subpoena for the medical records. The previous defense lawyer simply forgot to ask for copies of the records—her health issues just never came up—so the insurance company had no way of knowing that Vivian should not have been driving."

No wonder these guys wouldn't back down, thought the Mediator. Armed with this information, Michael clearly felt that the insurance company should pay full value for the catastrophic injuries his client sustained. "Now do you understand why we can't compromise this case? If we don't settle now, we're planning to seriously impeach the insurance company's experts at trial. I simply can't let them know about this information."

The Mediator was at a crossroads. He knew that the case would not settle until the insurance company learned of Vivian's condition. This was a strategic issue. Vivian's lawyers forgot to order a copy of her records because she wasn't the claimant. When the records were subpoenaed, Jamie's law firm didn't check the "Send Copy" box that would have ensured that a copy of the records was sent to Vivian's insurance company.

The Mediator looked at Michael intently. "Is there any way I can disclose this information to the insurance company? I have to think they will reassess the case if they see the medical files."

"I can't let you disclose this information because I simply don't trust the insurance company," he replied firmly. "They didn't do their homework on this case, and they are going to have to pay the price at trial. We would love to settle the case, but we cannot take the chance of disclosing this information. This new lawyer has won a lot of these big cases for the company. He'll work hard to find another sneaky way to get around this information and defend the case before the trial starts."

"Okay," said the Mediator. "I've got to take a moment to think this through. Hang tight and I'll get back to you. I need a few minutes to think."

Frustrated, the Mediator jogged down three flights of stairs and went outside the building to get some air. He walked around the block, running through all the clever ways he could think of to get the point across to the defense lawyer that the insurance company had exposure to a large damage award, without actually telling them about Vivian's condition. Then, suddenly, he had it. He ran back up the stairs and into the office where Jamie and Michael were waiting.

"Okay," he said. "Let's try something different. Michael, what do you think is the true settlement value of this case if liability were not an issue?"

"Given the gravity of our client's injuries," he replied, "we would still be willing to settle for $2 million—the limits of the policy."

"If I can get the defense to concede that the settlement value of this case exceeds the policy limits if Vivian admitted liability, would you consider disclosing the medical records?"

"That would be a start. I would have to think about it seriously."

"Good," said the Mediator. "I'll be back soon." He headed over to the office where he had stashed the defense lawyer.

"Let's try this, Dave," he said. "Without considering liability, can you evaluate the damage aspect of the case?" His answer echoed that of Jamie's lawyer: $2 million, policy limits.

The Mediator was on a roll now. Clearly, both lawyers were completely in agreement about the value of the case. The only disagreement was about who was at fault. His instinct told him that it was time to bring the lawyers into the same room to discuss the issue of damages. These two lawyers clearly had tremendous respect for each other and didn't need to prove anything at trial. He thought that if they only had a chance to confront each other directly—in a safe environment that didn't include clients looking over their shoulders—they would be candid about the case. He asked Michael to come with him back to the conference room. "Sit tight, Jamie," he told the young man. "We'll be back in a while."

The Mediator and Michael entered the conference room where Dave was waiting. As they all sat down around a small table, the Mediator turned to the defense lawyer. "Dave," he asked, "what would you recommend the insurance company pay on this case if liability were admitted?"

Dave thought for a moment. "That's a tough question. We are never going to admit liability, but—just for the sake of discussion—I would have to say that this could exceed the policy limits of our case. The injuries are quite dramatic, and I would have no problem recommending the policy limits if Vivian were at fault. But we all know that Vivian was *not* at fault here." Then he seemed to pick up on an undercurrent. "Are you aware of anything that would cause me to change my opinion?" he asked. He had tried to bury his reservations about the previous law firm, but now he wondered if his worst fears were going to prove true.

The Mediator said nothing, but gave Michael a look that said, *The ball's in your court.* Michael had heard everything he needed to hear—Dave's assessment was pretty close to his own. He felt his hard-fought case suddenly shift in a new direction.

Without missing a beat, he handed Vivian's lawyer the eye clinic file. "Dave," he said, "you're dead in the water on this one. Your client should never have been behind the wheel. I'm sorry you're finding out about it so late in the game. This is obviously an issue that your predecessor failed to discover, but would have, had he worked up the case thoroughly before turning it over to you."

Dave stared down at the file for what appeared to be an eternity. Finally, he looked up and spoke. "You got us here. I had no idea that Vivian had this problem. I want to spend some more time reviewing this file with my insurer, but I will recommend they pay the money to settle this case."

A short time later, the case settled in Jamie's favor—for the full amount. Jamie, now with a college degree and a tidy nest egg, invested in a Humvee—he wanted to feel an armored vehicle around him from now on. Vivian, who still carried the guilt of the pain and suffering she had caused Jamie, lost her license for good. And neither lawyer ever forgot again to check the little box that said "Send Copy."

WHAT HAPPENED?

The case seemed deadlocked until Michael disclosed an unexpected bit of information: Vivian was legally blind. The Mediator knew intuitively that if this information were used correctly, it could help settle the case before it got to court. Ethically, however, he could not bring this information to the defense himself, and he felt it would harm the negotiations if he tried to browbeat Michael into disclosing it. He needed to find a graceful way for both attorneys to deal with the new knowledge without feeling coerced or blindsided.

He decided to approach the problem from the inside out, skipping the locked-up liability phase altogether and starting with the endgame—namely, the cost of settlement. This approach allowed for recognition of a true settlement value and gave Jamie's lawyer a natural opportunity to show his hand.

The goal toward which the Mediator was moving was clear: to facilitate the dialogue between the parties in a directive way so that Michael would conclude for himself that in order to reach a settlement, it was more useful than not to reveal the information. He also wanted both lawyers to feel that they had been given the option of trusting their own instincts about the consequences of revealing the information. The Mediator read both lawyers as decent guys whose egos weren't caught up in the process. He trusted his intuition that if he were able to get them to this point, he could count on them to work things out together with minimal input on his part.

WHAT STRATEGIES CAN WE LEARN?

1. **Explore the motivation of the negotiator for withholding information.**

   Usually, the negotiator has an incentive to hide information or mislead the other party about it in order to win a bigger stake in the outcome. Question the negotiator carefully about how he discovered the information and why he is not disclosing it. This will help you understand how he plans to use it in the case and how you might be able to use it in the mediation to cause a party to shift positions.

2. **Explore whether there is a downside to revealing the information.**

   It is appropriate to discuss the advantages and consequences of disclosure. At the same time, you must remind the negotiator that you have a duty under the law to maintain the confidentiality of the information unless the negotiator gives permission to disclose it.

3. **Find a way to use confidential information legally and ethically in order to shift the negotiation.**

   Legally, you must maintain the confidentiality of the information that has been presented. Nonetheless, figuring out how to obtain permission to use disclosed information wisely can be the key to breaking a deadlock. For example, go through a series of hypothetical situations demonstrating how the information might be used and the potential reaction of the other negotiators. Consider role playing; the lawyer could experience how the other side might feel by playing the role of the person who receives the information. Another approach is to sketch out a simple chart (on paper or chalkboard) that outlines the advantages and disadvantages of disclosure.

4. **Get in touch with your instincts.**

   It's easy to get stuck in a single approach that's just not working. If you feel stymied, take some time alone to allow your gut feelings about the direction of the negotiation to surface. This will open up creative venues you have not considered.

5. **Demonstrate the settlement value to the parties that revealing the strategic information will provide.**

   Undisclosed information can be a weapon in court, but it can also be a tool in a negotiation. Remind the party that holding on to the information may serve a later purpose in court, but that revealing it now might cause the other side to shift positions. Project confidence; trust your instincts that the holder of the confidential information will see the value in disclosure.

6. **Use an endgame strategy.**

   Avoid the intermediate steps of the negotiation by asking the parties to agree on a fair value of the case. Secure the attorneys' willingness to recommend that value to their clients if liability were admitted. This should be done only when you have a strong understanding of the true jury value of the case or when the parties have already given you a sense of what they feel the damages are. Consider using jury verdicts in similar cases as examples of how the case might go if it went to the jury on damages only.

7. Let the answer come from the parties.

Direct the parties toward a common goal but allow them to reach the conclusion that you have already come to. This way they will not feel coerced. Ask the parties if they have tried similar cases with these type of injuries, or direct them to recent verdicts and settlements that have been published. Alternatively, list on a chalkboard all the economic damages and put a big question mark next to the issue of pain and suffering. Ask them to fill in the range of pain and suffering damages that could be awarded in this type of case.

CHAPTER FIFTEEN

THE SLOW DRIP

"I know you've already had a brief meeting with Edgar and his attorney," said Rexco's attorney. "I'm showing you this information in confidence, with the understanding that you cannot provide the information to plaintiff's counsel. Edgar's attorney is not aware that this file even exists, which explains why they brought this case in the first place." And with that, he handed the Mediator a personnel file bulging with papers.

When the Mediator had spoken to Rexco's lawyer briefly before the mediation, he had been alerted to the possibility that some explosive documents would be forthcoming. But now, as he read through the many memos detailing Edgar's employment history, the Mediator knew right away that he would have to take the "slow drip" approach to this case if he didn't want it to blow up in his face.

Tensions were high. Edgar, a hard-bitten fifty-five-year-old construction worker, was suing his employer for wrongful termination. That was somewhat ironic, because for most of his nearly twenty-five years in construction he'd held firm to his status as an independent contractor. He didn't like the idea of having to be *anywhere* every day, year in and year out, and he didn't like taking orders from anyone. Nonetheless, he'd spent much of the last eighteen years working with Rexco Construction.

Their history together had been anything but straightforward. For many years Rexco had hired Edgar on a per diem basis, as an independent contractor. Then, when his wife's health failed a couple of years ago, Edgar asked Rexco for a full-time position so that he could obtain medical insurance coverage to pay for his wife's medical bills. Rexco's management didn't think Edgar was the type of employee they wanted on a full-time basis—yes, he was a skilled worker who got the job done, but he wasn't always dependable. Still, they'd known him and his wife a long time. Out of consideration for his tenure with the company, and to honor his request for medical insurance, the company decided to hire him as a full-time salaried employee for the next year-and-a-half.

Edgar was grateful, but old habits die hard. He was basically a hardheaded rebel who didn't know much about office politics. He knew he had to take this job for the sake of his wife, but he didn't like it. Not surprisingly, once Edgar was hired his relationship with the company began to deteriorate. Some of Edgar's coworkers complained about his work ethic. He'd been written up by supervisors several times for not showing up to a job site on time, and now even his work product was below par. When new management came in, they quickly determined that Edgar was not the right material for Rexco and put plans into motion to terminate his employment. Those plans included memos from his supervisor to the human resources department and other documentation about his shortcomings. All of these memos were given to Edgar and then filed in his personnel folder, which was growing increasingly fat. Rexco had everything neatly lined up to fire Edgar, who was acting as though he weren't aware of his precarious status or didn't think the company had the courage to take action because of his long tenure.

But before anyone could tell Edgar he was about to lose his job, he was diagnosed with prostate cancer and took medical leave. While Edgar was at home recuperating from surgery, he received a letter from Rexco's human resources manager notifying him of his termination. Edgar was furious. He immediately hired counsel, who contended that Edgar had been terminated for unlawful reasons: discrimination due to his physical disability.

—◦◦◦—

At first blush, it had seemed that the timing of Edgar's termination was not good for Rexco. But the Mediator now saw that he was looking at a very different case. "As you can see," Rexco's attorney said as the Mediator finished reading the file, "the documentation in

Edgar's personnel file clearly reveals an intention to terminate well before the company became aware of the prostate cancer issue."

However—and this was the sticky part—because litigation had not yet commenced, this documentation had not been produced to Edgar's lawyer before the mediation. Edgar and his lawyer were both in the dark about Rexco's documented plans for termination.

The Mediator thought hard for a moment and then said, "You and I both know that nothing's going to budge in this case until Edgar understands his position. I'm not allowed to tell him, and that would probably be a lousy idea anyway. If I said, 'Edgar, you don't have a case—they were just about to fire you,' he'd explode, and so would his lawyer. But I'm pretty sure that if I can reveal this information to them bit by bit, it's going to get through in a way that will help us get this case settled." The Mediator knew from experience that the only way to approach this negotiation was to prevent the parties from initiating unstructured and wild accusations. The best tactic would be to discreetly reveal the confidential information in a manner that forced the parties to assess the liability realistically.

The lawyer thought it over. He was ready to go to court, but he knew that Rexco would much prefer to settle. "How would this work?" he asked.

"I'll select five or six key documents from the file that demonstrate the fact that Rexco had already decided to terminate Edgar's employment before the cancer surfaced. I'll schedule a series of meetings with Edgar and his counsel, and provide one document from the file each time. After three or four meetings, I'm fairly certain that Edgar and his attorney will come to their own conclusion about the realistic settlement value of the case."

"That sounds like a good plan," said Rexco's lawyer, happy that things were moving so well. "How long do you think this should take?"

"One very long day," responded the Mediator. And he was right.

—————

Several minutes later, all the parties gathered around the large conference table. The Mediator had initially met privately with the parties to build rapport and gather some intelligence as to what the impediments were to this case, and now he wanted to create an atmosphere where everyone felt safe. Edgar fidgeted in his seat, not saying much but looking disgruntled. The Mediator had already determined that he would meet in a series of private sessions with Edgar and his attorney over the course of the day, so this was the moment where the lawyers got to clear their throats and set forth their legal positions. It was a moment designed for the clients rather than for the Mediator, as he was well aware of the information deficits in this case. In a sense, this was the clients' day in court.

Edgar's lawyer spoke emotionally about the plaintiff's years of loyalty and his shock at being let go when the company knew he suffered from a disability. He even mentioned that this was a multiple six-figure case. Rexco's lawyer acknowledged Edgar's work history with the company, but gently implied that Edgar was aware of their dissatisfaction with his tardiness and lack of production. The lawyer did not mention any of the documents in the personnel file; he was going to allow the Mediator to "drip" them out over the course of the day.

�⚬⚭

During the first meeting with Edgar and his counsel, the Mediator began the slow drip. "I have something I'd like to share with you both that may come as a bit of a surprise," he said, passing them a copy of the first memo from the personnel file. Written months before the termination, it demonstrated problems with Edgar showing up late or not at all for jobs.

"As you can see," the Mediator continued deliberately, "Rexco feels that Edgar was well aware of the complaints about his behavior months in advance of the termination, and well before he came down with cancer."

Edgar looked stoic, but his lawyer furrowed his brow. This was the first time he had actually seen proof that there was some support for the defense position. "If you don't mind," he said to the Mediator, "I'd like to speak to Edgar in private about this memo."

"Of course," the Mediator responded, leaving them alone in the room.

He returned to the room a few minutes later and asked, "What do you make of these documents?"

"I'm in a bit of an awkward situation here," said the lawyer. "Since this mediation is prelitigation, Edgar told me he didn't think the memos were important and forgot to give me copies before we started this case. While it certainly has an impact on my evaluation, the company should have known better than to fire him when he had prostate cancer. The timing really raises some red flags for Rexco."

"I understand that the timing raises some questions," posed the Mediator. "But you told Rexco's counsel in open session, before you saw the memos, that this was a multiple six-figure case. I take it you have a different analysis now?"

"Of course. Edgar understands that his case did not get any better. I've advised him that it's quite possible he could lose the case," the lawyer said, shooting Edgar a meaningful look.

"Edgar," said the Mediator. "No one is blaming you for not providing the memos to your lawyer earlier. Most clients who have never been through this before don't have an understanding of what's relevant to a case. Nevertheless, your lawyer now has to reevaluate the case quickly if we are going to settle today."

"I'm sorry," said Edgar. "I apologized to my lawyer ten times already . . ." He stopped. "Look, I didn't take those memos seriously. Why should I? Everyone in the company gets memos. I had no idea they were going to use them to fire me. I'm sorry. Really."

"That's okay, Edgar," the Mediator replied. "If you didn't know, you didn't know. Unfortunately, the memos could be quite damaging to your case. But we're going to do our best to help you settle it quickly."

—ᗡᗡᗡ—

As one meeting followed the other over the course of the day, Rexco's attorney provided the Mediator with copies of other documents from the personnel file to deliver to Edgar. One document in particular looked as though it would have a devastating impact on Edgar.

"You won't believe this," said Rexco's attorney, somewhat gleefully. "Here is the final memo in which the company warned Edgar many weeks before his prostate cancer that another mishap would result in termination. Go ahead, read it!"

Clearly, things were starting to go downhill for Edgar as far as the evidence was concerned. "May I show this document to Edgar and his counsel?" asked the Mediator.

"We're getting a bit tired of this approach," responded Rexco's lawyer. "We don't mind you showing it to them, but we need to know that they're ready to get real in this case. Show it to them, but come back with a number that reflects the nuisance value of this case."

—◈◈◈—

By his fourth meeting with Edgar and his counsel, the Mediator could see that the slow drip had finally done its job. Edgar's lawyer, looking grim, spoke first. "These memos have made it exceedingly clear that Edgar's case doesn't have the appeal we thought it did. We're not going to turn around and go home, but we're ready to be realistic. I'd appreciate it if you could work with us on a reasonable demand for settlement so we can wrap this up quickly."

"Let me suggest that you ask for something in the five figures, maybe $50,000 to $75,000," said the Mediator. "I don't think they'll accept it, but it's not unreasonable to ask for it, and I expect to receive a response that moves this negotiation forward."

The lawyer consulted with Edgar for a moment. "We'd like to ask for $75,000," he said.

—◈◈◈—

Meeting privately with Rexco and their counsel, the Mediator advised, "I've got some good news. The slow drip approach has started to set in. Edgar has now demanded $75,000 instead of multiples of six figures."

Rexco's lawyer wasn't impressed. "If you think that's good news, you must be smoking something. This case isn't worth $75,000. We'll offer $15,000, but tell them we don't have much room to move."

The Mediator could see that the parties were now in a range that made sense. With just a little more shuttle diplomacy and numbers trading, the parties settled fairly painlessly at $30,000.

Edgar smiled for the first time that day, and went home happy; he knew he had been warned many times about his conduct, and this was a far better outcome than just being fired outright. His lawyer wasn't happy about the small amount, but he knew that any money was found money at this point, considering that his client had "forgotten" to tell him about the warnings.

WHAT HAPPENED?

This case was heard before litigation commenced, so there was no exchange of written information between the parties. As a result, the Mediator learned while scheduling the case that both sides were in the dark about what the actual testimony might be and what documents were available to support the case. During pre-mediation conferences with the parties to schedule the case, he began to start thinking about a game plan for the mediation. These premediation discussions are also known as the *convening* stage of a case.

In the convening stage, the Mediator determined that both parties were willing to come to the table, but he also learned that there was secret information from the personnel file that Edgar's lawyer might not know about. For this reason, he structured the case somewhat differently than he might have otherwise. Instead of beginning with a joint meeting of both parties, he scheduled separate meetings in order to diagnose exactly what the information deficit was and determine how he was going to handle it.

The second, or *opening*, stage of mediation is often done in a joint meeting with all parties present. The purpose is to set forth each side's statement of the case. Often, you will try to create a safe environment for the exchange of dialogue by coaching the parties beforehand as to what would be the most effective use of their time in joint session. In this case, during private meetings with the defense, the Mediator recommended that they not be specific about the documents in the personnel file so as not to embarrass Edgar and his lawyer during the joint meeting. He further recommended the slow drip approach: after the joint session he would deliver the documents to the plaintiff one at a time, in private caucus.

The case took on legs during the third stage of the mediation, the *communication* phase. This stage allows the parties to express whatever legal or personal issues might affect the negotiation. In this case, the information deficit with respect to the personnel file was exposed by the Mediator in a manner that took into consideration the timing of the disclosure. The Mediator paced the presentation of information until he was certain the plaintiff understood the impact of the documents. When that occurred, he moved the case into the fourth stage of the process, the *negotiation* phase.

The negotiation phase is the heart and soul of the mediation. Now you create an atmosphere in which you and the parties can be flexible and innovative. In this case, once the plaintiff understood the impact of the documents, he backed off from the predictable high demand for settlement, speeding up the negotiation.

This resulted in *closure,* the final stage of mediation. At this point, the parties are coming in for a landing: everyone is aware of all the relevant information, and you work to create an outcome both sides can live with.

WHAT STRATEGIES CAN WE LEARN?

1. **Deliver bad news with pacing and patience.**

   Most of us will actively resist accepting new or difficult information that is unceremoniously dropped on our heads, and parties in a mediation are no different. When you have bad news to deliver to a party in a mediation, parcel it out slowly to give them time to absorb it. This is all about timing. When a child asks a parent for a raise in allowance, for example, she knows instinctively that the best time to ask is not when her parents are worried or distracted but when things are comfortable in the house. The same holds true in mediation. The "slow drip" is one way to pace yourself, softening up the parties and ensuring they are receptive before you give them the bad news.

2. **Consider how to plan the session and understand the basic structure of a negotiation.**

   As the person who's running the show, you don't want to charge into a mediation without some prior thought and planning. It is your responsibility to give the parties a sense of what is supposed to happen during the session and how it will be structured. The easiest guideline for structuring a session is to remember that there are five stages: convening, opening, communication, negotiation, and closure. In real life, these stages don't always follow in precise order; but understanding this structure gives you a workable default when you are considering how to plan the session.

CHAPTER SIXTEEN

DEATH TAKES A HOLIDAY

"I'm so sorry, so sorry," sobbed Mary Partridge. "We just had no idea what we were signing." Her eighty-nine-year-old husband, Max, stricken by Alzheimer's, stared at the wall, uncomprehending. The Mediator, meeting privately with the plaintiffs, saw that Mary must have been stuck in this self-blaming loop for a long time, and he was already beginning to feel angry on her behalf.

"It's okay, Mom," their son, Bob, said, his arm around his mother. "We just want to get your money back."

"I'm *glad* your father can't understand what's going on," she said sadly, looking at Max. "He would be furious. Furious."

"Funeral Home Insurance should be forced to pay through the nose for what they've done," the Partridges' lawyer fumed. "These are honest people who were preyed on by scum!"

"Mary, would you mind telling me what happened?" the Mediator asked gently.

"Certainly," she replied. "Seventeen years ago, when we were in our early seventies, a very nice man knocked at our door and asked if we would be interested in purchasing low-cost funeral arrangements from a local funeral home. Well, we had just purchased cemetery plots and were thinking about all this anyway, so I invited him in. He offered to take care of our funeral arrangements at the funeral home of our choice—with flower arrangements, music, thank-you cards, caskets, everything. It would cost us only $9,000, which is really very reasonable, and we didn't even have to write them a check because they would automatically withdraw $200 a month from our credit union account. We had about $35,000 in savings, more than enough to cover it.

"Well, we were delighted that we could make these arrangements so easily, and we were so happy that Bobby and his sister wouldn't have to think about this when the time came. Of course at that time I thought we didn't have much time left. Who knew we'd keep going and going and going?" she smiled, shaking her head sadly.

"Then a few months ago, when Bobby took over paying our bills, he noticed that our credit union account was overdrawn." She stopped, on the edge of tears again, and turned to her son. Bob picked up the story.

"I couldn't understand it," he said. "They get Social Security checks every month, and they shouldn't have had to dip into their savings. My mom didn't know anything about it. When I asked the credit union where the money was, they told me that all the monies that were withdrawn from the account over the years went to Funeral Home Insurance. Mom said she had no idea who they were, but she did find some paperwork about their funeral arrangements." He pursed his lips tightly.

"When I looked at what they had signed, it turned out that they hadn't really bought funeral arrangements at all. That crook sold them a $9,000 insurance policy that they ended up paying $40,000 for!"

"Targeted marketing really works, doesn't it?" commented their lawyer in a sarcastic tone.

Funeral Home Insurance had used a classic targeted marketing strategy. The company knew its market (older people with a stable income, face-to-face with their own mortality), and it knew where they lived (in established residential neighborhoods). The company also knew psychology: these people were going to be worrying about their own deaths and how best to make things easy on their children when they were gone. If the company could promise to remove that pressure, it could make a quick sale. It had no trouble finding local funeral homes to sign on to the scheme, because the homes would get business they did not have to work for. The insurance company also knew that a door-to-door campaign was more likely to provide a consistently high return on its investment than a direct-mail campaign. This strategy worked perfectly in the case of Max and Mary Partridge.

The Partridges' lawyer was ready to do battle on their behalf, but their son didn't want to put them through any more pain. "I just want to make sure they get their money back," he told the Mediator. "That's all we're interested in."

"Okay," said the Mediator. "I'll see what I can do." He already knew the sad truth that these cases rarely make it to trial.

—◦◦◦—

"But we have the documentation!" said the Funeral Home Insurance representative. "It says right here that they were buying an insurance policy. They read it, and they signed it. I'm sorry if they didn't understand, but any judge will see that we're in the clear here." Sitting quietly in the background was the owner of Montgomery Family Funeral Home, which the Partridges had chosen to perform their funeral.

"A judge might see it your way," replied the Mediator, "but I think a jury—especially a jury of their peers—might view your marketing approach with some skepticism."

The man stopped blustering and thought it over, probably not for the first time. He spoke quietly with his attorney, who turned to the Mediator and said, "We're sorry for the Partridges, but we're not admitting any wrongdoing on the part of Funeral Home Insurance. However, we have no wish to cause them any more anxiety, and we would like to resolve this conflict without bringing it to court. What can we do to hammer out a financial settlement today?"

"I agree," said the Mediator. "I don't believe a jury trial will benefit any of you." He knew that the company wanted to make this case disappear; they didn't want to reimburse more than the premium for the insurance policy, but they also realized that the publicity factor in going forward would not bode well for their business. They had no wish to see their company name splashed all over the network news, described as a company that preyed on the unsuspecting elderly. The Mediator also recognized that the Partridges were far too old to invest in litigation and that their children simply wanted to unscramble a broken egg.

The Mediator was thinking to himself that it was a relatively simple case at that point, and he decided on a simple approach: a "one-step" negotiation, with the addition of a simple apology.

"Allow me to make a suggestion on an approach to wrapping this up with the minimal amount of conflict," suggested the Mediator. "First off, the Partridges feel very bad about having entered into this arrangement without understanding the consequences of their actions. Candidly, they are probably not going to understand the legal position you might take in the litigation, and I doubt if I could get through to them today on the technicalities of signing an insurance contract without reading it.

"Since the company has expressed a desire to make some financial remuneration to avoid the publicity and extensive costs involved in this case, I will spend some time with each side trying to formulate an understanding as to what both parties might find acceptable, then develop a written agreement based on my understanding. This way, you will not have to negotiate back and forth with the Partridges," said the Mediator.

"But," he continued, "there's one hitch: any settlement will have to include a verbal apology."

The company representative was surprised by this request. After all, the company was in the financial services business, and all it wanted was a quick deal. "Why would you need that from us?" he asked.

"Because it would address the Partridges' concern about having entered into a shaky arrangement with you, and could actually result in a financially attractive deal." Now the Mediator was touching a nerve that the insurer understood: money.

"Let me get this straight," said the rep. "You're saying that if we apologize to the Partridges, we'll be able to settle this case on terms that we find more agreeable?"

"That's my assessment," replied the Mediator. "It doesn't cost you anything to apologize, and it could have tremendous currency value for you."

"If you feel that we could ink a deal by such an apology, we're happy to do it," said the representative. "However, we don't want any apology in writing! We're a good company, and it would hurt our reputation if this kind of action got out to the public."

The Mediator then made a presentation to the company that focused on the damages of the case. First, he identified the amount of money that the Partridges had actually paid over the years for this insurance policy, and the cost of presenting the case in court. Next, he suggested that the Partridges' counsel would have to be paid if this case were to settle. Finally, he reminded the insurer that the Partridges still believe that they have paid for their funeral arrangements, and that it would be difficult to take that understanding away from them now.

"As you can see, since the Partridges paid approximately $40,000 over the years, and the lawyer will need to receive somewhere in the area of $25,000, it will take at least $65,000 to settle this case. That doesn't include damages for pain and suffering, but I think they might waive those damages if they know they can get closure today," observed the Mediator.

Counsel for the insurer turned to the owner of Montgomery Family Funeral Home. "Would you offer to provide the Partridges with the items they initially purchased, after we reimburse them the $65,000, at no additional charge?" The owner agreed eagerly. "If that would get us dismissed from this case, we would be open to that possibility."

"Well, then," the insurer told the Mediator, "we're open to some type of proposal from you in the range we discussed."

"Great," said the Mediator. "Let me meet with the Partridges to discuss the possibilities for settlement." He walked down the hall to where the plaintiffs were waiting.

———✿✿✿———

"Folks," he began, "thank you for your patience. I've been making some good progress with the insurer and the funeral parlor. We're almost ready to discuss what a fair settlement would look like. I realize you are primarily concerned about getting your money back, and I'll see what I can do for you. In the meantime, I would like a moment with your attorney privately."

The Mediator was keenly aware that the lawyer was on a contingency fee, and he didn't want to put him in an awkward situation with his clients. "Let's talk a moment about what we can do together to formulate an agreement. Obviously, your clients want to get their $40,000 back. That would be one component of a settlement. They also want and deserve an apology. How about the legal fees? How are they calculated?" he asked.

The lawyer was quick to respond. "Fortunately, we haven't done that much work on the case, so the fees are still modest. We figured we could settle this case for somewhere close to $100,000, and the fee would be one-third of that. Can you get it for us?"

"I'm not sure if they would pay that much, but if I can arrange to have the funeral parlor pick up the cost of the funerals, that would add value to the clients, though it might not help with the legal fees. What do you think?"

"I'm in favor of helping my clients in any way. These people really deserve a break. Getting the funeral parlor to pick up the costs would be tremendous. Please try and get that, and I'll be flexible with the fee," said the lawyer.

After consulting with each side a bit further, a deal memorandum was prepared. It gave the Partridges back everything they paid, plus legal fees in the sum of $25,000. The Mediator also arranged for Montgomery Family Funeral Home to agree to pay for all the funeral arrangements the Partridges had requested, free of charge. When he had the agreement written, he presented it simultaneously to all and asked everyone to agree to this arrangement without any negotiation. When everyone had agreed, he met privately with both the insurer and the funeral parlor and asked them to present their acceptance of the deal with an apology to the Partridges.

Finally, the Mediator called everyone together for a joint meeting, and he read the signed agreement out loud. All parties accepted the proposal, and the insurer's representative asked to make a statement.

"On behalf of our company, I would like to personally express my apology for any misunderstanding the Partridges had when they purchased our product. It wasn't our intention to confuse them about the nature of this policy. We are glad we could come to a meeting of the minds."

Mary then interjected, "We're just happy this is over. Our family is not sophisticated in these things. Thank you for seeing it our way."

The Partridges had their needs met and were pleased with the resulting agreement. Their lawyer, shaken by the experience and aware that the Partridges were just one example of many people like them whose goodwill and naiveté had been exploited, soon began putting together a class-action suit.

WHAT HAPPENED?

Early on in the mediation, the Mediator was aware of signals from both sides that no one was going to get stuck in the mud in this negotiation. The Partridges indicated a desire for closure by getting their money back. Although their lawyer might have wanted more, he was willing to defer to the clients' needs. The insurer was invested in finding a solution that worked, as they did not want the bad publicity (though they were adamant that their documentation was perfect).

Recognizing the magnetic drive toward some middle ground and the potential volatility if this were reduced to a typical distributive negotiation, the Mediator used a format that didn't allow for back-and-forth negotiations. This format can be used when there is trust in the mediator and an obvious desire on both sides to share their goals and objectives early in the negotiation.

Further, the Mediator wrote the agreement as his own recommendation based on the feedback he received from each side. This approach made it less offensive to each side, particularly because neither side wanted the Mediator to fail.

WHAT STRATEGIES CAN WE LEARN?

1. **Use the "one-step" approach—prepare a proposed agreement based on the ideas of all the parties.**

   This approach allows for the circulation of a draft agreement or memorandum that is subject to comments and criticism by both sides in a safe way. Neither side is being forced to accept the agreement, but you have prepared it with the knowledge that the parties will most likely accept it. You then present it in such a way that the parties are asked to accept or reject the proposed settlement as outlined in the draft.

2. Sweeten the agreement with an apology or an acknowledgment of misunderstanding.

When it is clear that teaching someone the law is not going to go anywhere, tap into the plaintiff's primary reason for bringing the case and try to get some value from the payer through a nonmonetary statement, such as an apology. It will bring down the dollar amount quickly and help achieve a durable agreement.

CHAPTER SEVENTEEN

IF THE SHOE FITS . . .

"Swap's a huge company, and they ripped us off," said Susan, tapping her foot. "It's as simple as that." She glared at Craig, Swap's VP for acquisitions. "You *know* Boingo was worth more than the $75 million you paid us—you paid Warble $80 million for a product that's not even half as good!" Swap! Boingo! Warble! The Mediator felt as though he were inside a video game.

The Mediator wanted to hear Boingo's side of the story from the beginning. "Susan," he said when she stopped for a breath, "before we get into that, help me to understand how this whole deal started."

"Sure," she replied. "I'm going to assume you know all about Swap, right?" She glared at Craig again.

"Of course," said the Mediator. Like most Americans, the Mediator was familiar with Swap. This large multinational clothing company, specializing in midpriced sportswear for teenagers and young adults, couldn't be doing better. Over the last few years the company seemed to have grown exponentially and had recently begun acquiring other companies. "Maybe you could start us off," he said, nodding to Craig.

"About a year ago," the Swap VP began, "our research team discovered that our target customers spent almost as much money on sports shoes as they did on clothing, so we decided to add shoes to our product line. We knew we couldn't compete with all the sports shoe manufacturers out there, so we decided to go for the simple solution: pick the shoes we liked most and try to acquire the company that produced them. All the buyers agreed that Boingo, a small company based in Ohio, made the shoes that fit best with our clothing line. They're fun, quirky, colorful, playful—just what we were looking for. So we did our homework on the company and decided to make them an offer. Susan seemed very excited about the idea," he said, looking at the CEO.

"Of course I was flattered when Swap made its offer," Susan said. Not only was she Boingo's CEO, but she had started the company based on her own designs. "But when we sat down to negotiate a deal, it turned out that we wanted to sell Boingo for more than Swap was offering. Swap explained that they were constrained by their board of directors and shareholders and couldn't give us more than they had offered. I was disappointed, but I understood all about shareholders. In the end, we decided to take their offer. Even at the price they were offering, we knew our shareholders would be pleased."

"So far it sounds great," said the Mediator. "What happened to bring you here?"

"A few months after we sold the company," Susan explained, "our CFO told me about another Swap acquisition he had just gotten wind of. It turned out that Swap had paid a lot more for Warble than it had paid for Boingo—even though our company was more valuable than Warble." Susan's voice was rising again.

Boingo's attorney swooped in smoothly and continued the theme. "It was obvious to us that Swap had lied to us about their financial constraints during the negotiations. We feel that Swap should have paid at least as much for Boingo as they did for Warble, and we're charging Swap with fraud. Under the circumstances, we feel that $100 million in damages is only fair."

Swap's attorney picked up the gauntlet. "Swap did nothing wrong," he said confidently. "They were telling the truth about their financial constraints during negotiations with Boingo."

"That's right," said Craig. "The fact is, no two acquisition scenarios are the same. We face a different set of constraints in each negotiation. That's why we were able to pay a higher price for Warble than Boingo. In any case, Boingo's claim for $100 million is outrageous. I don't even know what we're doing here!"

The conflict and rancor between the parties was escalating fast, and the Mediator could see that the meeting would soon become a shouting match. Time to be the referee. "Thanks for your input, everyone," he said. "I think I've got the general picture of your disagreement. You both seem to feel strongly here. At this point, I'd like to break up into separate sessions so I can get an idea of where this friendly deal went south. Craig, I think it would be helpful if I met first with the Boingo side, and then with you."

The two sides agreed, and went to separate rooms to wait for the Mediator.

—⟆⟅—

"Susan," the Mediator began, "help me understand how you arrived at your figure for damages."

"It's obvious we were ripped off," said Susan in a rush. "Swap took advantage of me. I'm sure it was obvious that I didn't know too much about the world of mergers and acquisitions. They sent their pros. Of course we got the short end of the stick." She stopped, fuming, and turned to her attorney.

"We're asking for $100 million because they lied to us about their financials and abused their position of power during the negotiations," explained the attorney succinctly.

"I see," said the Mediator. "Tell me, did you have a CPA or consulting firm conduct any due diligence before you got into this deal? Did you check Swap's financials before you signed?" The Mediator took note of Susan's furrowed brow. "Because, as I'm sure you know," he said, glancing at Boingo's attorney, "if you're claiming it was outright fraud, you have to prove that their conduct was intentionally designed to deceive you."

Susan gathered herself together. "We were anxious to do the deal. We trusted them—they're Swap, for pete's sake! We were thrilled about getting bought out by such a large company." She paused. "Maybe we didn't dot all our *i*'s or cross all our *t*'s."

"Okay, Susan. I get it. Let me talk to Swap and see what they have to say about all this."

—⟆⟅—

When the Mediator entered Swap's room, the team was ready: Craig was waiting with his arms folded and his jaw working tensely, while Swap's attorney was writing notes on a legal pad. Next to him sat their outside accounting consultant, her laptop booted up and spreadsheets at the ready.

"We did not lie during the negotiations to buy Boingo," Craig said evenly. "Susan was ecstatic. She got more money than she ever dreamed she would get for her shoes, and we got a great company. I can't believe she thinks we were out to screw her."

"Swap is absolutely not prepared to pay any damages," said Swap's attorney. "Swap did nothing wrong, and we don't want our shareholders or the public to get the idea that we were dishonest if we pay off Susan just to make her go away."

"I understand," replied the Mediator, "but Boingo is certain that you misrepresented your financials to them."

"How could that happen?" shouted Craig. "Our financials are an open book. All they had to do was go on the Internet and check out the forms we file with the SEC. Hey, they knew what they were getting into, they agreed, no one twisted their arm. They didn't have to do this deal." He paused to catch his breath and continued in a calmer voice. "Look, we're not going to take a loss because Boingo's got seller's remorse."

"Boingo feels that you had the advantage because you knew more than they did about finance going into the negotiations," said the Mediator.

"Maybe so," Craig acknowledged, "but so what? They had professionals they could call on. Boingo agreed to the terms of the deal. They were happy; we were happy. End of story."

"Let's go back a minute. What kind of support do you have for your position of being a public company, open book and all that? What did you provide them?"

"As a matter of fact," said Craig, "our accounting consultant was present during the meeting. She can tell you exactly what we presented."

On cue, the accountant turned her laptop around so that the Mediator could see the Excel spreadsheet. "I demo'd Swap's financials at the time of the agreement," she explained. "If you look at this spreadsheet, you can see exactly what they saw. We also have a copy of the minutes from a meeting of the Swap board of directors that instructed them on this purchase." She handed the Mediator several typed pages. "As you can see, it speaks clearly to their concerns about not paying Boingo more than $75 million because of

Swap's financials." She sat quietly while the Mediator read through the minutes and looked at the spreadsheet presentation.

"Was Boingo aware of these instructions during the meeting?" he asked.

"Probably not," replied Craig, "but we really didn't need to share this information with them at the time. These were our marching orders, not theirs."

"We felt that Boingo was a good company for Swap to acquire," the accountant continued. "Boingo was a good company with modest financial reserves, and a solid company like Swap backing them up could lift them higher than they could ever get on their own. It seemed like a good fit. And here's another thing Susan should know: if you compare Swap's stock prices when they acquired each company, you can see that they were a lot lower during the Boingo negotiations than later on, when they bought Warble."

"This is important information," said the Mediator. "I appreciate your thorough presentation. It seems to me that if Boingo was made aware of Swap's financial constraints going into this deal, they might be persuaded to reconsider their demands in this case. Would you mind if I brought the accounting consultant into the other room to show them this demo you just showed me?"

"Go ahead," said Craig, after consulting with his colleagues. "We think it would be helpful. We're not involved in a lawsuit yet, and we don't *want* to be involved in a lawsuit—we just want to clear up this misunderstanding and go forward with this deal."

"Okay, Craig. Let me steal your accountant for a bit, and I'll get back to you."

"Susan," the Mediator said, "I think we've got some information here that will help you see what happened in a different context." He explained to Susan about the Swap board's explicit instructions and the difference in Swap's stock prices during the Boingo and Warble acquisitions. After the accountant had shown her presentation to Susan and her attorney, they were very quiet.

"Susan," said the Mediator, "do you have a better sense of Swap's intentions now that you've seen their presentation?"

"Yes," replied Susan, shaking her head. "This whole thing has really made me see my limitations," she said, almost thinking out loud. "It's no secret that I'm a creative person; I'm not really interested in details, and frankly math was never my strong suit. Contracts and numbers make me want to run the other way. It's pretty ironic that I find myself in the center of a multimillion-dollar negotiation."

Susan had suddenly figured the whole thing out. "It's no secret that this was my first experience with being acquired. I thought it was pretty straightforward—you like us, you acquire us, and if we're worth more than Warble, then we get more money. But this presentation makes it pretty clear that maybe we should have drilled down a little further. Everyone in the company was thrilled to death. We were excited about being taken over by this big company, but even my financial people are new at the game. We thought we did our due diligence, but we were in a hurry. Should have dotted more *i*'s and crossed more *t*'s, I guess . . ." She trailed off, finally.

"Okay," Susan said, looking at the Mediator. "It's clear to me that Swap had good intentions. So what do we do now?" Susan now had a very different understanding of what had happened, and the Mediator could see that she needed some time to absorb it. "Why don't you and your attorney talk this over privately and give it some more thought? I think if we can all be a little more flexible, we might be able to work out something that benefits everybody."

"Yeah, that's a good idea," agreed Susan.

"Thanks. Give us a few minutes to get straight on our understanding of this case, and I think we'll have something for you," her lawyer added.

Fifteen minutes later, Susan popped her head out the door. "We want to go forward with the deal, and we're willing to be more flexible. But we still don't want to feel like we came in second to Warble. We'd like to hear what Swap has to say."

"Hang tight—I'll get right back to you." The Mediator walked back down the hall, pleased with the way things were going.

———∞———

"Craig," he said, "Boingo was impressed by the financial presentation, and they'd like to talk about how you can all bring this deal forward."

"That's good to hear," Craig said, smiling for the first time that day. "We really just want everybody to be happy here—that's kind of our company's mission. Maybe we could come up with a way to bring up Boingo's returns without having to take a loss or pay damages."

———

When Susan heard this, she was pleased. "Look, it was never really about getting revenge money. We don't really care *how* we're compensated. We just want Boingo to be valued at least as highly as Warble."

"Let's get you guys together and see what we can come up with," suggested the Mediator. "It sounds like you're all on the same wavelength now."

———

The atmosphere in the second joint meeting was light and friendly. They brainstormed back and forth for a while, and the Mediator just sat back and facilitated. After a short time, Susan came up with a creative solution. Susan said, "I think I've got it!" she said, looking intensely at Craig. "Swap has bought a few smaller manufacturers like Boingo over the last couple of years, right?"

"Right," Craig agreed.

"Well, then, pretty soon, you're going to have to build a state-of-the-art factory to deal with all this expansion. In the meantime," she continued, her voice rising with excitement, "why don't you use one of Boingo's existing production facilities? We're all tooled up, our employees are skilled—we're ready to go!"

"Yeah," Craig nodded readily, "that makes a lot of sense. If we don't have to invest money in a new plant right away, Swap can increase its return to Boingo on the overall investment."

"Plus," Susan added, "our workers could keep their jobs while we make this transition." Treating her employees fairly was clearly important to this young entrepreneur.

In the end, Swap agreed to keep manufacturing at Susan's plant for the time being, and offered to pay an addition $5 million for the brand—bringing them even to what they paid for Warble.

In so doing they avoided litigation and created some goodwill with Susan and her people. With this arrangement, Swap would have no net loss, and Boingo could claim a higher value for its operation. The compromise also allowed both Swap and Boingo to save money. Perhaps more important, the agreement allowed them to get back on friendly terms and to preserve their good business reputations.

WHAT HAPPENED?

This negotiation began in conflict: Boingo held a fierce perception that Swap had "ripped them off" when acquiring them and had valued them less than a rival company, Warble. Swap was equally adamant that they had paid a fair price for Boingo and were being unjustly accused. Ultimately, the Mediator's challenge would be to search for a way to help both sides arrive at a deal that each felt benefited them. First, however, he would need to deal with their perceptions and help them look at things through a different lens. His strategy was to break the case down into three parts: reports, inferences, and judgments.

In exchanging information, the basic symbolic act is to *report* what we have seen, heard, or felt. Boingo reported that Swap lied about its financials when it paid significantly less for Boingo than it paid for Warble. The way to challenge a mistaken report is to seek to verify its truth. In this case, the Mediator reviewed the financials that Boingo had access to at the time of acquisition, and the minutes of Swap's board meetings in which the discussion of purchasing Boingo took place. The Mediator also helped Boingo look at the stock price of Swap at the time of the purchase to give Boingo an idea of Swap's financial position. With this relatively easy and verifiable information at hand, Boingo saw right away that it had jumped to an inaccurate conclusion about Swap's motives.

An *inference* is a statement of the unknown based on the known: "Swap paid more for Warble than for Boingo [known], so they must have defrauded us [unknown]." Making an inference is akin to reviewing a patient's symptoms and reaching a diagnosis: a trained doctor might be able to reach the right diagnosis, but someone untrained in medicine might misdiagnose the problem. When dealing with a party's inference, you can run the appropriate tests to confirm or verify the accuracy of the diagnosis—in this case, by gathering information that proved Boingo's inference was faulty.

Judgments are conclusions that evaluate previously observed facts and either approve or disapprove of something. Boingo's conclusion (based on a faulty inference) that it had been defrauded is a judgment that stops further thought and discussion, as it wasn't based on fact. It was up to the Mediator to verify the facts, accomplished through the review of the board minutes.

WHAT STRATEGIES CAN WE LEARN?

1. **Manage preconceived notions.**
   Preconceived notions held by both parties are the raw material of which disputes are made. Identifying them is an important first step in identifying the barriers toward settlement. Dealing with such preconceived perceptions about others and their intentions requires information management. You must slowly acquire enough information about the subject matter to allow the party with the incorrect perception to revise their thoughts in a way that transforms the context of the dispute.
2. **Trust your intuition and see where it takes you.**
   Dealing with preconceived notions also requires you to improvise. Effective improvisation is a product of skill (education plus experience) and intuition. If you trust your intuition that one of the disputants reached a conclusion based on inadequate or inaccurate information, you can follow that intuition and seek to verify the facts.
   You can then use these facts to turn a perception around and open the conversation to a discussion of a principled agreement for both sides.
3. **Break perceptions into component parts: reports, inferences, and judgments.**
   Observe how the disputants report their beliefs. If they report them without much factual backup, that's your first clue to seek verification from the parties to either support their belief or demonstrate that it is incorrect. Do the same when a party draws a conclusion about the dispute from an inference that lacks foundation. When parties use

judgment-laden words like "fraud" and "guilty" to describe their opponent, it is a good sign that you should explore the parties' underlying factual support.

4. **Look for leverage in the parties' desire to continue their business relationship.**

Even though they are involved in a rancorous dispute, it's often the case that both parties would prefer to continue the business relationship; many times, they are looking for a way out that allows them to save face and feel good. As mediator, you can work to create a mutually satisfactory outcome for everyone by finding (or creating) ways for both parties to feel that they gained from the deal.

CHAPTER EIGHTEEN

THE STAGGERED APPROACH

"If he'd just told me the house was infested with mold in the first place, I'd be participating in the Ironman Triathlon right now, and we wouldn't be here hassling over money." Carol was furious, and she wanted to make sure her landlord, Al, knew it. Al, well-worn and leathery, stared miserably at his hands. He looked like he'd rather be anywhere but here. He had clearly dressed up for the occasion, but his best clothes still looked out of place in the context of this downtown office.

Carol had a right to be angry: the insidious aspergillus mold that had infested her rented beach house had given this formerly healthy woman an alarming litany of medical problems.

Aspergillus is a fungus, a type of mold that grows in wet places and wreaks havoc on the body's immune system. When it finds its way into the bloodstream, it causes watery eyes, sneezing, hives, and many other nasty reactions. When it finds its way onto clothing and furniture, those items often have to be destroyed. One of the worst aspects of an aspergillus infestation is that people often don't know it's there until they've been sick for quite a while.

That's what happened to Carol. At first, she thought she just had a cold. But after months of recurring colds, she developed sinus problems and a cough that never really went away. Carol was upset and concerned. She was nearly forty, but she had always competed (and won) against much younger women. She had started with great genes and took pains to eat only organically raised foods; her exercise regimen was beyond reproach. She attacked this problem with her usual determination, consulting doctor after doctor, but her symptoms just got worse—and multiplied. Finally, she found a doctor who thought her cluster of symptoms suggested mold. Test results confirmed the doctor's suspicions: positive for aspergillus.

Carol was floored. Where could she have encountered *mold?* Her doctor suggested she have her house tested immediately—and to move out if she wanted to keep what was left of her health.

When Carol learned that the home she had been renting for seventeen years was a veritable aspergillus factory, she was hopeful that her landlord would help repair the property, patch up whatever leaks were causing water intrusion into the house, and perhaps show some sensitivity to her physical condition. They'd never been the best of friends, and she considered Al something of an odd duck. He was never rude, but he kept conversation to a bare minimum. He seemed almost pathologically shy. But he had always been a fair landlord, and they'd had a cordial relationship over the years. So she was stunned when Al told her to either move out or get a lawyer. Offended and shocked by his unfeeling response, she did both.

She was puzzled by Al's belligerent position. She was even more puzzled when she drove by the house a week after she had temporarily moved in with friends and saw that he was busy repairing the house and eradicating the mold. Did he want to get rid or her and rent the house to someone else?

Apparently not. Three months later, Al called Carol's lawyer as if nothing had happened. "I've had an expert inspect the property, and I've got a report that says the house is mold free," he said matter-of-factly. "Carol can move back in whenever she likes." Carol's lawyer asked Al for a copy of the expert's report, but it never arrived. What kind of game was Al playing?

Even though her friends pleaded with her to find a new place to live, Carol wanted to move back into the house she had lived in for almost two decades. This house had been her *home.* It was a beautiful property, right on the beach, with clean air and an unbroken expanse of sand to run on. But she was suspicious: Why wouldn't Al turn over that inspection report? Maybe he'd just torn out the carpets, patched the holes, and repainted, leaving the mold to reproduce. She had no faith whatsoever that the mold was really gone; she couldn't *see* the microscopic spores, so the report was all she had. She decided she would have to go to court to force Al to prove he was telling the truth. But the courts were crammed with cases, and before the judge would hear her case, he had asked Carol to see a mediator.

―――∽∽∽――

The Mediator had learned all of this information in premediation discussions, before he met the parties in person for the first time. Given what he had heard, this case looked as though it could get very emotional very quickly. How could he shake things up so that the inevitable didn't even have a chance to happen? He chose to use a staggered approach: instead of proceeding in the usual way, he would stagger the presentations of each side in between an active negotiation. He'd give one party the opportunity to let off steam and then—instead of allowing the other party to respond and shuttling back and forth between them—he would immediately solicit an offer from the other side to jump-start negotiations. He'd used this unusual technique before, and the results were always interesting. It was a bit like setting off fireworks at seemingly random intervals: at the very least this strategy would unsettle the parties' expectations.

So instead of beginning with gentle understanding or objective listening, he wanted to start off with a bang—creating a visceral reaction that was actually painful. The natural person to start things off in this direction would be the plaintiff.

"Carol," the Mediator began, "I'd like you to describe your symptoms for us so that we are all clear about exactly how the mold has affected your life."

"How has it affected my *life?* My life is *wrecked,*" said Carol, her hands clasped together so tightly that her knuckles were already white. "I'm a top amateur triathlete. I made the U.S. Olympic team *three times.* But now I'm dizzy; I have vertigo, which means my balance is shot, which means that half the time I can't even walk a straight line let alone ride a bike, swim, or run. I have excruciating fungal infections. My lungs have been affected, so I have trouble breathing. Not great for a runner, is it?" she said, looking around and making sure everyone was paying attention.

"My memory has been affected too. Makes it kinda hard to hold a job. I'm tired all the time. I'm too tired even to be frustrated with how tired I am. I feel like I'm losing my mind, if you really want to know. I'm a frigging basket case. I've had more medical tests than I can recall, including more than one colonoscopy. *That* was delightful." By the time Carol finished reeling off her horrific list, she was sobbing loudly. Her attorney put her arm around her client's shoulders, consoling her softly.

Even though there had been no discussion about who was at fault, Al and the lawyer for his insurance company were shifting nervously in their seats, clearly shaken by her bitter recitation. "Omigod," Al muttered over and over. "I had no idea."

"Thank you, Carol. I know this is tough for you, but I appreciate you hanging in there. Al, I'm sure you have something to say, but I want you to hold on to your thoughts for a few moments—I have some other ideas to explore with each side separately. I promise we'll have a chance to hear your side of the story in a few minutes. Carol, I'm going to ask you and your attorney to wait here while I speak to Al and his lawyer in another office."

—◦◦◦—

As soon as they were alone, the Mediator set off another small explosion designed to shake things up. "Al," he said, "I'd like you think about making Carol an offer."

"An offer?" said Al and the attorney in unison. The attorney protested, "We haven't even had a chance to respond to Carol's allegations yet. Isn't this a little out of order? I've been involved in a number of mediations, and I can tell you I've never done it this way."

"I realize you haven't had a chance to respond to what Carol had to say, and I'm going to give you an opportunity to do that soon. But my experience tells me that it would be more effective to set up your position with an underlying monetary statement." Al and his lawyer looked puzzled. "That way," the Mediator explained, "your position will set the agenda for the mediation, and when you do make your statement it will have more of an impact."

The lawyer wasn't convinced. "But we don't know yet what Carol's expectations are with respect to the negotiation." Clearly, this was not the style of mediation he was accustomed to. *Good,* thought the

Mediator. "I know this is a little irregular, but after all, you did receive a large demand package before the mediation, so you have a general idea what they are looking for. Trust me—this approach works."

"Well, okay," said the lawyer. He thought for a few minutes. Then, clearly having decided to be magnanimous and make the first move, he said, "We can offer Carol $25,000."

"Great! That's a good start," said the Mediator. This relatively low number would allow him to anchor Carol at a certain level of expectation and let him open the dialogue about the value of the case—which was the entire point of this little exercise. "Let me take that back to Carol and see what she says."

The Mediator plunged right in. "Carol, I'd like to report that even though you haven't heard from the defense, they're willing to put some money on the table. That's a first for me! Usually they want to start by casting blame on the plaintiff, but I guess they're ready to play. I need to caution you that this is just the start of the negotiation, and I would expect that we'll have several other discussions that lead to a larger offer. So I have to ask you to stick with this process no matter how you view the offer. Is that acceptable?"

"Yes, I'll stick with it. But I don't have to like it."

The Mediator proceeded. "Okay: they've offered you $25,000."

Carol was underwhelmed. "You've got to be kidding!" she said, looking disgusted. "Is that supposed to be a real offer? It's an insult. Tell them we appreciate the gesture, but we thought they'd offer more. I'm looking for an offer in the millions. I know Al looks a little marginal, but he owns a lot of properties. He can afford it."

"Look," the Mediator responded. "I realize you view this as a modest first offer. Why don't we all get back together and let them explain their side of the story? That way, you'll have a better understanding of how they came up with this proposal." Carol and her lawyer looked dubious, but they agreed. The Mediator knew that this would give the defense an opportunity to put some meat behind their offer. The Mediator intended to manage Carol's financial expectations and send the plaintiff and her lawyer off to see how they could control the damage.

—ᔓ᷍—

Before the parties gathered together in the conference room, the Mediator took the insurance company's lawyer aside. "I want you to give them an overview of your position. They need to hear it, and I think it will help them understand exactly how far you're willing to go."

"No problem," said the lawyer, and Al added, "Whatever it takes."

So, when they were all together, the attorney made a detailed statement on the question of what caused Carol's injuries. "We sympathize with Carol," he concluded firmly, putting his palms on the table, "but she's asking for *way* too much money." The lawyer's body language made it absolutely clear that Carol would never get what she was asking for.

"Look," the lawyer continued in a more conciliatory tone. "Al's an old school kind of guy. He's got several properties in the beach communities, and he's always done his own work. Beach houses are damp, and mold has always been a problem. But killer mold? That just wasn't on his radar." The Mediator was well aware that mold complaints had recently become the "tort du jour" for some lawyers, and he could see that Carol's attorney was working hard to look impassive.

"So when the report came back and said the mold was no longer at a dangerous level," the landlord's lawyer continued, "he just got back to work finishing his cleanup. The simple truth is, he just couldn't get it through his head that the report, and not his word, was what mattered to Carol." He looked at Carol. "It was just an oversight on Al's part. We'll be glad to give you the report; honestly, we have nothing to hide here."

After the defense had finished its presentation, the Mediator separated the parties again. From this point on, he would stagger the moments in the meetings during which the parties were permitted to confront each other. This approach would prevent the typical conversation from taking place, in which one party or the other is afraid of making the first move and the negotiation bogs down. Instead, he hoped, things would move along faster, and the time apart would give both parties space to contemplate the progress of their negotiations and the direction in which they were headed.

"Do you think that the information provided by the insurer's counsel might have an impact in court?" the Mediator asked Carol's lawyer. He was curious to see what she had learned, what kind of impact the defense statement had made, and how she felt about the legal risk.

"We understand that health problems related to mold infestation are hard to prove," she replied, "but it's no secret that my client suffered a lot of damage."

"I realize that," responded the Mediator. "But I think we both know that it's going to cost you a lot of money to bring in doctors to support your claim that the damage was actually caused by the mold in the house. I'm trying to acknowledge that the damage is there—no one's disputing that—and focus on your investment in proving the cause of the damage in court. I wonder if you can put a percentage on your chances of winning this case."

"Well," the lawyer said after some thought, "I'd say we have at least a 50 percent chance of winning."

The Mediator nodded and turned to Carol. "Your lawyer is very practical," he said. "There's always a cost attached when you go to court with experts to prove your case. In mediation, we often try to look for a situation that lets both parties leave satisfied—or at least equally unsatisfied!" Carol rewarded him with a wry smile. "But in court," he continued, "there's always a winner and a loser. And as your lawyer has said, even though it's clear that you suffered and are still suffering, you will not necessarily win." And then he set off another bomb: "I'm going to ask you to lower your demand."

Carol's lawyer jumped. *Right on target!* the Mediator noted to himself. "We recognize there's some serious risk here," the lawyer protested, "but we think this is easily a six-figure case."

"And don't forget that mold report," said Carol, although at this point that refrain was losing steam.

"When you say this could easily be a six-figure case, do you mean a *low* six-figure case?" asked the Mediator.

"To be realistic, we would consider an offer in the low six-figures, but I can't guarantee that my client would accept it."

"Why don't I see if I can get their commitment to looking at this as a six-figure case?" said the Mediator. "Let me see what they say. I'll get back to you soon."

———

"As you know," the Mediator said to Al and the lawyer, "coming in, Carol and her attorney were looking at this as a seven-figure case. We've made a tremendous amount of progress with our approach today," he said, with a smile and a nod to the lawyer. "They still think they have a strong case for damages, but they're willing to concede some of the liability. My read on it is that if you were able to come into a range somewhere in the low six figures, you would probably get their attention."

"We didn't want to go that high," replied the lawyer, "but we might be able to get close."

"Around $75,000 to $90,000?" ventured the Mediator.

"If you could get them below six figures we would probably consider that range," the lawyer conceded.

This told the Mediator that the case would settle for something over $75,000 (the defense's bottom line) but for less than the $200,000 he suspected the plaintiff was considering demanding. *Now I've got this case into a reasonable zone,* he thought.

———

Back with the plaintiff, however, he didn't talk about money: right now, they needed to confront Carol's lack of trust about the mold report. Until that emotional roadblock was removed, he knew, the case would not proceed. But Carol started off with no prompting. "Look," she said, "I'm really concerned about this mold report and what it means to me. Why didn't they tell me about this at the beginning? I still don't believe them."

"Maybe there's more to this than meets the eye," the Mediator suggested. "Let me see if I can get Al to discuss this with you." And with that he trotted back down the hall.

—⁂—

"Al," he began, "I don't know what's up with this, but it might help move things along if you would meet with Carol and apologize for not letting her know about the original mold report."

"Sure," Al shrugged. "I wasn't trying to hide it. I can't believe she's making such a big deal about this. I guess the insurance company didn't send it on. And then I was busy with the repairs, and it wasn't something I really thought she needed. She's the renter. It's my property, and I was dealing with it. I *told* her it was okay. But if you think it will help, fine."

"Great," said the Mediator. "I'll get Carol, and we'll meet back in the large conference room in five minutes."

—⁂—

"Al," said the Mediator, "please let Carol know what happened with this mold report."

"Carol, I wish I had understood how important this was to you," Al said earnestly, thrusting the report at her without ceremony. "We've known each other for years. I was just following the advice of the insurance company. They sent somebody out to check it, and the report just got filed. I should have given it to you, but I didn't, and I'm sorry. Honestly, I wasn't trying to hide anything. I guess I was just being clueless," he said, suddenly inspired. "Please accept my apologies."

Carol didn't say anything, but as she read through the report her shoulders dropped about an inch, and she tried not to smile. She wasn't going to let him off the hook so fast. "Yeah, Al, you've been pretty clueless about this whole thing. You know, if you'd just been straight with me from the beginning, we could have avoided all this."

"Believe me, Carol, I would love to have avoided all this. You know, I really didn't get it until today how sick you got from all this. I really am sorry I didn't show you that report."

"Okay. We've known each other a long time. You've always been a decent landlord. I've always liked living there, and I miss it.

I accept your apology." For the first time that day, Al and Carol exchanged a friendly look.

The Mediator had created a nice human moment, but he knew there was more to it than that. Such an emotional appeal was actually a shrewd negotiation move because it caused Carol to feel that her landlord was not as bad a person as she had painted him to be in her mind.

Emotional component handled, thought the Mediator. *Now for the money.* "I'd like to meet separately with each of you," he said. "Carol, would you and your attorney mind waiting in the small office while I speak with the defense?" He hoped that Carol's new, more lenient frame of mind might lead her to talk to her counsel about accepting a settlement recommended by the Mediator in the next round.

—◦◦◦—

"Al," said the Mediator, "it's time to be realistic. It's going to be difficult to get Carol to accept a number under $100,000. She's got medical bills and lawyer's fees, and she wants to end up with something when she's paid everyone else. If I suggest a number in the low ones, say $125,000, would you consider that?"

But before he could answer, the lawyer said, "Al, we need to talk privately about this."

"No problem," said the Mediator. "I'll leave you guys alone."

—◦◦◦—

The Mediator, however, didn't wait to see how the conversation would come out. He had expectations to manage in the plaintiff's room. "Carol," he said, "I realize you want to settle for over $100,000, but I'm getting a lot of pressure to go *under* that number. I can't guarantee they'll pay $100,000, but I might get close. Would you consider something under that?"

"We didn't come here to settle for five figures," said Carol's lawyer, running her hand through her hair. "If they're willing to go to $100,000, they'd be willing to go a little higher—Carol has expenses, you know."

Now the Mediator knew intuitively that the case would settle for between $100,000 and $125,000, with about one-third going to the lawyer.

—⁓—

The insurer's lawyer was firm. "We won't go higher than $125,000."

—⁓—

"Carol, they just won't pay $150,000," the Mediator said. "I *might* be able to get them to go for $125,000. Will you accept that if I can get it?"

She thought for a few moments and consulted with her lawyer. "Tell them yes, but not a penny below that number," she said.

The Mediator smiled. The staggered approach had worked its magic. Both parties signed off on the settlement, and as Carol shook hands with Al, she was already talking about hiring a moving van and getting back to her life.

WHAT HAPPENED?

The staggered approach is a counterintuitive technique that runs contrary to virtually all the literature of negotiation. In this completely artificial setup, the Mediator intentionally staggered the presentations to make it appear that the balance was favoring first one side and then the other. He also broke with tradition by having the defendant make the first move—making a settlement offer directly after the plaintiff's opening presentation and before the defense had a chance to respond.

This strategy was a wakeup call for the plaintiff and her counsel that allowed them to see in stark terms exactly how the defense valued the plaintiff's presentation of the case. In choosing this strategy the Mediator was taking a chance: it was entirely possible that Carol would have been so frustrated by the small amount of the offer that she would threaten to leave the proceeding. That's why it was important for the Mediator to get a commitment in advance from the plaintiff to stick with the process, no matter what the numbers might be.

Following the initial offer, the Mediator built empathy with the plaintiff by agreeing that the offer was too low. He then swung the pendulum the other way by encouraging the defense to explain their reasoning to the plaintiff and her counsel. This helped Carol and her attorney understand how the defense had arrived at their number—that it wasn't meant as a thoughtless insult.

The Mediator continued negotiations until he saw they were about to stall, then blew up Carol's emotional roadblock with Al's apology, letting the anger escape from the case. Once both parties had been disarmed, they were forced by the momentum of the process to make larger moves in shorter periods of time. The anger release also forced the parties to take a more businesslike approach now that the personal issues had been taken care of.

Finally, when it became clear that the traditional back-and-forth negotiation would not end in complete closure, the Mediator took it upon himself to recommend to each side a number he thought each should consider. When both parties agreed to his suggestion, the matter was concluded.

WHAT STRATEGIES CAN WE LEARN?

1. **Stagger the presentations to shift the balance of power and keep the parties off balance.**

   Staggering the presentations creates a situation in which the balance of power quickly shifts from one side to another. This is contrary to traditional mediation theory, which generally holds that in order to create balance and procedural fairness, each side should have an opportunity to make a statement to each other at the same time. But when it's clear that this traditional approach will result only in each side's shooting bullets at each other, it makes sense to stagger the presentations so that the focus is on one side only. Then, after negotiations begin, you can redirect the focus to the other side.

2. **Consider a counterintuitive approach when you feel it's called for.**

   A mediation is always an improvisation. If your intuition tells you that the traditional approach you planned will lead to disaster, have the confidence to try your own counterintuitive approach. In this case, for example, the Mediator suggested that the defendant make the first offer in the negotiation even before he had explained his position in the case. You don't always have to be the messenger, the referee, or the understanding social worker!

3. **Appeal to the parties on an emotional level to help them understand each other's position.**

   When you appeal to emotions, you are seeking to get the parties to acknowledge some sense of responsibility for their actions. By the time a case comes to mediation, parties are usually fairly well entrenched in their beliefs about who's right and who's wrong. An emotional appeal forces each party to consider how the other might feel and what that person might have gone through as a result of the conduct alleged. Some people, in fact, operate more through "emotional" intelligence than through reasoned logic. For them, connecting emotionally with the situation helps them better understand the other party.

CHAPTER NINETEEN

TIME-SHARE

Mike was furious. "I can't believe they fired me just because I asked for more money. I wasn't just some flunky in their operation. I've been their top guy for years." He'd been fuming for weeks, and for good reason. At age forty-nine, Mike was a heavy hitter for TimePlus, a time-share company with resorts in prime vacation locations all over the world. In fact, he was the lead broker whose license the company used with the Department of Real Estate to sell these nifty little lifetime commitments.

The Mediator let Mike's anger drift out the window, determined not to let it affect him. He was dead tired. He'd had three complicated cases back to back, working without a break. In contrast, this one looked relatively simple—he should be able to wrap it up by the end of the day and go home and sleep for what was left of his weekend. In fact, he thought, it's almost as simple as the time-share business itself: convince a relatively young couple on vacation to come to a meeting where they will receive cocktails and a free digital camera, then sell them on the concept of investing in holiday rentals for the rest of their lives. Once they make the commitment, they're stuck with the property. All the time-share company has to do is make sure the resorts are clean and stocked with fresh linens.

Mike was great at his job, and when he had asked TimePlus for a salary increase, he expected to get it with no problem. But the company blindsided him: not only did they refuse to give him more money, they found a reason to terminate his services. Mike was insulted, in shock, and angry, and he wasn't the kind of guy who walked away from a fight. He found his own reason to sue the time-share company for wrongful termination.

"They had no right to fire me," Mike told the Mediator when he had first met with Mike and his lawyer privately that morning. "We all know that they found someone younger and less experienced who would work for less money. That's not a good enough reason in my book."

The Mediator pondered the working agreement between the parties. "Mike, this agreement says that the company can fire you at their own will, without any reason. Are you aware of anything that would change the terms of the contract, or any fact that would show they discriminated against you?"

"Absolutely. First off, they hired a much younger person to replace me. On top of that, we had many discussions over the years in which they assured me of lifetime employment—especially since I let them use my broker's license."

"Okay, Mike. Wait here while I talk to the company and see what they have to say."

"Make it quick," said Mike's lawyer, Ryan. "I don't want to work straight through my tee-off time tomorrow morning." He laughed to show he was joking, but the Mediator knew that Ryan was a rabid golfer, and there was probably more than a grain of truth in there.

—⁊⁊⁊—

But it wasn't going to be quick. TimePlus's side of the story was succinct: "We don't owe Mike an explanation. You've read our agreement. We don't owe him a reason for letting him go."

The Mediator then began a series of separate discussions with each side. Mike and Ryan emphasized the fact that Mike was almost fifty years old and had been replaced by a much younger person, giving rise to his claim of age discrimination. TimePlus contended that Mike was simply not as productive as he used to be and that a change was necessary in order to keep the business moving forward. The idea that TimePlus could be held liable before a jury for hiring a younger person to replace Mike, coupled with statistics provided by Ryan demonstrating that the company had a pattern of hiring younger people, struck home with TimePlus's president; clearly, he didn't want to see this point brought out in open court. So, little by little, they negotiated back and forth through the Mediator until they were only $15,000 apart—a relatively small percentage of the total. Mike was willing to settle for $150,000, and TimePlus said they wouldn't pay a cent more than $135,000. Deadlock. The Mediator asked Mike and Ryan to wait in another room while he spoke to TimePlus privately.

———

"There must be some creative way we can get around this," he said to the president of TimePlus. But the man shook his head. "We're not putting any more money into this deal. We would rather pay our lawyers at this point." The Mediator said nothing. He had heard this line many times before from people who were frustrated with negotiations. Usually it was a placeholder in the conversation that meant they just didn't know what else to do, or didn't want to ask their board for more money to negotiate with. He waited a moment to give the president a chance to reconsider.

"Look," said the president, laying his palms on the table for emphasis. "I'm not giving him any more money. But if Mike wants to settle, maybe there's something else we can do for him."

"What do you have in mind?"

"Well, maybe Mike would like to take his family to one of our resorts for a few weeks. We'll comp him for everything. He just has to get his family there—wherever he wants—and they can enjoy a luxury vacation on us. We'll give him carte blanche. A package like that is easily worth $15,000, and he knows it."

"Sounds like an interesting opportunity," replied the Mediator. "Let me present it to him privately right now and see what he says." The Mediator got a second wind. They finally seemed to be making progress.

———

As soon as he entered the small office where Mike and Ryan were waiting, he started right in. "Mike, the company's made you an interesting offer. While the cash doesn't add up to $150,000, the value of the deal does." Mike stopped drumming his fingers on the table and looked up. "What's the catch?"

Uh oh. The Mediator had a sudden sinking feeling. "In exchange they'll give you and your family a four-week, all-expenses-paid vacation in any of their resorts—anywhere in the world you want to go!" He put as much enthusiasm into his voice as he could muster, but he knew he'd made a wrong turn.

"Screw them and screw their resorts," Mike shot back, his face red. "They think they can buy me off with a *vacation?* I don't want any of their product. I don't want to see them again. Tell them they can take their vacation and shove it. It's cash or nothing."

Damn. The Mediator knew he had made a huge error in the way he had presented this proposal. He chalked it up to being dead tired, but still, it was no excuse. He knew better. Fortunately, he thought he had a way to save the situation.

"Mike, I'm sorry I brought it up. I thought it was worth a shot, but I can see I was dead wrong. Ryan," he said, turning to Mike's lawyer, "come for a walk with me, and let's talk about options. Hang tight, Mike. We'll get this sorted out." Mike looked dubious, but he leaned back in his chair to wait.

———✺———

Ryan and the Mediator walked down the hall to another small room and sat down. "Here's the story," said the Mediator. "We're $15,000 apart; TimePlus tells me that they're done negotiating, and I believe them. Mike won't take their free vacation because he doesn't want to take *anything* from them at this point. I hate to bring this up, but is there anything you can do with your fee to make this deal work?"

The Mediator thought that Ryan might be open to the idea of reducing his contingent fee to settle the case. That was a fairly common maneuver for lawyers who would rather walk away with a slightly smaller fee and have the case settled rather than gamble on a larger percentage that required spending a long time in court. Once again, however, the Mediator had miscalculated. "If you're asking me to discount my fee, I don't think so. I've worked hard for Mike. Why should *I* be penalized?"

"I know you've worked hard," replied the Mediator. "I'm just telling you that you will have to work quite a bit harder to get paid, because the time-share company is stuck. This case will have to go to court unless we come up with another way to divide the pie here," he said.

They stared at each other for a long, blank moment. The Mediator was thinking hard. Suddenly, he remembered an earlier conversation in which Ryan commented that he was a scratch golfer and had played some of the time-share's many top-rated courses. The Mediator started to put two and two together: he could use the same settlement dollars and free vacation, but spend it a bit differently.

He shot up out of his chair, energized. "Wait right there, Ryan. I've got one more idea. Let me talk to TimePlus and get right back to you."

———

The TimePlus team looked like they were about ready to go home. "Thanks for waiting," the Mediator began, "but I've got some bad news. Mike has rejected the offer. Still, we're really close financially. It's a shame Mike didn't take the vacation package," he mused. "It seemed like the perfect solution. I asked Ryan to reduce his fee modestly so that Mike could net the same amount at $135,000, but he was offended that I even asked. But if you'll agree with a slightly different approach, I think I've got a way to resolve this deadlock. Why don't we offer the vacation to Ryan? I happen to know that he's a scratch golfer, and he likes to travel. Perhaps he'll reconsider the fee reduction if he thinks the vacation opportunity has value to his family. Mike nets the same amount. If it's all right with you, I'd like to present the idea as coming from me so Ryan's more receptive to it."

"That's a great idea!" replied the company president. "I don't care how the product is used as along as we don't have to come up with any more cash." Then he smiled magnanimously and said, "And we can sweeten the pot with some free rounds at one of our resorts with one of the top hundred golf courses in the world attached to it. His choice."

"Great," said the Mediator. "Wait here." He walked quickly down the hall to see what Ryan would say.

—◦◦◦—

"Ryan," he began, "TimePlus absolutely refuses to kick in the additional $15,000 to settle." At this, Ryan started putting on his jacket. "But I've got some good news." Ryan sat down again. "The company is willing to give you and your family the same free vacation they offered to Mike. They tell me that they have some of the top golf destinations in the world. World-class courses, in the top one hundred. They're offering four weeks, all expenses paid—rooms, food, spas, the works—for you and your family at any of their resorts."

"Whoa," Ryan said, sitting back, his eyes wide open. "Do they still have that magnificent resort in Cabo? I've never played that course . . ."

"The only caveat," continued the Mediator, "is that you need to consider reducing your fee so that Mike nets the same amount as if the company were paying the additional $15,000. I really appreciate the hard work you've done for Mike on this case, and I know you said were averse to fee reduction, so I'm not going to push this on you. But in light of the uncertainty in the outcome of this case, and your penchant for golf, it seems like a pretty sweet deal."

Ryan thought hard. He knew they were running out of options and that looking at the outcome differently was the only way to settle this case. He was also sorely tempted by the offer. But instead of accepting the proposal, he said, "Hold on; I need to make a phone call."

Don't let this fall apart now, thought the Mediator. Nervously, he asked, "Who are you going to call?" The lawyer quickly grabbed his cell phone and headed out the door. "My wife!" he called over his shoulder as the door slammed shut.

Minutes later, Ryan came back into the small office. He'd held up pretty well over the course of the long negotiation, but now he looked a bit disheveled.

"What happened?" asked the Mediator.

"My wife accepted the deal," Ryan replied sheepishly. "We're going to Cabo—with a two-week beach layover in Tahiti."

—∽∾∿∾—

When Ryan told Mike about the deal he'd brokered, Mike just laughed. "Hey," he said, "as long as I get my money, there's no reason why you shouldn't get some pleasure out of the deal too. Just promise me one thing," he said seriously.

"What's that?" asked Ryan.

"Promise me that you'll stick it to TimePlus for everything you can get."

WHAT HAPPENED?

When both sides in a negotiation are stuck, it's up to you to help the parties come up with new ways to solve the problem. This often involves thinking outside the box. The idea of trading dollars for vacation time was a good one, but Mike's anger at TimePlus predisposed him to reject out of hand anything the company might suggest. As soon as the words were out of his mouth, the Mediator knew he had made a rookie mistake. Had he presented the idea as his own, Mike might have jumped at it.

Fortunately, his next instinct was a good one—to offer the deal to Mike's lawyer. He led the TimePlus president to a place where the president suggested this idea himself, which allowed him to feel a sense of ownership in the settlement, as opposed to having it shoved down his throat. However, the Mediator presented the idea to Ryan as his own because the parties had developed intense emotional barriers during the negotiation, which prevented them from trusting each other.

After all this intricate deal making, they settled. But what the Mediator didn't realize was that the main deal maker was not even in the mediation room—she was at home with the kids!

WHAT STRATEGIES CAN WE LEARN?

1. **Search for other currency besides dollars to trade.**
   Sometimes, showing the parties where the opportunity for progress is can be better than monetary finagling. By thinking outside the box, the Mediator was able to

exchange one form of currency (dollars) for another form of currency (vacation) in order to make this deal.

2. **To avert resistance, make sure that all unusual proposals appear to come from you, rather than the parties.**

When somebody views his adversary as always wrong, he will react by rejecting any offer the adversary presents; this phenomenon is known by the psychological term *reactive devaluation*. The devaluation of seemingly reasonable offers creates an impediment to the settlement. In this case, the plaintiff wouldn't accept free time-shares because the offer came from his hated former employer. If the Mediator had presented this as his own idea, Mike would have been much more likely to accept it. Even if the great idea in a negotiation is not yours, it can pay off to present it as your own.

3. **Create a mosaic of interests.**

The parties in the dispute are not always the only people who have a stake in the negotiation. In this case, the Mediator had to manage the attorneys' needs as well as both internal (that is, across the table) and external negotiations (such as the one between the lawyer and his wife); ultimately, he learned that the real constituency who was necessary to make the deal (the lawyer's wife) wasn't at the table. As a mediator, you always try to identify a mosaic of interests with attorneys, plaintiffs, and defendants. Once you have all the pieces, your task is to arrange them into a coherent whole so that everyone feels that his or her interests have been addressed. For example, when it comes to addressing the interests of attorneys, it's pretty much a given that they always want to make money, impress the client, fulfill their professional duty, and not look foolish in the process. Your job is to try to give them a way out that's successful. In this case, the plaintiff's lawyer, Ryan, gets money (his fee, somewhat discounted but still large) plus a free luxury vacation. Mike, the plaintiff, gets the amount of money he wants plus closure. The defendant gets closure on the case that avoids going to trial and doesn't exceed the budget he had allotted to settle the case.

4. Use the "net to client" approach.

The "net to client" approach is a relatively simple one; it allows the client to receive the same amount of money even if the settlement of the case is a little bit less than offered. In this case, the client was going to receive 60 percent of $150,000, or $90,000. The lawyer was going to receive 40 percent, or $60,000. The employer offered only $135,000. For the client to receive $90,000, the lawyer had to be willing to accept $45,000 plus the dream vacation valued at $15,000. Because the lawyer accepted that deal, the client ended up netting the same amount as if the settlement had been $150,000.

CHAPTER TWENTY

THE SILENT MOVER

"Marian," the Mediator said gently, "you are a very wealthy woman. It seems clear that this dispute is not about money. Is this about Thomas, or did something else bring you to this point?" As Marian sat silently, her sad dignity was apparent. The Mediator let her sit quietly for a moment as he reflected on the case.

Thomas had died a lifelong bachelor and left his considerable estate to four charities. He had spent many happy years with Marian, his companion, business partner, and lover, and together they owned an apartment building; Thomas owned two-thirds and Marian owned one-third. On his deathbed, Thomas felt guilty that he had never married Marian as he had always promised her, and he drew up a handwritten agreement to transfer his share of the apartment complex to Marian for one dollar.

Unfortunately, Thomas's will did not specifically mention the agreement, and the estate—including the two-thirds ownership of the apartment complex—was divided among the charities at probate. Marian filed her claim and spent a large chunk of time, money, and energy in court. The charities saw her as a wealthy woman who was greedy. They were prepared to offer her a settlement, which was lower than the true value of the property. There had already been extensive litigation, and both sides were firmly entrenched in their positions.

Marian confided in a friend that she had spent over $100,000 in legal fees and was frustrated with her attorney and confused about what to do next. Her friend put Marian in touch with a more sympathetic attorney, Deborah. Deborah suggested that mediation might be a good idea at this point. Marian was skeptical, but she agreed, and so did the lawyers for the nonprofits.

Until now, the case had been all about the money. And because both parties were so wealthy, they could afford to pursue the case. Deborah, however, felt that Marian truly wanted to resolve the case but that something was holding her back. Deborah had hand-picked this mediator because she had confidence that he could deal with the money issues and also relate to people and listen for the client's underlying needs.

The Mediator had chosen to meet privately with each side instead of beginning with a joint session, and his first meeting was with Marian. He could see from the legal briefs that this case was all about money and property, but he knew that Marian already had plenty of money; her one-third share of an apartment building was really a small drop in a big ocean. He agreed with Deborah: there must be more to the story. He wondered what the silent mover would turn out to be, and he knew he would have to open up the Pandora's box of Marian's emotions to find out. So instead of beginning the conversation by saying, "How much do you want?" and sticking with the legal concerns, he chose to view the case through a "relationship lens" and to play the role of therapist, discussing issues that had no legal relevance to the dispute.

"Marian," he tried again, "I understand it's important that you receive a fair settlement, and we will work toward that goal. But for the life of me I can't imagine that the money you receive for this apartment is going to change your lifestyle. What's this really about?"

Marian became emotional and tearful. "Look," she said, "I'm tired of this litigation. It's not for me. I'd like to settle, but they haven't offered anything. I don't know *how* to settle it, I don't know what I want—" Marian had reached her limit.

"Well, you've asked for your share of the estate," said the Mediator. "Is that what this is all about?"

"No," said Marian. "It's not." She sat quietly for quite a few minutes, clearly struggling with something. Finally, she came to a decision. "I've lost two people who were very dear to me. Thomas, of course, and Robert—my son from my first marriage. I'd like to tell you about my son." *Ahh,* thought the Mediator. *The silent mover.*

"Robert had learning problems, emotional difficulties, and health issues since the moment he was born. For years I took him from doctor to doctor. They gave him every test imaginable, but none of the doctors were ever able to agree on a diagnosis. His particular constellation of problems never seemed to fit into one of their neat categories, so they didn't know what to do," she said bitterly. "Of course, that made adequate treatment impossible.

"He was a dear boy, but he was quite sensitive and had a great deal of difficulty making friends or even holding a social conversation. He was miserable; he knew how people looked at him. They treated him differently, and he hated it. And I think his emotional suffering made his physical problems worse. He was in a great deal of pain most of the time. He was a very intelligent, caring soul, but he couldn't hold down a job or have any kind of social life at all. He had failure after failure, and there was nothing I could do about it." Marian paused, pulling herself together. "I've never told this story before," she explained, looking at the Mediator intensely.

Finally, she picked up her story. "Well, there you have it. Two years ago he took his own life. I was devastated. Even though Robert wasn't his son, Thomas had always been very kind to him, and his support after Robert's death was all that kept me going." She paused and said quietly, "And then, of course, Thomas died." Again a silence, and then, "I've been thinking that perhaps we could convert the apartment house into a home or treatment facility for children like Robert . . . a place where they could get help, with programs and people who cared and who understood what they were going through! I don't want one more child to suffer the way my son did."

"Marian, that's a wonderful idea. Do the people representing the charities know about your wishes and what you and your son endured?" asked the Mediator, affected by her deep feelings and passion.

"No," replied Marian, taken aback. "Of course not. I never discuss my private life. And don't ask me to tell them. I won't."

"Marian, what if the Mediator and I shared the story with them?" Deborah suggested tentatively. "You wouldn't have to be in the room."

"It will just make me look weak," Marian replied quickly. "I don't trust those people. They're the most *uncharitable* people I've ever met!"

"I think your counsel is on the right track here," said the Mediator. "I know it's difficult, but allowing us to tell this side of your story will help the other parties understand where you're coming from. These charities might actually have a heart," he smiled. "Let's see if we can tap into it."

The Mediator knew that Marian's story really had nothing to do with the case, but it had everything to do with why Marian was fighting so hard. She needed something to hold on to. She had lost her son; she had lost her lover and dear friend. And now they wanted to take this last little piece of Thomas—which he had wanted her to have—for absolutely no reason except that they could.

"We don't need to tell them the entire story," he continued, "but maybe if they understood how meaningful this was to you, they'd start looking at this case in a different way—and you could wrap this up and be done with it."

Again Marian sat and thought. "I *am* sick to death of this litigation," she said at last. "If you think it will help end this mess, go ahead. But leave me out of it."

In a private meeting with Deborah and the lawyers from the nonprofits, the Mediator explained Marian's motivations.

"I don't know if you're aware that Marian's son committed suicide shortly before Thomas died," he said. A ripple of surprise passed over their faces. This was news to all of them.

"Obviously," the Mediator continued, "the money is important, but fighting about that doesn't seem to have gotten you anywhere except here." He smiled. "Deborah and I are in agreement that her feelings about her son's suicide have become entangled with her feelings about Thomas and the property he wished her to have. Clearly, these feelings are an emotional impediment to her settling the case. I feel very strongly that if we could allow Marian to believe that the outcome of this case in some small way allows her to bury her son and honor Thomas at the same time, you might be able to wrap this up today."

"We had no idea," said one of the lawyers. "What can we do?"

Deborah told them about Marian's idea of converting the apartment house into a facility for children like her son. Three of the charities were involved in work for disabled and disadvantaged

youth, and they immediately began rolling out ideas about programs and projects and activities that could assist these kids and
their families.

"I like it," said one of the attorneys. "That's an honorable
approach that's not just about dividing up the real estate."

"Yes," said another, looking to the others for agreement. "This
is something we can get our arms around and embrace."

"Speaking for my nonprofit," said another, "that goes along
with our mission—to help people."

The Mediator left them alone to discuss the plan privately.

—◦◦◦—

"We'd like to do it," the lawyers said when he came back. "We
absolutely support the idea of a residential and outpatient treatment facility for children with multiple physical and emotional
issues that don't fit into any other funded category."

"Great," said the Mediator. "Let me take this idea to Marian
and see if it's something she'd be willing to do with her share of
the property."

—◦◦◦—

Marian was startled when she heard the offer, and pleased. "I can't
believe it. Of course. I'll give my entire share to fund that center."

What an incredible difference it had made for such a compas-
sionate story to be shared. The charities agreed to establish such a
program and asked Marian to become involved in the project and
sit on the board of directors. They proposed to name the center
after Robert, as a memorial. Marian was overwhelmed. For the first
time in a year, she had something to care about.

WHAT HAPPENED?

The parties walked into this mediation having defined the issue in
the case as whether Marian would get the apartment or not. There
was no room for movement. A discussion of issues that are tangible and measurable sets the agenda for the negotiation. Once the

agenda is set, the parties take a position on the issues, which is their way of identifying their perspective on how or whether the pie should be divided up. This approach will often start an adversarial and argumentative process in which each side tries to convince the other that it is right, but the process obviously didn't work in this case.

When the Mediator recognized that the parties were on a path of destruction, he decided to focus on the less tangible, more abstract concerns that underlie motives. This is what silent movers are all about: they don't represent the actual value of the item in dispute, but they do represent the motivating force behind the perspectives of each party. They are very real to the parties, maybe even more real than the desire to a good deal. In this case, the Mediator was able to gather more information about Marian's interests, and that information allowed the parties to be creative in coming up with solutions—far more creative than they could be when merely negotiating from their original positions.

The Mediator also chose to act completely transparently in exchanging information with the parties. In other words, he shared with the parties what he believed was the best task to focus on and why he thought the task was appropriate. In this way, he helped ensure that the parties were clear about the process, their goals, and their roles. This approach also provided a window into the Mediator's thinking and analysis.

WHAT STRATEGIES CAN WE LEARN?

1. **Steer away from the legal issues temporarily if you believe that doing so will move the negotiation forward.**

   Almost every mediated case is presented in a way that requires you to evaluate legal issues and each side's perspective on how the pie should be divided. Although these issues are critical in reaching agreements, following the legalities unswervingly—especially when the legal outcome of the case will not change the financial standing of the parties—can lead to a breakdown in the negotiation. Setting aside the legally relevant information for a moment and allowing parties to talk about the broad relationship issues can open up more creative solutions and give the parties a better sense of satisfaction with the process.

2. **Use the silent mover to shift the parties toward mutual under-standing and closure.**

   The silent mover—an unspoken deal-breaker that one party
   holds as vitally important in the negotiation—can impede
   progress. But once you identify it, you can use it to stimulate dialogue that will bring closure. First, reinforce the
   party's beliefs about the silent mover by suggesting that
   they reveal those beliefs to the other side. By doing this
   you are affirming that what the party is thinking is useful
   and important to the dispute, even if it might not change
   the legal outcome. Bringing the silent mover out into the
   open transforms the process from a game of demands and
   offers into a fruitful discussion of appropriate settlement
   options.

3. **Create an open negotiating environment.**

   In some cases, there's no quicker way to reach an impasse
   than by insisting that parties stick to the legal issues. When
   you create a more open and supportive negotiating environment, one that encourages parties to share ideas that
   don't have anything to do with the legal issues in the case,
   you can often elicit suggestions from both sides that
   unlock the doors to settlement.

Chapter Twenty-One

A Small Deception

"Nell," the Mediator began, "why don't you tell me what happened?"

But instead of answering, Nell looked to her attorney for help. "Walter?" she said. When the Mediator heard that, he knew that this old-fashioned, grandmotherly woman had essentially turned over all her personal power to her lawyer. *If it were up to her,* the Mediator thought, *she'd probably settle for the minimum. On the other hand, I bet she'd follow her lawyer straight to the courthouse steps if that's what he advised.*

"Go ahead, Nell." Walter nodded gently. "You can tell your story."

"Well," she began tentatively, "two years ago my husband, John, died of pancreatic cancer. It was so quick. He only had five months after the doctor told him." Her eyes began to well with tears at the memory.

"May I finish the story?" asked her attorney. Nell nodded her assent, dabbing at her eyes with a tissue.

"When John died," continued Walter, "he had recently transferred his life insurance from one company to another, hoping to secure a better rate. He purchased a $1 million policy from Household Life Insurance. As you know, all life insurance policies have a two-year contestability provision. So when Nell submitted the claim within two years of the policy inception date, Household Life asked to review John's medical history."

"That's right," interrupted the Household Life claims examiner. "We just wanted to confirm that John didn't know about his pancreatic cancer condition when he applied for insurance." She tried making eye contact with Nell, but Nell was taking knitting needles and yarn out of a large bag, and seemed to have disconnected from the conversation.

"If it turned out that he did," explained the Household Life attorney, "and he failed to disclose it, then naturally Household Life would decline payment on the policy."

Nell looked up suddenly. "We had no idea he was so ill," she said, shaking her head. "No idea at all. He looked fine, he felt fine . . ." Her voice trailed off, and she went back to her knitting.

"Thank you," Walter said, continuing with his story. "Naturally, Nell was distraught and overwhelmed after her husband died. When Household Life asked her to come to their office to sit for a three-hour meeting and sign new medical authorization forms, she called me to ask what she should do—I've been John and Nell's family lawyer for many years. I advised her not to sit for the meeting and not to sign any forms. She had no legal obligation to do so," he said, looking pointedly at Household Life's lawyer.

"Rather than simply use the medical authorization forms John had signed when he applied for insurance," Walter said in some irritation, "the insurance company filed a *lawsuit* against Nell seeking a court order compelling her to provide background information on John's health. At my advice, Nell responded with a countersuit asking for the $1 million policy benefits *and* the emotional distress and punitive damages she deserved."

He talked on, but the Mediator already knew the rest of the story: the court had declined to issue a definitive ruling as to the rights and responsibilities of the parties under the life insurance policy, so the parties had been forced to sit down and work out their problems in mediation.

"Nell has been suffering, waiting in limbo on this matter for two years," her lawyer concluded. "We believe Household Life should pay her a *minimum* of $5 million."

The Household Life claims examiner and her lawyer both rolled their eyes in response. It would have been hard to miss this loud and clear cue, and the Mediator asked, "Would you like to make a statement?"

"Yes, I would," said the claims examiner, with a nod of okay from her lawyer. She sat forward and looked directly at the Mediator, speaking firmly and with some heat. "We did nothing wrong. We investigated the claim, we gathered basic information, but we were rebuffed by Nell's lawyer. What are we supposed to do? When we don't investigate we get in trouble. When we do investigate they don't give us the information we need!"

The Mediator felt that Nell's deference to her lawyer, and the basic facts of the case, pointed to Walter as the driving force behind the lawsuit. Two years had passed since John's death, and Nell seemed accustomed to living without the $1 million insurance proceeds. Yet her lawyer was convinced he had a multimillion-dollar lawsuit. The Mediator decided he could gather more intelligence about the case if he could talk to the parties privately. He would begin with Household Life.

—❧—

"I'll be honest with you," said Household Life's attorney to the Mediator when they were settled in a small office. "We don't think John knew about his condition, and we think we should pay the claim. We *would* have paid the claim if we'd had the information we asked for. But at this point we don't want to be penalized for the lawyer's conduct. We think that he set us up to create a case. We want Nell to have her policy benefits, but there's no way we're paying $5 million. If she suffered at all because of the payment's being withheld—and we don't think she did—that wasn't our fault, and we're not paying punitive damages. We're really hoping that you'll be able to negotiate this deal for us so that she gets her money today and we can all go home. We just don't think we could offer the limits at this point, or Walter will ask for more, and we're not in a position to pay more."

"I understand your position," the Mediator smiled. "It sounds like you were able to verify that Nell's husband did not have cancer when he applied for the insurance, and you're prepared to pay the policy limits. You just don't want to be penalized for reaching this conclusion through litigation. Let me talk to Nell and her counsel."

—❧—

When the Mediator spoke to Nell's counsel privately, the lawyer held his ground, as the Mediator had suspected he would. "This company has treated Nell very shabbily," he said. Nell was absorbed in her knitting. "We're not willing to negotiate under $5 million." This stance effectively ended the possibility of a realistic negotiation, so the Mediator thought hard to come up with a strategy he could use to bring Nell's counsel into a zone that might be acceptable to the defense.

He knew Household Life was being reasonable. They didn't feel they owed any punitive damages, but they admitted they were willing to pay the premium price. This admission of willingness to pay was a rarity in the Mediator's experience, but he also knew from experience that he couldn't simply offer Walter the million and expect him to take it. Intuitively, Walter would feel that the process was a little too easy and would automatically ask for substantially more—and the Mediator knew from his discussions with Household Life that such a move would result in a failed negotiation. Instead, the Mediator needed to deal with the lawyer's expectations and ease him into a settlement zone slowly. To do this the Mediator had to go along with Household Life's desire to conceal their true intention, which was to pay the policy limits, until the time felt right to offer the money. Negotiating in a competitive environment often involves stretching the truth or quietly concealing known positions in order to guide parties to a common ground. This type of deception can often drive the negotiation: it allows parties to overcome barriers and make concessions. So when Household Life asked the Mediator to conceal its desire to pay policy limits in order to get the deal done, the Mediator was willing to look for a way to use this information as an aid in the negotiation.

—◦◦◦—

First, the Mediator wanted to clarify Nell's intent: Was she prepared to make her own decisions? Or would she continue deferring to her lawyer, as he suspected? He shut the door behind him and entered the small private office, where he found Nell knitting what now looked like a yellow baby blanket while her attorney shuffled through some papers.

"Nell, it's just the three of us now, so we can talk frankly. I'm wondering how the insurance company treated you when you first submitted the claim."

"Oh, they were great," Nell replied, looking up with a smile. "They helped me with the process. They were very kind."

"So what happened? What stopped the process from finalizing?"

"John had just died. It was a terrible time. I had *so* much to deal with. I could hardly think straight, and there were some complications with the estate. . . . When this came up I felt that if I had to do one more thing, well. I just couldn't. So I called Walter—we've known him forever—and just turned it all over to him. I was so grateful," she said, smiling at her attorney. "When the insurance company sent me a letter asking for more information, I gave that to Walter too. I assumed he would take care of it."

"I see," said the Mediator. "Do you know why they didn't pay the claim?"

Nell shook her head, bewildered. "I have no idea. Ask my lawyer. He was in charge of it all." She picked up her knitting again.

Whether or not these discussions were really over Nell's head was debatable; she seemed to have decided it was none of her business. So the Mediator proceeded to the second stage: even though Nell was still in the room, he would conduct this negotiation with Walter. He went over to the whiteboard on the wall, picked up a marker, quickly sketched in four columns, and began labeling them: (1) Life Insurance Contract Benefits, (2) Emotional Distress, (3) Interest and Attorney Fees, (4) Punitive Damages.

"Let's break this claim down and see what we dealing with," he said as he wrote. "Okay, you've got a million bucks in life insurance benefits, right?" He wrote "$1 million" in the benefits column. "Right," Nell's counsel agreed.

"Emotional distress . . . well, they haven't yet *declined* the claim, so how much can you really get?" He left the column blank. Nell's counsel narrowed his eyes slightly, sat very still, and said nothing.

"Interest on the million and attorney fees . . ." The Mediator stopped and looked at Nell's lawyer. "What's your deal with Nell?" he asked.

"Nell has retained me on a flat contingency fee," he replied. "I'll get a percentage of settlement."

The Mediator started writing. "Let's say $1.4 million, okay?"

"That's about right," agreed Nell's counsel, as the Mediator wrote the figure in the third column.

The Mediator pressed on. "Now, you're asking for punitive damages to punish them for the despicable way they handled the claim. But how are you going to prove this? They never denied the claim; they were just asking for more information." He stopped writing and looked at the lawyer calmly. "Think about this for a while," he continued. "I think it represents a reasonable recovery for you." Nell's counsel nodded, but said nothing, and the Mediator came in for the finish. "If you still want me to go back and demand $5 million, I will—that's my job. It's possible Nell could walk out of here at the end of the day with all her benefits—but a proposal like that isn't going to end this negotiation." The room was very, very quiet.

"I think I see where you're going with this," said Nell's counsel.

"I'm going to let you talk all this over with your client," said the Mediator, and left the room with a much better idea of Nell's true settlement range—much less than the $5 million they were demanding. Now it was time for stage three: getting Household Life into settlement range.

—⁓⁓—

"I've spoken to Nell's lawyer, and I think he's lowered his sights a bit from his original demand," the Mediator said frankly. The Household Life claims examiner let out a deep sigh and smiled. "It would be very helpful if you could allow me to present your offer of $1 million—the actual policy benefits—so I could drop the anchor at that level."

"We only want to offer it if you think it would either settle the case or come awfully close," said the attorney. "You know where we stand. We'll leave it up to you."

"Okay," agreed the Mediator. "Let me figure it out." He was pleased: he was ready to return to Nell and her attorney and move on to stage four, which would be the key to moving these negotiations to endgame.

—⁓⁓—

During stage two, the Mediator had learned something important: Nell's lawyer was working for a flat contingency fee. He would be paid only if he won the case. The Mediator knew he could use this knowledge to push the attorney—who, it seemed more and more clear, had orchestrated this case for his own benefit—into a corner.

Nell's blanket project had grown by several inches, and her attorney was smiling expectantly as the Mediator entered the room. But the smile disappeared when the Mediator said, "Walter, have you thought about what would happen if another lawyer had to come in to try this case?"

"What are you talking about?" The lawyer was dumbfounded.

"I've been thinking about this," the Mediator continued, "and it's not so far-fetched. Because it was you who recommended that Nell not sign the medical authorizations, there's a very good possibility that you could be asked to serve as a witness to the insurer's defense that Nell failed to cooperate under the insurance policy. As the mediator here, I'm concerned that you will have to turn this case over to somebody else. . . ." Walter said nothing, but his forehead was suddenly damp. The Mediator pressed on. "I'd like you to take a look a little further down the road. I think we can avoid all that if we play our cards right now."

"What do you mean?" asked the lawyer.

In response, the Mediator said, "Nell, would you mind if I had a word with Walter privately?"

Picking up a dropped stitch, Nell said, "Of course not."

The two men stepped out into the hall. "Look, Walter," said the Mediator, "I didn't want to create a controversy in front of Nell, but I've learned from Household Life that they plan to move the court to recuse you if this case goes to trial. They have made it very clear that they will call you as a percipient witness if they have to." The Mediator enjoyed this role sometimes—mediator as trickster, making things happen by alternately causing and resolving conflict. True, the insurance company hadn't said anything of the sort. But legally, this was a very real possibility, and Walter would know that. In the world of mediated litigation, such small deceptions—as long as they are not fraudulent and no laws are broken—are all part of the culture of confusion that occurs in a litigated case.

The Mediator could almost hear the wheels turning in Walter's mind. The lawyer could either compromise now or see his fat contingency fee reduced to very little. "Hang on," said

Walter. "You know my basic concern is for Nell's well-being. I'm sure she doesn't want to see this case drag on any longer than it already has. We're prepared to come down a bit, just to move things along."

As they walked back into the office where Nell was waiting, the Mediator made a bold move: "What if I can get the insurance company to pay Nell's full benefits and another $250,000 on top of that for attorney fees? Would you consider that?"

Walter sat tall and straight. "If you're telling me that's their offer, I will need to discuss that with Nell." This signaled to the Mediator that Walter was ready to consider an offer closer to the policy benefits.

The Mediator had permission from the defense to offer the policy benefits, so he took the opportunity to make that move. "I can't tell you that they would offer $1.25 million, but I can tell you that they are prepared to pay the policy benefits of $1 million."

"I think that gives us something serious to chew on. Please give me a chance to discuss this with my client," Walter responded.

—⁓—

Things are moving right along, thought the Mediator. He went back to Household Life and advised them that the offer of $1 million had been made.

"Now what?" asked the claims examiner.

"I should have a response in a couple of minutes. I only made the offer after I was certain Walter and his client would consider it—or something close to it—seriously," said the Mediator.

"What do you mean 'close to it'?" asked the claims representative.

"As you know, they were seeking punitive damages. I believe they're committed to releasing those damages—but there's still the issue of Walter's getting paid."

The claims representative was not too thrilled about paying additional monies for Walter. "If it wasn't for him," he grumbled, "this case could have been settled years ago. I hate the idea of paying him anything, but if we have to pay something to get this case settled, we would consider it."

—⁕—

Shuttling back into the room with Nell and Walter, the Mediator asked, "How are things going in here?"

"Well," said Walter, "I have authority from Nell to reduce our demand to $1.5 million. We can't answer your question about settling for $250,000 over the policy benefit because we have no way of knowing if they would pay it."

"I understand your concern," said the Mediator. "It sounds to me like if you were certain they would pay the extra $250,000, you might be interested in that deal, but you don't want to send them any weak signals."

"Exactly," said Walter.

—⁕—

By the end of the day, the Mediator had suggested a Solomon-like solution: Nell would receive all her benefits—$1 million—plus two years' interest, and her attorney would be paid his fee—$250,000, over and above the benefits. And Nell had finished knitting her blanket—a gift for her next grandchild. After just a little discussion, the proposal was accepted by all parties, and the mediation concluded successfully.

WHAT HAPPENED?

At the initial meeting with the plaintiff and her lawyer, the Mediator was able to assess that Walter was calling the shots. His years of experience in the field led him to conclude that the demand for settlement of the case was very likely based, not on the client's needs, but on the lawyer's desire to achieve a windfall. It was also clear that the lawyer had allowed the dispute to mushroom out of proportion by refusing to provide basic information to the insurance company. If this fact were not addressed quickly, the negotiation would go nowhere.

The Mediator was at a turning point: he could blame the lawyer for his actions, which would probably have angered Walter and ended the process, or he could handle things objectively.

He decided on a multistage technique in which each stage was designed to manage and downsize Walter's expectations. By separating the damage claim into its component parts, the Mediator was able to demonstrate that the large demand for settlement far exceeded the potential value of the case. This opened up the avenue for Walter to make a more realistic assessment of his prospects.

The clincher was a small but pointed move that enabled the Mediator to demonstrate the loss of revenue Walter would suffer if the case were referred to someone else to pursue. In fact, the move was akin to bluffing in poker. In both poker and mediation, technique and skill are often more important than a great hand—provided the trick is not a material misrepresentation. In this case, the scenario painted by the Mediator was a real possibility, albeit one the defense hadn't yet considered!

Walter finally accepted the concept that this would not be the windfall he had hoped for, and he was prepared to negotiate at a realistic level. He was now much more receptive to a frank discussion of value in a way that provided full compensation to his client and himself.

WHAT STRATEGIES CAN WE LEARN?

1. **Identify the key decision maker in the negotiation.**

   Identify the key decision maker as soon as possible: this is the person around whom you'll be tailoring your strategy. Sometimes, of course, it's the client; but at other times, as in this case, it's really the lawyer who's calling the shots. This preliminary determination is critical to directing the balance of the negotiation.

2. **Be prepared to play the role of trickster if you think it will move the case along.**

   In myth and legend, the trickster plays the role of reconciler of immovable objects and the manager of conflict. To play this role requires you to be able to work in a world of confusion and ambiguity and to be willing to help the parties transform their perspectives so that they can reach a turning point in their decision-making process. It often involves managing the white lies that parties use against each other in a way that keeps the dialogue moving forward and away from extreme positions. Tricksters are shape-shifters, playing whatever role is necessary at the moment to create a dissonance that ultimately leads to a fruitful discussion on common ground. As trickster you may simply appear as humorist, judge, and listener, or you may even assume the guise of heckler, fool, or deceiver.

3. **Use the techniques of the trickster sparingly.**

The constructive use of trickster techniques like deception and humor is the key to success. People often don't understand these approaches when they are in the midst of an anger-laden conflict. Your choice to use words that disrupt the dialogue of the parties can often cause the negotiation to lock up, because the parties lose confidence in you. Other times, using trickster techniques to redirect the parties toward a positive move or concession can be a turning point in the negotiation.

CHAPTER TWENTY-TWO

THE LADDERED APPROACH

Marla sat quietly at the conference table, somewhat distraught but holding it together, compulsively stroking the diamond heart necklace that her husband, Richard, had given her for their thirtieth anniversary. In front of her were displayed the memorabilia of their life together: photographs of their wedding, family holidays with their children and grandchildren, and their second honeymoon in Italy; love letters; scrapbooks . . . symbols of the "love, comfort, and care" necessary to bolster a wrongful death suit, and mementos of an orderly, pleasant world that was now gone forever.

The Mediator listened intently as the lawyers jockeyed for position during this first joint session, their positions predictable—and predictably far apart.

"Richard was living free of pain and looking forward to an active retirement," Marla's counsel stated. "He and Marla had just purchased a retirement home in the desert and scheduled a cruise to the Caribbean. He was a person who looked forward to each day. We can prove that the injuries he suffered in the accident were the direct cause of his death."

The lawyer for the insurance company, of course, claimed the precise opposite: "This was a relatively minor incident that in no way could have contributed to Richard's suicide. We believe the evidence will show that he was predisposed to taking his life because of his years of depression resulting from his prior back problems."

The story was a sad one. Richard, a decorated veteran and career soldier, had recently retired from the military. He and Marla were still relatively young, in their early fifties, and they were looking forward to filling their hard-won leisure time with traveling, looking after their grandchildren, and playing daily rounds of golf.

The only hitch was Richard's aching back. A chronic medical condition in his spine had recently degenerated to the point where the pain was excruciating, and he had no choice but to undergo major back surgery. Still, he was glad to do it, confident that the surgery would allow him to enjoy his leisure years. So, like the good soldier he was, on Monday he went in for the spinal laminectomy, and by Friday he was already up and about, well on the way to what he hoped would be complete recovery. The next weekend he was feeling so good that he and Marla flew to Las Vegas to visit their daughter. But on the way home from the airport, the shuttle van they were riding in was lightly tapped by another vehicle. It wasn't much of a collision, but it was more than Richard's unstable back could take. An ambulance rushed him to the hospital, where he was treated and given pain medication.

A couple of days later, Richard saw his neurosurgeon, who pre-scribed physical therapy and rest. But things got worse instead of better. Richard's medical condition began to spiral downward. It became so bad that he had to undergo another back surgery a cou-ple of months later. After the second surgery, however, he still was not improving. The constant and unrelenting pain was taking a real toll on his normally stoic attitude. Marla was very worried as Richard lost more and more weight. He was beginning to look like an old man, and they both worried that the nightmare would never end. They tried everything—painkillers, therapy, medical appointments—but nothing helped.

Richard began to worry that he would end his years as an invalid, with Marla having to care for him, and he couldn't bear the idea. So one morning, when Marla had gone grocery shopping, he wrote his wife a note expressing his love for her and setting her free. Then he put his service revolver in his mouth and squeezed the trigger.

Richard and Marla's original lawsuit, which had sprung from the moderate car crash case, was now amended to include allega-tions of wrongful death. And it was this suit that brought Marla and her attorney to mediation today.

—⦇∾∾⦈—

As the lawyers took their opening shots, the Mediator was already thinking about what his best strategy would be. He knew what would happen if he sat back and let things take their own course. Experience had taught him that in a wrongful death case such as this one, the plaintiff would always make a demand based on the value of a human life. That's what Marla's mementos were there to demonstrate. In this case, such a demand was very likely to be in the multimillion-dollar range. The defense would strongly resist such a high number, citing Richard's severe preexisting physical problems at the time of the accident. If the Mediator allowed this kind of sparring to begin, the two sides would soon be so far apart that it could take days to calm them down and move them closer together. After just a few minutes, he decided to adopt a gently directive strategy he called the "laddered" approach. He would walk the parties up or down the rungs separately until they met at a mutually agreeable middle point.

<hr />

He began at the top of the ladder in a private meeting with Marla and her attorney. Marla sat tensely as her attorney spoke. "We believe Richard's life is worth $10 million in compensation," he began, "but just between you and me we're willing to come down to $5 million. He was a decorated war veteran, a loving husband and father." But the Mediator didn't want to give him a chance to ask for this amount, because he knew it would quickly lock the mediation up in an impenetrable impasse. Clearly, he needed to start moving this guy down the ladder right away. First, however, he front-loaded the case by empathizing with Marla, knowing she was feeling a powerful mix of strong emotions about her husband and apprehension about this strange process.

"I'll never be able to walk a mile in your shoes, Marla, but I can appreciate what you've been through. I want to thank you in advance for sticking with us today. I know it's difficult to sit here while we try to put a dollar value on your husband's life."

"Thank you," she said softly.

"Unfortunately," he continued, "we're dealing with the civil justice system, which may not understand the causal link between the accident and your husband's suicide. Would a jury really be able to feel that this accident caused him to lose control and kill himself? Honestly, I've never seen anything like this happen. But I'll be happy to present your case in whatever way you want."

The Mediator held Marla's gaze for a moment and then turned to her attorney. He could tell that the man had understood his subtext. The lawyer had already lowered his emotional tone a notch. "I think we both know that you're trying to get us the best possible deal," he acknowledged. "That's why we agreed to come to mediation in the first place."

"You know that I can't take an extreme demand to the defense," the Mediator said firmly. "Realistically, the highest a jury is going to go is probably two to three million. And you also know that Richard's preexisting back problems, not to mention a recent major surgery, are going to have to figure into their calculations. Your likelihood of success if this thing goes to trial could be less than 50 percent. If you want to get this negotiated, let's start with a reasonable demand."

The lawyer thought hard but said nothing.

"Listen," said the Mediator, "I don't expect you to make a new demand right now, but think about it. I'm going to leave you here to discuss it with your client while I see what's going on with the defense."

Although the Mediator wasn't bringing a demand to the insurance company, he wanted to create the expectation that one might be coming. "You know how these death cases go," he said. "It's entirely probable that the plaintiff is going to ask for a few million dollars on this at least. I'm just trying to get a feeling for where everyone stands right now."

"Candidly," the defense attorney replied, "we're prepared to pay Richard's medical bills. But we don't want to send a message to the plaintiff's counsel that he can expect us to come up to the amount we're sure he wants on the wrongful death. We think there's a good likelihood that we could succeed in court when the jury hears about Richard's surgery and preexisting condition."

The Mediator said, "If that's the case, then I think it might be a gesture of goodwill for you to begin by offering to pay the medical bills." What he didn't say was that this would set the stage for the negotiation and allow the insurance company to take the first step up the ladder.

"Fine," agreed the lawyer. "We'd be much happier offering $60,000 for medical costs than millions in damages we don't think we're responsible for."

"That's a good move," said the Mediator. "I'll take it to them and see what they say." He was pretty sure that starting with an offer, even a small one like this, would mollify Marla and her lawyer and keep them from climbing back up the ladder.

———

"Good news," the Mediator told them. "Although the defense hasn't received a demand, they have offered to start these negotiations by offering to pay Richard's medical bills. I realize it's not a huge amount, but at least it's a start." Just as the Mediator had hoped, Marla's lawyer was surprised and somewhat pleased.

"Look," the Mediator continued, "it's a good bet that $3 million is a long shot if this case ever gets to a jury. It's going to be a real challenge proving that Richard's death was a direct consequence of accident so minor that it barely dented the van." To the Mediator's surprise, the plaintiff's counsel immediately decided to take a giant step down the ladder. He and Marla must have had some serious discussion while he was talking to the defense. Instead of dropping from $3 million to $1.5 million, the logical next step, the attorney said, "Let's show them we're serious. We're willing to go under seven figures. Tell them our demand is $950,000 and see what they say."

———

Because the Mediator had set the stage by creating the expectation that the plaintiff would ask for several million dollars, the six-figure demand was well received by the defense. It didn't seem like an over-the-top amount, which they would have seen as insulting and unrealistic. Released from the necessity to resist, the defense took their second step up the ladder, offering $100,000.

After a few more trade-offs, the defense continued to move up while the plaintiff continued to move down. Soon the case reached a level of $250,000 offered and $500,000 demanded—just a few steps apart. *We're finally in the zone of reason,* thought the Mediator, *and the momentum is here. Let's close this deal.*

Now the Mediator had some choices. He could offer to split the difference. Or he could pick a number (say, $350,000), write it down, keep it to himself, and say, "Here's how I feel about the case. Each of you pick a number, and the closest to my number gets it." Both of these simple strategies had worked in past cases. In the end, he decided to create a sense of tension between the two parties.

"Would you split the difference if we got it into the threes?" he asked the defense.

"We don't want to go that high," said the defense attorney, "but if you get it to our number I'll make a phone call to the insurance company and see what we can do."

This concession told the Mediator that if the defense attorney knew they could definitely settle for $300,000, he'd make a phone call to see if he could get the extra $50,000. "Let me see what the plaintiff has to say," the Mediator said. "I'll be right back." They were only a step apart now.

——⁓⁓⁓——

Marla was staring out the window at the traffic below, her hand still on her diamond heart. Her attorney was going through papers on the table. They both looked up expectantly. When the Mediator told them what he had in mind, Marla and her counsel exchanged glances, wordlessly confirming an early discussion. "That sounds good," the lawyer said. "Tell them to go ahead and make the call. If the money's there, we'll consider it."

Now both parties were standing on the same rung. The defense attorney already had his cell phone out. He made the call, and they soon struck a deal at $300,000. Both parties knew that the dollar value they had put on Richard's life was not a real reflection of his value to Marla, but everyone left the office feeling good about what had transpired there.

The Mediator put the ladder away until the next time he needed it.

WHAT HAPPENED?

Even though Richard's story was a sad one and Marla's feelings needed to be considered, this was basically a dispute over money. The key here is that the Mediator immediately came up with a strategy to bring the two sides together. He didn't wait for the parties to control the negotiation—he was proactive and took control.

As a mediator, you always need to adopt a style that is appropriate to the particular case. In some cases you can control the room less obtrusively by acting as facilitator, asking questions, and serving as the messenger who passes information back and forth. In other cases, like this one, it pays to be more directive, guiding the parties and instructing them on what could get them a deal. In this role you can give your own opinion, be pushy, and even tell people where the negotiation is going next. It can be somewhat dangerous to take this extreme approach, however, because you run the risk of alienating one or both parties.

In this case, the Mediator wanted to be on the directive end, but he also knew that because of the emotions involved he had to be gentle—the iron fist in the velvet glove. He decided to begin by demonstrating to Marla that he understood her situation, thus gaining her trust. At the same time, he was indirectly sending signals to her lawyer about the value of the case. His gentle handling of Marla showed that he understood the emotional tone of the situation and gave the Mediator tacit permission to be direct with her lawyer.

WHAT STRATEGIES CAN WE LEARN?

1. **Anchor both parties in a potential settlement range as soon as possible.**

   If prior experience allows you to estimate the potential settlement range of a particular case at the beginning, this evaluation can sometimes help you set a more realistic top and bottom limit to the negotiations. First, check in with the parties to discover if they are looking at the case with a figure that is higher or lower than you had in mind. Then float the number or range you are aiming toward; when

the negotiation commences in earnest, that figure will
serve as an anchor toward which you can guide the parties.

2. **Lead the plaintiff lower by evaluating what the case is worth at
the top of the ladder.**

It's easier to determine a fair settlement range if you have
reached agreement with the plaintiff on an evaluation of
the top end of the ladder—for example, "I think we can
agree that the most a jury would award your client is $2
million." Because most cases do not settle at the highest
end, you can use the number to reduce the expectations
of the parties by underscoring or discounting various factors, such as the likelihood of winning the case in court
and the fact that juries rarely award amounts that high in
this type of case.

3. **Jump-start the defense offer by leading them to expect a high
settlement demand and then shattering that expectation.**

Give the defense the impression that the plaintiff will be
seeking multiples of the true value of the case, and assure
them that you will do your best to persuade them of the
risks inherent in such a strategy. Once the defense sees
that you have been successful in getting the plaintiff to
demand a reasonable sum, they will have confidence in
your abilities to resolve the case and will be more flexible
in their approach toward settlement.

4. **Ask the plaintiff's counsel to make a settlement demand below
the maximum value of the case.**

Once you have led the defense to expect that the plaintiff
will start with a large number, seek a more reasoned
demand that is based on the likelihood of success and the
argument that it will be met with a more moderate
response.

Chapter Twenty-Three

The Confidential Listener

"I understand that Mary is heartbroken about her son's death," said the attorney representing United Insurance, "but unfortunately she failed to supervise him properly, and we feel that her negligence contributed to his death in Mr. Harper's pool."

Mary leaned toward her lawyer, trying to avoid the brutal gaze of her ex-husband, Brian, by hiding behind her curtain of long blonde hair. Brian's lawyer, whom the Mediator knew to be a classic "ambulance chaser," smirked when he heard the insurance attorney's assessment of the case. Even though both Brian and Mary were the plaintiffs in this wrongful death suit, Brian's percentage of the settlement would probably be higher if Mary were found to be somewhat at fault. At the same time, however, the two of them would get a smaller overall settlement, so he had to be careful with what he said in front of the defense team.

"My client is also heartbroken over the death of his son," said Brian's lawyer, looking at his client. Brian bowed his head.

"That's a bit absurd, isn't it?" countered Mary's lawyer. She was standing up for her client, but she recognized the difficult position they were in: shooting bullets at Brian would only cause the insurer to reduce its value of the damage portion of the claim. "Brian is hardly on a par with Mary as a parent—he has not been the primary caregiver for many years. In fact, he left Mary when Glen was six months old, showed up on her doorstep three-and-a half years later asking for money for drugs, and then disappeared again. But this case is not about Brian and Mary. It's about Mr. Harper's complete lack of concern for safety and about his choosing to sneak around the building codes. A simple fence with a locked gate would have prevented this tragedy entirely. We feel completely justified in asking for large damages—"

"As do we!" Brian's lawyer put in.

"—and we're sure that a jury would see this heartbreaking accident as we do."

"We disagree."

This sounds more like a divorce case than a damages case, thought the Mediator. With one ear tuned to their bickering, he reviewed the facts quickly in his mind.

During a freak heat wave in early spring of the previous year, John Harper had decided to invite his neighbors to a barbecue and pool party in his backyard. Mary, a single mother, was grateful for the opportunity to get out of the house and socialize with adults for a few hours. She brought her son, eight-year-old Glen. Everyone had a great time, and after swimming and hanging out at the pool, they went inside to have dinner. After dinner, the adults stayed in the living room enjoying each others' company. Glen told Mary that he was going to the playroom with the other kids to play video games.

After a few hours, Mary was ready to go home. But when she went into the playroom to find Glen, he wasn't there. The other children said he had gotten bored and wandered out a while ago. She looked all over the house but couldn't find him anywhere. In a panic, she ran outside and found him lying at the bottom of the pool. Mary dove in and brought him to the surface. Emergency services tried to revive him, but it was too late. He had drowned.

Mary and Brian had both been approached by lawyers after a story about the tragedy hit the evening news, and had filed suit separately against John Harper for "premises liability" because there was no safety fence around the pool. But even though they were coupled in this lawsuit, they were far from being a couple.

Brian was a former drug addict and petty criminal who had been in and out of jail. Mary had struggled to raise her son on her own, with no help from Brian. In fact, Brian hadn't even contacted her or Glen for several years. Nonetheless, Brian felt that because he had fathered the deceased child, he was entitled to 50 percent of whatever the insurance company was prepared to offer. Mary felt strongly that because Brian had not shown much interest in Glen during his life, he should not profit from the boy's death.

The Mediator could see that the animosity between Mary and Brian was going to make it difficult to split the settlement pie, whatever it might be. Whatever one of them said, the other would say the opposite. He needed to create a structure that lulled them into a sense of security and would allow each of them to feel that he or she was not being backed into a corner by the other. So, rather than stall the negotiation at this point, he decided on a strategy called the "reversible recommendation." He felt certain they would arrive at a number—after all, they were here for the money.

"Here's what I'd like to suggest," he said, addressing the lawyers. "I'll talk to each plaintiff privately. Each of you will discuss with me the number you would recommend to your clients, with the understanding that they can reverse or withdraw the recommendation at any time." Turning to Mary and Brian, he explained, "This will allow either of you to back out of a number you don't feel comfortable with, without having to make a commitment to a specific proposal. Does that sound reasonable for all of you?"

Mary and Brian, puzzled, looked to their lawyers for advice. Neither of the lawyers had ever worked in quite this way before, but they both agreed to go along with the Mediator's strategy. Brian's lawyer said, "We're putting ourselves in your hands. If you tell us this is going to get us to the money, we'll go along with your recommendation."

The Mediator's plan was relatively simple, and he hoped it would help them avoid the internal bartering that was sure to ensue if he allowed things to take their normal course. Because the demands would be couched as "recommendations" and the parties could change their minds at any time, they would feel more in control. In reality, however, the Mediator doubted that either Mary or Brian would actually invoke their right of reversal—they would just feel better knowing that they could. The Mediator planned to turn the pressure on high, gently moving each party off their numbers by suggesting that the other side might recommend something in a range that appeared closer to what the particular party was looking for.

"Right now," said the Mediator, "I'd like to ask each party to go to a separate office so we can talk privately."

—◁◁◁◁▷—

As he began working his way through the private rooms, the Mediator decided it would be helpful to see if he could get Brian on board first.

"Thank you for speaking to us privately," said Brian's lawyer, shaking the Mediator's hand. "I didn't want to say this in front of Mary, but Brian has long suspected his ex-wife of being a neglectful mother." The Mediator knew this was a rather transparent ploy to reduce Mary's share of the settlement.

"This is probably not the best time to be attacking each other," said the Mediator. "I understand your point, but it seems to me that it's in your interest to work together with Mary to negotiate the best possible deal with United Insurance. Once that's done, *then* we can decide how to split up the pie."

"We agree," said Brian, slapping his palm on the desk. "Let's get the money on the table."

"Okay, then I propose that you and Mary put your differences aside and negotiate a number or range you can live with, and I'll work with the insurer to see if they'll pay it. I know you have some issues with Mary, and I know you have some ideas about what kind of number is reasonable. But I encourage you to be fair and reasonable here. If you try to overnegotiate this thing, you might miss an opportunity with the insurer," warned the Mediator.

And with that, he went to speak to the United Insurance executive and his lawyer.

—◁◁◁◁▷—

"Now that we're behind closed doors," the Mediator said, "tell me what your thoughts are about this case." He was curious—they seemed anxious and tense, and more concerned about the case than they let on in the joint meeting.

"We can see that taking this case to court will only cause the parents more pain," the lawyer told the Mediator, "and we're prepared to offer them some serious money to settle. But we're concerned that if we put any money on the table, Mary and Brian will get into a fight about how to split it up, and we don't want to be involved in that mess."

"Are you saying that you'd prefer to have an advance understanding between Mary and Brian that they would speak with one voice before you start the negotiation?"

"As I said, we don't mind making an offer. We simply want some assurance that we're not wasting our time. It seems clear that Mary and Brian have a long history of personal conflicts, and it's not up to us to solve them." The lawyer sat back in his chair with a sigh.

"I understand your concern," said the Mediator with some sympathy. "So before we plunge into negotiations, let me try to arrange an understanding between the parents so that they speak with one voice."

"Thank you," said the lawyer, clearly relieved.

—⁓—

The Mediator shuttled back and forth between Mary and Brian in a series of meetings. He asked Mary to step out for a moment so he could talk to her lawyer privately.

"I understand you made a demand before the mediation for $1.25 million," the Mediator said to Mary's lawyer.

"Yes, we did," she replied. "I actually spoke to Brian's lawyer"— and here she rolled her eyes—"and the one thing we could agree on to get the ball rolling was to ask for a number over a million dollars."

"Did you have a sense that the insurer would pay seven figures on this case, especially in light of the claims of parental negligence against Mary?"

"We recognized there would be comparative fault issues here, but we didn't want to leave anything on the table! How high do you think you can get them?"

"Right now, I'm just trying to get Mary and Brian to agree on which way is up," the Mediator laughed. "Beyond that, my sense is that a number over seven figures will cause this negotiation to fail. What's your evaluation of a reasonable range Mary would consider?"

Mary's lawyer thought for a moment and replied, "Honestly, we think this is a high six-figure case. See what you can do with Brian and his so-called counsel."

—◦◦◦—

The Mediator moved between Brian's and Mary's caucus rooms a few more times and eventually concluded that they would be willing to accept a settlement of the entire case for $850,000, subject to final approval from the insurer. Splitting up the proceeds would be the bigger challenge, but that would come later.

—◦◦◦—

The United Insurance executive and his lawyer had been waiting impatiently for about an hour-and-a-half while the Mediator worked out the issues with Mary and Brian. By the time the Mediator came back into their room, they were understandably cranky.

"What took you so long?" asked the lawyer without preamble.

"As you can imagine, I ran into some problems getting Mary and Brian to agree on anything. I'm happy to report that we finally reached consensus on what they would settle the case for," said the Mediator.

"I'm sure you'll tell us so that we can let you know if we have the authority."

"It's not that easy," the Mediator explained. He was about to embark on another strategy, that of the "confidential listener," and he explained the premise. "I don't have permission to reveal their bottom-line number yet, but there's a way around that. If you agree to share your number with me confidentially, I'll act as sort of an escrow person who holds everyone's number in my head. Again, all of this is in the strictest confidence—I'll only reveal the numbers if they fall within $100,000 of each other. If the numbers overlap, then I suggest we split the difference."

"What are we playing here, wait and hurry up?" the insurance executive raised his eyebrows.

"We were expecting more of a negotiation," the lawyer said, "but we understand the difficulties you have in dealing with the plaintiffs. Give us a few minutes to consider your suggestion."

The Mediator left the room and allowed them an opportunity to chat. After a few minutes, they invited him back in the room.

"To be honest," said the insurance representative, "I hate giving mediators our bottom line because they always ask for more. But I don't see much of a choice here. I do trust you—you've never let us down in other cases. We'll go along with your proposal. So here it is: our bottom-line authority is $700,000. There are liability issues here, as you know, and Mary could be held comparatively negligent.

"We're trusting you," the insurance representative reiterated.

"I appreciate your trust," responded the Mediator. "It's going to make these final negotiations go a lot more smoothly. And I can assure you that there's no crossover in this case: your number is definitely lower than their number. Unfortunately, you're farther apart then I had hoped, but not so far apart that this case can't settle. I think it would be helpful if you allow me to reveal your bottom line to Mary and Brian—provided I get their permission to reveal theirs to you."

"Wait a minute—does that mean you're going to ask us to pay more than the $700,000? We told you that was it for us!" exclaimed the insurance representative.

"I would hope that neither side draws a line in the sand, but if that's your endgame, then I'll make sure they understand it. I do believe it will be worthwhile doing it this way."

"As we said earlier, we're trusting you here," said the lawyer, not sounding quite as sure this time.

—◦◦◦—

The Mediator called a joint meeting with Mary, Brian, and their lawyers to discuss the status of settlement.

"As you know, I've been working hard to discover what the insurer would pay to settle this case. I now have that information, and I'm convinced that they've given me all of their authority," the Mediator said, turning his confidence level up to high. "I'd like to propose that I simultaneously disclose your number with their number, so we can determine together whether this case can settle."

The parties seemed confused by this approach—even the lawyers. They were still in the dark, and didn't think the insurer would pay the $850,000.

"I take it they don't have the $850,000 we were looking for, or you would have told us already," said Mary's lawyer flatly.

"I'm not going to say either way. But I think when you hear their number it will certainly be worth talking about," said the Mediator.

"All right," said Brian's lawyer. "We're in. How about you?" he raised his eyebrows in the direction of Mary's lawyer.

"Mary?" she looked at her client, who was making a great effort not to look at her ex.

"Whatever's right," Mary replied, with a shrug.

"Okay, go ahead," her lawyer said.

"Great. You know your number. I'm going to write their number on the whiteboard here." He wrote "$700,000" in large black numerals. "Now I'm going to go to the insurer's room and write your number on *their* board. While I'm gone, you can discuss your options."

—⋙⋘—

Back in the insurer's caucus room, the Mediator wrote "$850,000" on the board.

"Close, but no cigar," said the insurance executive. "I've already made our bottom line crystal clear.

"Hang on," said the Mediator, "we're not done yet. I'll be right back."

—⋙⋘—

When the Mediator went back into their room, he could see that Mary and Brian had reached the outer limits of their patience with this negotiation and were ready to deal. Mary seemed especially energized. She was sitting up straight and had pushed her hair back from her face.

"We've talked about this long enough," she said, finally looking Brian in the eye. "I want to take the $700,000 and put this behind us. I can't stand the idea of going to court and dredging up this situation again," she said, shaking her head slowly from side to side.

"Do you think you can get them up a *little* bit?" Brian whined. But it was clearly a last attempt. "We were hoping for a little more."

"Folks, I'm afraid they are truly at the end of their rope," said the Mediator, getting tough. "Candidly, if you're not happy with this, you don't have to take the money now. You could litigate this further. But there are some problems with the case, as we already discussed earlier, that could cause the value to go down further."

"Maybe we should talk it over," suggested Mary's lawyer.

"Fine," said the Mediator. "Let me know your decision."

Fifteen minutes later, they called him back in. "We've agreed. Tell them we accept their offer," said Mary's lawyer.

"Excellent," said the Mediator. "I'll ask the insurance company to prepare the documents. While they're doing that, we can figure out how Mary and Brian will divide the settlement."

———

By this time, Mary and Brian seemed to be working well together, so the Mediator was optimistic that this part of the negotiation would go quickly. He was wrong.

"So what did you each have in mind?" began the Mediator.

"Right down the middle: 50-50," said Brian. "That's $350,000 for each of us."

"Forget it, Brian!" Mary shouted. "Were you even there for half of Glen's life? You can have $100,000. That's it." She sat back, her arms folded across her chest for emphasis.

"Yeah," Brian spat back. "You were there *all* the time—great job of keeping him safe. Thanks for nothing."

Mary was tearful and angry. "Screw you, Brian. You're only here for the money, and we all know it."

With Mary and Brian bent on mutual destruction, the Mediator realized he would have to take the reins. "Whoa," he said, holding up his hands. "I can see this wasn't such a great idea. Mary,

Brian, I'm going to put you each back in a private caucus room with your lawyer, and we'll see if we can work this out. Mary, you're first."

—◦◦◦—

In the caucus room, the Mediator saw that Mary had calmed down a bit.

"Mary, if we're going to get this done, you're going to have to put your feelings aside for the moment and accept that Brian is going to end up with more than you think he deserves."

"I know, I know," replied Mary. "He's just so infuriating!"

"And that's going to mean coming closer to his number than you'd like to."

"Okay. I'll give him 25 percent—that seems fair."

"Do you really think he'll go for that, Mary?" asked her lawyer.

"I have to tell you, *I* don't think he'll go for that," said the Mediator.

"Try it," Mary insisted.

—◦◦◦—

Brian was still worked up. "You've got to be kidding!" said Brian. "Give *her* 75 percent? After she killed my kid? I don't think so. No."

"Frankly, I'm not surprised by your response," the Mediator said, ignoring the invective. "I know it's pretty far off from what you had in mind. But we all know that 50-50 isn't going to happen." Brian shrugged but said nothing.

"How would you feel if I were to recommend a 60-40 split—that's $420,000 for Mary and $280,000 for you."

"I'm not real happy with that number," said Brian.

"Well, think it over. I would like to at least float it past Mary to see if there's some common ground here. I won't make it a proposal from me, just an idea to see if she'll be flexible."

—◦◦◦—

"I guess I would agree to that," said Mary. "I just want this whole thing over with. And I never want to have to deal with Brian again!"

"Mary seems receptive to the idea of a 60-40 split, Brian. Before I seal the deal with her, I need to know if you can accept that."

Brian shook his head stubbornly. "No. It's 50-50."

"Brian," the Mediator said slowly, looking hard at Brian's lawyer, "I'm sure your lawyer has advised you about your options. You can opt out now and let a private arbitrator decide this for you. But that means you give up any control over the outcome. And it also means that the arbitrator will be looking closely at how you performed as a father when Glen was alive." He let that sink in for a moment. He was pretty sure that Brian, the former drug addict, wouldn't be able to walk away from the instant gratification of a quick-fix settlement. It had been clear from the beginning that he was much less concerned about the loss of his son and more concerned about putting money in his pocket quickly. The Mediator decided to push Bran to closure by sweetening the deal just a little.

"Brian, be honest: How much were you expecting to receive from any potential settlement when you walked in here today?"

"Well," said Brian, thinking hard, "I was expecting to walk out of here with about a quarter of a million after I paid off my lawyer here."

"Ahh," said the Mediator, "now I get it. You have to pay your lawyer one-third of the overall settlement, and you can't net $250,000 if your portion is $280,000."

"Right," Brian nodded.

"I have an idea, but it will require a small discount on the $250,000. Here's my question: Would you be satisfied netting $225,000 after your lawyer gets his one-third fee?"

Brian looked puzzled. "I wouldn't be thrilled, but I'd consider it just to get this nailed down now. But I don't understand how you're doing the math on that one."

"That's $225,000 in your pocket, right now. Does it matter how I do the math?" asked the Mediator.

"No," said Brian, "I guess not. As long as you make sure I walk out with $225,000, you can carve it up any way you want."

"I need to talk to your lawyer privately, Brian. We're going to take a walk and be back in a few minutes."

But a walk wasn't necessary. As soon as the two men were out in the hall the lawyer said, "Are you sure you can do this?"

"Well, I may not be able to get this in a range that will net you the $95,000 or $100,000 you wanted. Do you have some flexibility?"

Brian's lawyer paused for a beat and said, "A little. But do what you can to protect me."

"Absolutely," the Mediator replied.

"Then why the hell not? Go for it!"

The Mediator wasn't surprised that Brian's lawyer jumped so quickly at the lower sum. It was a sure thing, and a lot easier than trying the case in court. He went to talk to Mary and her lawyer.

"We're almost done, Mary," said the Mediator. "If you'll agree to accept $400,000," Brian will sign off."

"That selfish bastard," she said, wiping sudden tears off her cheek.

"Mary, I know this doesn't feel good, but realize this: the fact that the insurer is willing to pay out $700,000 is really their acknowledgment that John Harper was negligent and that you are a good mother." He waited while Mary digested that idea. "If you take this to trial, you may get a bigger portion of the settlement than Brian, but it will mean you'll have to dredge all this up again and deal with Brian and his accusations again. And the judge will look very closely at your behavior the night of the party, asking you how much you had to drink and so forth. Do you really want to go through all that?"

Mary crossed her arms around her chest and hugged herself tightly, rocking back and forth. "No," she said finally. "I've had it. Tell Brian I'll take the $400,000."

All that was left was for the Mediator to confirm with Brian's lawyer that he would accept $75,000 for his fee so that Brian would net $225,000. The parties settled for $400,000 and $300,000 respectively.

WHAT HAPPENED?

The Mediator created a safe, flexible structure for decision making, a device that would allow Mary and Brian to make decisions about their side of the case such that they could change their mind if they didn't like what the other said. It wasn't so much a tactic as a mind-set that allowed them to feel that they were not being hammered into submission; they could say no to each other at any time.

This approach sidestepped the usual back-and-forth haggling between plaintiffs that often occurs in litigated cases, but allowed the plaintiffs the liberty to back out without ever making a commitment to a specific settlement proposal. In short, any settlement numbers discussed would be couched as recommendations as opposed to formal offers. The Mediator understood that people tend to base big decisions on emotion, not logic. It was clear that Brian and Mary couldn't agree on anything between them, and never had; nothing he could do in one short day would change that fact. So he based his approach on their customary way of doing things. The whole idea of the "no-commitment" approach was to create a context in which Mary and Brian felt safe. Ironically, they never used it.

Next, the Mediator acted as a "confidential listener" to each side, getting them to commit their bottom-line numbers to him in exchange for his agreement not to share them with the other side unless they were within a certain range. If they were within the range of $100,000, they would reveal their numbers. The Mediator was certain that the gravitational pull of such close numbers would cause one or both of the parties to stretch to make the deal. But when the parties ended up $150,000 apart—a little too far to stretch—the Mediator had a problem. He had promised not to reveal the numbers. To get around that, he chose to ask each side for permission to reveal their numbers simultaneously, knowing that the numbers were too close for comfort. Seeing the numbers in stark black and white made the plaintiffs realize that $700,000 on the table was too much money to walk away from, and the case resolved.

WHAT STRATEGIES CAN WE LEARN?

1. **Use the reversible recommendation to create a safe atmosphere for negotiation.**

   When dealing with multiple plaintiffs with similar interests, it is critical that they speak with one voice. If the individuals involved are in conflict with one another, you need to create a context in which they feel safe operating. In these situations, you can gently suggest that they propose a number or range, with the understanding that they can back out of the arrangement at any time. That way, they don't feel locked in or pressured to accept a particular number.

2. **Serve as a confidential listener.**

   Obtain a proposed final settlement offer from each party. Without disclosing the content of the offers, you, the confidential listener, advise the parties if their offers are within a specified range. The range usually is agreed on by the parties in advance, along with a mechanism for dividing the difference in the event that the offers overlap. If the offers are outside the specified range, you can help the parties bridge the gap and achieve a final settlement.

CHAPTER TWENTY-FOUR

DROPPING THE BOMBSHELL

Chris, in his mid-thirties with a wife and three children, liked his life. He'd been a meter reader for the Green River Gas Company—one of the best, according to him—for ten years. When he was fired for taking an extra day off, he was furious—especially because he had hurt his neck a few days earlier. He felt he was being unfairly discriminated against, and filed suit for wrongful termination. In a premediation meeting with the Mediator, he explained his position enthusiastically.

"I'm great at my job," Chris grinned. "Anyone will tell you I can read more meters in one day than anyone else they've got. Heck, I've been at this for ten years—I ought to be good by now!"

"So what happened?" asked the Mediator.

"Damned if I know," Chris replied, turning his hands palm up and looking bewildered. "I've had trouble with my neck for years, but I try not to let it slow me down. Still, when it flares up I need to take care of it. This time, I hurt my neck on a Thursday—couldn't even look over my shoulder, it hurt so bad. So I called in sick on Friday. Fortunately, the next day was the beginning of the Fourth of July weekend, and I got Monday off too. I spent the whole damn weekend in bed, and when I went back to work on Tuesday, ready to go, they fired me."

"You can see how poorly Chris has been treated here," said his lawyer. "We're justified in asking for $750,000. We could easily get that for lost wages, emotional distress, and attorneys' fees when we win this case in court."

The Mediator's first thought on hearing this story was that Chris seemed quite satisfied with himself and that his narrative seemed a little too pat, but he'd heard a lot of even less likely scenarios over the years that had turned out to be true. Still, as he walked over to the room where Chris's employer was waiting, he wondered what he would learn. As it happened, he was in for a surprise.

—◦◦◦—

"I'd like Chuck here to tell you his side of the story," said the Green River Gas Company's corporate attorney. "He's been Chris's supervisor for a decade now, and he's got plenty to say."

Chris's boss was disgusted. "Yeah, Chris has been with us for ten years, and it seems like when the weather's fine he always manages to take a day off or get an extra vacation day or call in sick. He *is* a good employee, and he seems to think he deserves it. To be honest, we've cut him some slack—but he's been warned many times over many years. In fact, just a month before this all happened, I couldn't take it anymore. I gave him an ultimatum: if he took advantage of the system or my goodwill one more time, I'd fire him."

"I understand from Chris that he hurt his neck and called in sick," said the Mediator. "Is that what happened?"

"Not exactly," replied Chuck, rolling his eyes. "It's a pretty good story. On the Friday before the Fourth of July holiday, Chris called in at 5:30 in the morning and said he could barely move his neck and wouldn't be coming to work. I was pretty suspicious, but what could I do?

"Then I got lucky," Chuck continued. "Our other meter readers have been getting pretty fed up with Chris wangling all these paid days off. One of our guys, Dale, lives right across the street from Chris. He really resents Chris, and he's always trying to catch him out. On Friday morning he was eating breakfast and staring out his window, and he saw Chris get into his truck with his family at 9:00 A.M. and start hooking his boat onto the boat hitch. Dale called me right away, and I asked him how quickly he could get out his video camera and start taping what Chris was doing. Then I called a private investigator and hired her to go down to the river and follow Chris around."

Chuck produced a videotape and pushed it across the table toward the Mediator. "We have a really entertaining date- and time-stamped tape here of Chris driving his speedboat and water-skiing all weekend. His neck looks like it works just fine." Chuck laughed.

"When Chris came to work on Tuesday, I asked him how he was feeling. When he told me he'd spent the weekend in bed due to his neck condition, I told him I knew he was lying, and I fired him."

"That's quite a story," said the Mediator. "Do Chris and his counsel know about the videotape?"

"No," said Chuck. "He just yelled at me and stormed out. I never got a chance to tell him about it."

From his meeting with Chris, the Mediator could see that the meter reader was an accomplished bluffer who had managed to get away with murder for years through audacity and sheer force of personality. He was asking for a hefty settlement, and the Mediator was sure they were in for a lot more of that kind of behavior if he asked the plaintiff to present his case first. *If ever a case has called for reverse direction,* thought the Mediator, *this is it.* So he asked Chuck and the Green River attorney, "I wonder if you'd mind if we did something a little different to jump-start this mediation?"

"What have you got in mind?" asked Chuck's counsel.

"Well, you've got a real bombshell here. Rather than hit Chris over the head with this evidence, which is sure to shock and embarrass him, I think it would be helpful if we could meet privately with his lawyer and have you demonstrate what you have. I will not ask him to respond to the tape. I just want to give him a chance to see it, evaluate it, and then speak privately with his client," said the Mediator.

"That's fine with us, but we're not going to respond to a $750,000 demand in light of this evidence. We'll stick with our original position: we offered him a modest severance package to resign instead of firing him outright, and we're still willing to discuss that. See what you can do."

—◦◦◦—

The Mediator knew Chris's counsel was not prepared for what he was about to see, so he pulled him out into the lobby for a quick conversation away from his client.

"I realize you're ready to present an overview of a strong damage and liability case to the other side in a joint meeting, and I don't want to get in your way of doing that. But I've just learned that the defense has obtained some significant evidence, and I'd like you to see it before we go off in a direction where positions harden and the case can't settle," said the Mediator.

"What are you talking about?" The Mediator could see that Chris's counsel was in the dark about his client's activities.

"Green River Gas has some surveillance tape of Chris that he doesn't know about. Rather than have them play it in front of you and Chris in a joint session, I thought you'd appreciate the chance to preview it before we get too deep into the negotiation. I think a private meeting of counsel makes more sense here. You can just tell Chris we are going to review some evidence before we get started with the formal presentation of the case."

"Isn't that a little unusual?" asked Chris's attorney, clearly disconcerted. "I've been involved in many negotiations, and in every one the plaintiff has always presented the case."

"Yes, it is unusual," replied the Mediator. "But I think if you bear with me you'll see my reasoning."

"This better be good," said the lawyer, "or we're going to be asking for a hell of a lot more money than $750,000!"

―――≈≈≈―――

And with that, the Mediator took Chris's counsel into the meeting room, dimmed the lights, and signaled Green River's attorney to start the video. As they watched Chris laughing, water-skiing, and craning his neck around to check behind him as he drove the speedboat, the Mediator kept his eyes on Chris's lawyer. He clearly seemed to be shocked by what he was seeing.

As Green River's lawyer stopped the tape and turned on the lights, the Mediator jumped in.

"I need a few minutes with plaintiff's counsel here. We're going to take a walk outside, and we'll return in a few minutes."

—

"I can't believe Chris didn't tell me about this," said his counsel.

"I was pretty sure this tape was going to take you by surprise," said the Mediator. "What do you want to do?"

"We're cooked," the plaintiff's counsel said. "I'm going to need to speak to my client alone for a few minutes." And with that, the lawyer walked back inside, straight into his caucus room, and shut the door. The Mediator waited patiently in the hallway.

Several minutes later, counsel opened the door. "Come on in," he said to the Mediator, ushering him into the caucus room. "I'd like you to tell Chris your impressions of the tape," he said.

"Well, Chris," said the Mediator, looking him straight in the eye, "I'll cut to the chase. What they've got is pretty damaging. It certainly goes against everything you've testified about your medical injuries, and it would be used dramatically in court as impeachment."

"What does *that* mean?" asked Chris.

"It means it takes the guts out of your case. My advice is to try to get as much as you can out of Green River Gas now—assuming they're still prepared to pay anything."

Chris was rocking back and forth in his chair, agitated. "They taped me without my knowledge! Isn't that entrapment or something? I don't think they had a right to invade my privacy like that." Chris stood up and sat down again. "That's just not right. Can't we sue them for what they've done to me?" Chris's face was beet red.

"Chris," said the Mediator. "There's an old saying: if you're going to live outside the law, you've got to be honest."

"Meaning what?" moaned Chris.

"Meaning that when you bring a legal case like this, you have to be prepared for anything that happens in the battle, and if you're proved to have presented something that's not true, it's better to take the hit and move on."

Chris's counsel agreed. "We need to settle this thing now, Chris. If you want to keep spending money to take them to court, I advise against it, but it's your money. Just know that it's entirely possible you could end up with less than you had when you walked in here."

"Are you kidding me?" Chris wailed. "I can't believe how these people screwed me over! I want to take them to trial. We can get the judge to say they can't show the tape."

"Wake up, Chris," said his attorney, clearly running out of patience. "That's not going to happen! If you pursue this any further, your reputation's going to be shot so full of holes you'll *never* get another job."

As Chris mulled over that possibility, he suddenly ran out of steam. "How am I supposed to support my family?" he whined. "My wife'll kill me." He looked at the Mediator. "I need money to tide me over until I find another job." Chris was near tears, feeling very sorry for himself.

Chris's lawyer turned to the Mediator and asked, "Do you think you could get them to pay him some severance, maybe six months' salary, so he can get on with his life?"

The Mediator knew that Chris needed a way out that would preserve at least a shred of what dignity he had left—for the sake of his family if not for himself—and he was pretty sure the company's offer would hold. "I think they'd be open to that type of approach," he replied, "provided that's what you and Chris want me to do."

"Just get me out of here," said Chris. "I want this nightmare to go away. I'll take six months' severance—and not a penny less."

—✿—

"Chris understands that the surveillance tapes put him in a bad light," the Mediator explained to Chuck and his attorney.

"I should hope so!" the attorney said.

"And I've asked him to reconsider the severance package you offered him before the mediation."

"The company is still prepared to give him the six months' severance pay we offered him in the first place," said the attorney. "He did do good work for us for ten years."

"When he bothered to show up for work!" Chuck said, shaking his head in disgust. "I just hope he understands how lucky he is to walk away with that package," he added. "But I doubt he even thinks he did anything wrong."

WHAT HAPPENED?

When the Mediator heard about the secret videotape evidence, he knew he had a chance to short-circuit hours of posturing by an accomplished pretender, get the numbers into a more reasonable range, and wrap up the mediation quickly. He took a calculated risk by springing the tape on Chris's counsel without his client present, but he also knew it was possible that Chris might have taken offense and stormed out, or worse. Fortunately, Chris's attorney quickly came to the conclusion that they were better off cutting their losses and looking for the exit as quickly as possible. In the end, Green River Gas Company was happy to pay the price of a small settlement to finally get rid of Chris, and Chris was grateful to be able to get a little cash to support his family and save his reputation—he'd need it the next time he looked for a job.

WHAT STRATEGIES CAN WE LEARN?

1. **Consider using "reverse direction" when the defense holds very damaging evidence, but drop the bomb carefully.**
   This technique is a very directive approach that reverses the usual order of presenting information. Instead of having the plaintiff outline his case in the first joint meeting, you begin with the defense. The purpose is to test the plaintiff's reaction to the revelation of damning evidence before too much posturing takes place. It's a dangerous approach because it is quite confrontational—when faced with such direct evidence, the plaintiff might take offense and walk out of the room. Nevertheless, it does set the stage for a negotiation that has less posturing and more sensible discussions. Consider using the approach with counsel alone. Doing so gives the attorney the chance to assess the potential damage to the client and analyze an exit strategy.
2. **Look for the language of concern.**
   During the presentation, always look for body language or verbal communication from the plaintiff's counsel that would indicate concern. If you detect concern, you can suggest that the parties negotiate in a much more reasonable

range than what was initially set forth in the plaintiff's
demand.

3. **Provide parties with a dignified way out that softens the realization that their initial unrealistic expectations will not be met.**
When you discover damaging evidence that could clearly
embarrass a party, discuss the evidence with the lawyer
first: never drop the bomb on someone without warning.
At the same time, obtain a settlement proposal from the
defense that gives the embarrassed party an opportunity
to save face.

Chapter Twenty-Five

Worth the Wait

"What is *wrong* with you? I thought you were my friends. Don't you have any humanity at all?" By now, Margaret's tears were cutting streambeds through her makeup and running down the ridges of her face. The Mediator was seriously worried about the elderly woman's health. But just as he was considering calling a halt to the negotiations, the former waitress beat him to the punch.

She dried her tears, and when she spoke again, Margaret's tone was flat. "I've had it," she said. "I'm going home. I guess I'll see you in court." And with that, she picked up her coat and walked out. The owner of Thelma's Restaurant, Sheryl, and her trusted manager, Ted, were in shock. Even Margaret's attorney was speechless.

The Mediator felt terrible. The case had barely started, and it had gone suddenly, terribly wrong. As Margaret slammed the office door, he turned back to those who were left at the conference table and took up the reins.

"That's a first for me," said the Mediator. "I've never had a party storm out before."

"Now you can see what we're up against," said Sheryl, shaking her head.

Erin, the Employment Practices Liability (EPL) lawyer from Sheryl's insurance company, tapped nervously on her briefcase. She was there because if this case didn't get settled today, there was a real possibility that Margaret would file an age discrimination case against Thelma's. That possibility was getting more real by the minute.

The Mediator turned to Margaret's lawyer. "Larry, maybe you can get Margaret to change her mind and come back," he said.

"Please see what you can do. While you work on that, we'll take a break, and then maybe Ted and Sheryl here can fill me in on their perspective."

"I'll see what I can do," said Larry, hastening after his client.

—◦◦◦—

During the break, the Mediator reviewed the case. Margaret, almost eighty, had worked at Thelma's for nearly four decades. The original owner, Thelma, had died some years ago, and her daughter Sheryl had been the owner for almost fifteen years. The old restaurant's homey food and retro decor had suddenly gotten trendy again, and the place was packed with customers. That was fine with Margaret—she'd worked there so long she felt like she owned the place herself, and liked nothing better than chatting with old customers she'd known for many years. She openly disagreed with Ted, the manager, when she thought something could be done better, but despite her forthright style Ted always gave her solid evaluations, and the customers adored her.

So when she had been let go—without even a retirement party or a pension—she was shocked and hurt.

"I spent half my life working at Thelma's," Margaret had said when the meeting began. "Thelma never would have treated me like Ted and Sheryl did. She's turning over in her grave, I know it." She barely stopped to take a breath.

"I was their best waitress for almost forty years. The customers love me, they love me—I still get calls from them asking when I'm coming back. But do Ted and Sheryl show any appreciation at all? No! They just got rid of me. They didn't even have the nerve to fire me outright or give me a retirement party—Ted said if I wanted one, I could have one at my own cost." Margaret seemed in danger of hyperventilating, but she went on.

"Cutting off my health insurance was the last straw. I decided to get myself a lawyer and sue."

In her complaint, which had been provided as a courtesy copy but not yet served on the parties, Margaret asked for well over $1 million. She asked for lost wages because they cut her hours back, and front pay for money she would have earned at Thelma's until she got another job. Margaret also claimed that Thelma's was discriminating against her because of her age, and said that the restaurant should have to pay a very large penalty for breaking the law. Most important, Margaret was asking for damages for emotional distress.

Sheryl thought Margaret's claim was ridiculous and refused to pay her anything. As the owner said to the Mediator, "We've been carrying her for years; we should have fired her long ago, when she started slowing down, but she was like a fixture at Thelma's. We just didn't have the heart to do it. We've already gone above and beyond the call of duty by paying her a monthly stipend when she didn't even work there anymore! And now she's asking us for front pay? She's eighty years old—she can't expect anyone's going to hire her now."

"We let Margaret go because she was no longer a good worker," said Ted, backing up his employer, "not because she was old."

"That's right," said Sheryl, gathering steam. "What are we supposed to do, keep her on until she dies on a shift?"

And that's when Margaret left the negotiation.

"Ted," said the Mediator after the break, "it looks like Larry is still trying to track down Margaret, so maybe you could fill me in a little more about the background. What exactly happened to bring things to this point? From what I've heard, Margaret was a loyal, long-time employee."

"I've worked with Margaret for years," said Ted, "and in her prime she was the best. Even when she started slowing down a bit about ten years ago, she worked as hard as anybody. But at about age seventy-two, her arthritis started to give her problems. Still, she made it clear that she had no intention of retiring any time soon. The other staff covered for her—everyone loves Margaret—but it was clear that she couldn't handle the pace anymore. We need a faster turnover than she was able to provide."

"We didn't want to fire her outright," explained Sheryl. "My mother hired her herself; she's practically a legacy. So we decided that the kindest thing would be to try to phase her out gradually. We reduced her hours to two-thirds time and figured she'd catch on and bow out gracefully."

"But five years later," Ted continued, "Margaret was still work-ing two-thirds time. She wasn't bad when things were slow, but we just couldn't count on her when the restaurant was full. She also spent more and more time talking to the regulars who were her friends and neglecting other customers."

"She started treating the place like it was her home, and they were her invited guests," said Sheryl.

"I tried to talk to Margaret about it many times," said Ted, "but she wouldn't listen. Finally, I got fed up. I had a restaurant to run. Sheryl wouldn't fire her because she didn't want to hurt her mother's memory. All I could think of was to put her on vacation—indefinitely—and I passed the word around that she wasn't return-ing to the restaurant."

"It's not like we turned her out into the snow," said Sheryl. "We continued to pay her something every month, and we covered the cost of her health insurance for a while. Finally, my accountant asked me where all that money was going. It just seemed crazy, so we stopped paying for her health insurance."

"Margaret went ballistic," said Ted, shaking his head.

"We didn't want to drag the poor old lady to court." said Sheryl. "We thought mediation would be the best course. For all the good it's done."

At that moment Larry walked back into the room with Margaret.

"Larry," the Mediator said quickly, "why don't you and Margaret come with me to a smaller room so we can talk privately. I'll get Margaret some tea."

"Two sugars, no milk," Margaret snapped.

—⁓—

Margaret drank her tea, subdued and silent. "Margaret," said the Mediator carefully, "I know this is tough on you, and I'm sorry you have to go through this. But I think if you hang in there we can work through this and avoid going to court. Ted and Sheryl filled me in on some of the details while you were gone, and now I'd like to hear your side of the story. Can you tell me what's going on for you?"

Margaret was still very emotional, and all of her feelings of betrayal and disappointment quickly surfaced. "I just don't understand why they treated me so coldly," said Margaret. "They never *once* told me what was going on. All of a sudden, I was working fewer hours. That was okay, I guess, but then when they put me on 'vacation'—forever!—I was mystified. Was I fired? Retired? I didn't even get a chance to quit. I was in some limbo place. I was just gone, disappeared. Like I never worked there. Some of my old customers said there was gossip about me—I'd had a stroke, I'd gone senile and stolen the silver—because Ted and Sheryl never said a word." She stopped and thought for a few minutes, then continued, almost thinking out loud. "I know I'm old. I'm not a fool. If they'd just come and talked to me like a human being we wouldn't be in this mess."

"That's an interesting insight," said the Mediator. "May I discuss your concerns with Ted and Sheryl?"

"Sure, why not?" replied Margaret.

"Please do," her lawyer added.

"But good luck to you," said Margaret, as the Mediator was leaving the room. "All those two think about is how many customers you've got, how many tables you're turning over, and how many drinks you're selling."

—⟪∾⟫—

"Sheryl," said the Mediator, "as you no doubt noticed when Margaret ran out of here, she's clearly reached the end of her rope on this thing. I thought it was important to separate everyone so we could avoid another meltdown. Now we need to really figure out the best approach to resolving this thing."

"I agree," said Erin. Sheryl looked down at her manicure, and Ted bit his lower lip. Clearly, they felt horrible. They knew that they didn't really owe Margaret anything, and they genuinely felt that they had treated her very well under the circumstances. But they also found it hard to sit and hear about her anguish.

"Margaret told me that she wished the two of you had just talked to her about your concerns. It seems that all of your maneuvering, no matter how well meant, just succeeded in confusing her and ultimately in making her feel hurt and angry."

"Yes, but the customer turnover at her tables was dismal," Ted persisted. "People would sit there for hours, chewing the fat with Margaret."

"Have you thought that maybe some of those customers were coming for Margaret rather than for the meatloaf?" asked the Mediator quietly. "And that with Margaret gone, they might go elsewhere for a friendlier restaurant?"

"My mother would have understood that," said Sheryl, near tears. "God, I've known Margaret my whole life. I feel awful. There must be something we can do." She looked at the EPL lawyer. "We can pay her something, right? What can we give her that will make her drop this case? And help support her, of course," she added quickly.

"I have the insurance company available by phone," said Erin. "Actually, I'd like to call and let them know what's going on. In fact," she said, turning the Mediator, "maybe you can help me by sharing your assessment of the case."

"Of course," said the Mediator, "I'd be glad to."

Erin got the company on speakerphone and introduced the Mediator to the insurance representative. The Mediator said, "We've spent a lot of time with Margaret today, some pretty emotional stuff. And I can tell you it's been pretty hard on her—in fact, she bolted out of here at one point. The whole thing is just more than she can handle, and frankly, considering that she's almost eighty, it's more than she should have to handle. Age discrimination might really resonate with a jury—it's hard to accept that Thelma's fired a woman whose life's work has been the same job for more than forty years." He looked pointedly at Sheryl and Ted. "There may have been a better way to handle this."

"It sounds like we might have some exposure here," said the insurance rep. "Let me talk to my lawyer—privately."

After a few minutes, the insurance rep called back and Erin said, "My adjuster wants to offer Margaret some significant money."

"What have you got in mind?" said the Mediator.

"We don't mind putting six figures on the case, but we absolutely need Margaret to reduce her demand dramatically."

"When you say 'six figures,'" inquired the Mediator, "are you talking $100,000, $200,000, or more?"

"We're in the low end of that range," Erin replied.

"That's a lot of money!" said Sheryl.

"Yes, but if Margaret takes this to court and she wins, she can recover her damages *and* attorney fees—and the insurance company is worried that it might be a pretty substantial amount."

Sheryl and Ted sat back and took all this in. They were playing in the big leagues now.

"Can I take an offer of $100,000 back to Margaret?" asked the Mediator.

"Sure," said Erin, "go ahead. But remember, we're trying to be reasonable here. They need to appreciate our efforts!"

"Good news, Margaret. I spoke to the insurance company for Thelma's. They've reviewed your case in detail and are willing to offer you $100,000."

"Hell, no!" said Margaret. "What do you think, Larry?"

"I think it's a good start, Margaret. You can come down a little. Let's go to $780,000," said Larry.

"Okay," said Margaret, with a sigh. "I trust whatever my lawyer tells me. I'll come down as far as $780,000, but that's it." She looked exhausted with the effort. It was clear to the Mediator that this was all too much for Margaret to handle. She didn't understand this type of negotiation over dollars and cents, and it wasn't really addressing why she was there.

Suddenly, Margaret stood up. "I can't do this anymore!" she exploded, and walked out again.

"I'll go after her," said Larry. But Margaret never came back. The session fell apart before the tough negotiations began.

Over the next few days, the Mediator placed several calls to Margaret's lawyer. Finally, he called back.

"Margaret's depressed," Larry explained. "She knows she doesn't have the stamina to make it through a trial, and I've encouraged her to come back to the table."

"That's good," said the Mediator, "but I have to be able to assure the other side that she won't run off again."

"She won't," said Larry. "I'll make sure of that."

"Well, if she's willing to reduce her expectations, I think the other side is prepared to put some serious money on the table. But it seems to me that the real sticking point is that she needs some recognition that they handled her termination badly, and she wants some tangible appreciation for her years of service to Thelma's."

"Absolutely. You're right on with that assessment," replied Larry. "That would go a long way toward getting this thing settled, provided the money was right."

⌇⌇⌇

As the second session began, both sides were determined to compromise. They didn't want to go to trial, and they didn't want to have to spend another entire day thrashing this out.

The Mediator began by having a private caucus with Ted and Sheryl.

"I think it's pretty clear that you're going to need to come up with something creative to let Margaret know that you really do value her life's work. I can't say it any more clearly than this: your insurance company is going to have to come up with some serious money, but as her employer you have to do something special beyond that. For example, you might want to recognize her forty years of service. That's what will likely make her stay in the negotiation."

"Yeah," said Sheryl, "we got the message loud and clear. Even our own customers have been telling us that. They miss her, and they wish she was still there."

"Maybe you could do something that makes it possible for Margaret to feel good about coming to the restaurant once in a while," suggested the Mediator.

"I told Sheryl that we should just offer her free meals for life," said Ted. "She can come in and eat whenever she wants, no charge."

"That's a great idea," said the Mediator. "What other ideas have you got?"

"Well," Sheryl offered, "we were thinking about having an Employee of the Month award named after Margaret—you know, in her honor—and then we'll give her a special lifetime achievement award at our company picnic next month—engraved trophy, a big party, the whole works. Do you think she would get the picture that we really do care about her?"

"Along with the money from your insurance company, that should do it," said the Mediator. "Erin?"

"I'm authorized to go up to $300,000," said the EPL lawyer. "But we don't want you to offer it until you can assure us it will settle the case."

"Okay. I'll go into the other room and do a little more intelligence. I won't offer any money without your permission," said the Mediator, and went to talk to Margaret and Larry.

—⁓⁓—

The Mediator approached Margaret with relentless cheerfulness. He told her about the awards, the party, and the lifetime of free meals, and how bad Sheryl and Ted felt about the thoughtless way they had treated her. Then he added the kicker. "And guess what? Their insurance company wants to offer you some significant money that will allow you to visit with your friends at Thelma's anytime but never have to work another day in your life. I'd like to talk to Larry about that privately, if you don't mind."

Margaret was relieved and happy. "I don't mind work, really. But I know my stamina for carrying trays isn't what it used to be. Sure, do whatever you have to do."

Meeting separately with Larry, the Mediator suggested, "Larry, I think it would be helpful if you indicated that your client would come in under $500,000."

"So fast?"

"Look, Larry—cards on the table. This has been going on for days! You know the insurer has lost its patience on this negotiation. They only came back to the table after I assured them we would work quickly to get into a range you both find satisfactory. I'd like to help you find out what their range is ASAP. I think they will respond if you signal that your client is in a reasonable zone."

"Okay," Larry agreed. "Normally I wouldn't do this, but Margaret wants this settled."

"And we don't want her to change her mind," said the Mediator, smiling.

———

"Margaret likes your ideas," the Mediator told Ted and Sheryl, and they're willing to settle under $500,000."

"Now that is good movement. I think my principal will be pleased!" said Erin.

"Yeah," said the Mediator. "As you can see, the range of settlement is somewhere between the $100,000 offer and the $500,000 demand. Based on our prior conversation, if I can get them down to $300,000, do I have permission to offer it?"

"Well, now that you have got them down so fast, maybe we can save some money on our authority," said Erin, trying to gain some points with the insurer.

"Erin, I'm not willing to play that game," exclaimed the Mediator. "I relied on the $300,000 authority when I convinced Margaret and Larry to come down under $500,000. They'll lose confidence in me if you try to push this negotiation downward."

"Look," said Erin, "we're obviously here to settle this case. Any time I can save my company some money I'd like to do it. If you think that would not be a wise move, then let's get this done at $300,000. But don't forget that $300,000 was and is my top dollar. I can't make any more phone calls."

"So, can I infer that you might be receptive to meeting halfway?" asked the Mediator.

"Yes, but don't put us in a spot where we have nowhere to go!"

———

"Larry, I've had a chance to speak further with the insurance side," the Mediator explained. "Rather than playing verbal Ping-Pong, I've asked them to consider meeting you and Margaret halfway at $300,000. My question to you is, if I can deliver $300,000, would that do it?"

"If I tell you it would, can you assure me you won't come back and try to offer something less?" asked Larry.

"I wouldn't be making this inquiry unless I thought I could deliver it."

―∽∿∾―

Just a few short minutes later, the case settled for $300,000, two awards, a celebratory party tribute, and a lifetime of free meals at Thelma's so that Margaret could meet and greet her friends whenever she wanted to. Margaret finally felt that she was being treated the way she should have been, given all her years of hard work. When she thought about an award being given out even after she died, she felt very important and valued. She also knew that $300,000 would go a long way on her budget, and she looked forward to eating meals with old friends whenever she liked—not to mention being waited on by someone else! So Margaret accepted Sheryl's offer. She got what she needed—which, as she said, was well worth the wait.

WHAT HAPPENED?

The initial problem with the Mediator's approach in this case was that instead of meeting separately with the parties and learning about Margaret's deep pain right at the beginning, he immediately put them into a joint session and let the emotions roll. Unfortunately, Margaret's emotions were at the breaking point, and she soon lost control and bolted out of the session. A short amount of time spent separately with the parties ahead of time would have allowed the Mediator to choose a different approach and avoid having the case fall apart before it ever got started. When Margaret returned to the session, the Mediator kept the parties separated, and they were able to exchange information in a more structured fashion.

Unfortunately, Margaret had not really recovered from her earlier breakdown, and the continued tension prevented her from understanding the importance of patience during the negotiation process. She was so distraught that she immediately rejected anything she saw as an attack—and because nothing had been done to disabuse her of the idea that Sheryl and Ted were out to get her, that was how she viewed everything coming from their camp.

Although the initial offer of $100,000 was not, in the scheme of things, unreasonable, Margaret mistook it as another slap in the face. She fell apart and left again. This put an added burden on the Mediator to maintain an upbeat attitude and stay with the process, even as it required follow-up telephone calls over a period of days. This follow-up demonstrated to both parties that he was committed to settlement and helped get them back on track.

Once back at the table, the Mediator recognized that a long, drawn-out negotiation would not be suitable for either side. Separating Margaret's lawyer for a private conversation about the money helped accelerate the negotiation and caused the insurer for Thelma's to quickly reveal their top dollar to the Mediator. At the same time, the Mediator addressed Margaret's nonmonetary concerns, helping her achieve her vision of a positive ending to her career as a waitress.

WHAT STRATEGIES CAN WE LEARN?

1. **Demonstrate your belief in the process.**

   Demonstrate your belief and commitment to the process at all times, even (perhaps especially) when things break down. Negotiations can be stressful, and some people rely on avoidance as their only tool for dealing with conflict. Avoidance does not necessarily represent a rejection of the negotiation process, but may simply be the only way the person knows to manage conflict. When you are faced with skittish participants, your best tool is to remain steady, be persistent, and keep reminding the parties (verbally and nonverbally) that you know where you're going and how to get there.

2. **Turn the walkout situation around.**

   Paradoxically, parties who walk out on or even flee a mediation session are sending a message that they have an underlying desire to settle but just don't know how. By removing themselves so dramatically, they are actually making a statement that they are unique and that their uniqueness has not been recognized. It's important to view the walkout move as the raw material for future deals, not as an abandonment of the process. To turn it around, follow up quickly by phone or email, and make it clear that the door is still open for continued dialogue and regrouping when the person returns.

CHAPTER TWENTY-SIX

CREATING VALUE

"When Apex Consulting sent it's consultants on a three-week cruise to the Bahamas and then charged the trip to Golden State Grocers as a business expense," the plaintiff's attorney explained, "naturally we refused to pay."

"What Golden State doesn't understand," explained Apex's lawyer, "is that this is the way business is done in our industry."

"I'd like to thank you for summing up your clients' positions," said the Mediator. "Right now, I'd like to ask counsel to take a low profile so I can hear from the parties themselves." The large conference room was packed with high-powered executives. Golden State was represented by Jerry and Louise, the company's vice president of operations and IT chief, respectively; Apex Consulting's two founding principals, Raj and Peter, were also present. With so many decision makers in the room, the Mediator had high hopes that they would be able to work out their differences. As it turned out, with his help they were able to do that and more.

"Jerry," he said, "you're the VP of operations for Golden State; why don't you begin by telling us what happened so we can get a better idea of everyone's point of view?"

"As you know," he began, "Golden State is one of the oldest and largest retail grocery operations in the state. We've always managed all of our own internal processes and programs, but times change. A few years back it became apparent that we needed to computerize more and more of our operations. We decided that the most efficient way to handle this would be to contract with an outside computer consulting firm to organize and computerize our data processing system and then to operate that system.

"We did our homework, and chose Apex Consulting. They're a young company, but relatively well established, and we've been very pleased with their work—except for this. We had no idea when we hired Apex that they were going to send their consultants on a Caribbean cruise and bill us $30,000 for the privilege!"

"Can you tell me the nature of your contract?" asked the Mediator.

"Certainly. When we signed the contract last year, Apex became responsible for all of our computer-related activities for a period of ten years—that includes vendor management, purchasing, and payroll. We agreed to pay them a consulting and administrative fee of more than $1 million per year. Until now, it's been a good partnership. To be honest, we were relieved to have experts handling our computers so that the retail staff could focus on management issues. And Raj and Peter made it clear that they were pleased to have such a significant contract with one of the largest retail operations in the state."

"Thanks, Jerry," said the Mediator. "Raj?" he said, turning to one of the Apex principals. "How does the partnership look from your side?"

"As Jerry says, we've been quite happy," Raj began. "Of course, we had to come up to speed on the grocery business. When we analyzed Golden State's needs, we saw right away that in order to do the best job, some of our employees would need additional training to learn about the food delivery business. We wanted to make sure they were developing the right kind of systems for Golden State." He looked at Jerry and Louise and then returned to the Mediator.

"We felt they were such an important client that it was worth getting the best training available. We did our own research and found out that the guru trainer of the retail food business—yes, there really is such a person," he grinned, "was Daphne Simmer. She's something of a legend. By age twenty-five, she'd already made a fortune with her computer start-up and retired. But she got bored pretty quickly, and looked around for an interesting way to do business. She was totally hooked into her PDA—her personal digital assistant," he quickly explained, noting Jerry's quizzical expression. "With PDAs, laptops, satellite, cell phones, and all her money, she knew there was no reason to be tied down to an office.

So she bought a yacht, hired a crew, had them sail it around the Bahamas, and offered her trainings there."

Peter continued the story. "I went to the trainings along with Stephanie and Karim, the consultants who would actually be designing the software for Golden State. Yes, we spent two weeks sailing in the Bahamas, but we were doing the trainings 24-7, learning everything we could about the retail food business—personally, I couldn't believe there was so much industry-specific information. We worked extremely hard, but Daphne made it interesting. When we got back we couldn't wait to get started, and Stephanie and Karim went to work immediately designing and implementing new programs and systems for Golden State. And, from everything we've heard, Louise is very pleased."

"Yes," agreed Louise, "I have to admit Apex's systems have really given us a more efficient way of doing business, and it's tailored to our needs in a way I wouldn't have thought possible. I'm just sorry we were so slow to implement this new technology."

"That's all well and good," said Jerry, "but they had absolutely no right to stick us with the bill!"

The Mediator was slightly puzzled. *Why were they making such a big deal out of such a relatively small sum?* he wondered. But he kept his questions to himself for the moment. "Peter," said the Mediator, "I know you're in charge of the financial end of Apex. What happened?"

"Well, not much, from our point of view," replied Peter. "At the end of the first year of our contract, we presented Golden State with a bill for $30,000 in addition to our $1 million annual consulting and administrative fee. This covered travel to the Bahamas, the cost of the seminar, and individual consultations with Daphne. But they refused to pay."

"And why not?" said Jerry. "When we got that bill we were furious. We felt they had taken advantage of us. We wrote them a letter advising that we could find no term in the contract that required us to reimburse Apex Consulting for the charges. As a matter of fact, since this firm began many years ago we have had a strict policy against reimbursement for such expenses by our own employees, and we weren't about to reimburse Apex for expenses they had never even discussed with us."

"As I have already explained to Jerry," said Raj evenly, "this is standard practice in our industry. We always need to get up to speed on new clients, make sure we understand their needs before we go ahead and design a system. The purchasers of computer consulting services routinely reimburse these kinds of training expenses. It never even occurred to us that Golden State wouldn't understand this." The Mediator could see that both sides were now furious, so he took the focus off them by asking Apex's attorney to summarize his client's issues.

"Apex Consulting never intended to pay for the seminar," he explained readily. "Their clients *always* pay for trainings, and Apex Consulting didn't want to jeopardize its relationship with other clients by making an exception for Golden State."

"Golden State feels that they've been taken for a ride by Apex," countered the grocery chain's lawyer. "They were being asked to pay for these consultants to fly thousands of miles to the Bahamas and then pay a premium price for what amounts to a vacation cruise, when they don't even pay to train their own employees in their home state."

Clearly, both sides were upset and unwilling to see the other's position. Still, they had signed a ten-year agreement and had nine years to go. If they could not resolve this dispute now, they were in for a rocky decade, and they both wanted to salvage the relationship. They had all been enthusiastic about the possibility that mediation could resolve their differences, and nobody really wanted to go to court.

The Mediator decided to let them keep talking, creating a safe environment in which both sides had permission to say what they really felt and get everything out in the open without being directly confrontational. So the first hour of the meeting was spent with both sides reiterating their positions and not really hearing what the other side had to say. Eventually, and inevitably, the dialogue ground to a halt.

"Let me see if I can summarize where you're both coming from," said the Mediator. "Raj, what I'm hearing from you and Peter is that this kind of training is critical to your success in providing quality service to Golden State. You feel that it's crucial to understand the ins and outs of your client's business, how the industry works, and the details of the retail food management industry, and there's no better way to do that than this particular training. The fact that it happens in a lovely place and environment is icing on the cake. Is that about it?"

"Yes," Raj smiled in response, "and we appreciate the fact that you took the time to listen to what we had to say beyond the fact that we sent our consultants on an all-expense-paid cruise!"

The Mediator then turned to Golden State. "Jerry, from your point of view, you had entered into a contract with an agreed-on budget. Had you known about the training up front and that they expected you to pay for it, you may or may not have agreed to it. But I think what really sticks in your craw is that they submitted their bill after the fact."

"Exactly right," said Jerry, clearly pleased that the Mediator understood his position.

The Mediator had used a simple strategy to build the parties' trust, one that had worked many times before: let the parties dig themselves in, then bring them out by expressing complete understanding of what had brought them there. He could use that trust to guide the rest of the process.

But at least one of the lawyers had other ideas. "This is a complete waste of time," said Apex's counsel, shaking his head.

"Wait a minute," said Peter, with some annoyance. "I think the mediator really gets it. I want to let him help us—don't you, Raj?" Raj nodded his agreement. The Mediator watched with interest as Raj and Peter rolled right over their lawyer's negativity.

"So tell us," said Raj. "Do you have any ideas how we can get through this impasse and get moving again?"

"I do," said the Mediator. "But it's been a long morning. Now that we have a good idea of what's going on, and where we all stand, let's take a few minutes' break to freshen up."

"That's a good idea," said Louise, voicing everyone's relief at being able to escape the tension.

"My assistant will show each of you to a separate office, and you can talk things over privately. I'll meet with each of you separately in about fifteen minutes," the Mediator said, rising from his chair. "We'll see what we can work out."

—◦◦◦—

When the Mediator entered the Apex room, Raj and Peter looked glum. *Uh-oh,* thought the Mediator, *they've been talking to their lawyer.*

"I appreciate what you're trying to do here," Raj said, "but I have to agree with counsel here. So far, it's been kind of a waste of our time."

"Look, what you did in this training seems extremely valuable. On paper, though, it really did look like a vacation. I think you can understand why Golden State sees it that way, but we need to get them past that perception. I think I can turn this thing around if you can arm me with a few bullet points about precisely how this training works to Golden State's benefit."

"Sure," said Peter. "We can give it another shot.

"We're a general consulting firm," he began, "which means we serve all kinds of clients. We can't know as much as Golden State knows about their business. For that matter, I don't think there's any other consulting firm that does. These trainings were a crash course in the grocery industry and in best management practices. For example, we learned all about the competition so that we could bring a broader perspective to our client when we give them advice. We learned how we can utilize certain cost-saving measures in purchasing and delivery that we—and they—were not aware of. I'm talking about computer purchasing methods, operations that Daphne is an expert on that could potentially save them millions. Their $30,000 investment in this type of training is miniscule compared to the profit they'll get via that knowledge base.

"Look," said Peter, "I was on that cruise, and believe me, this was *not* an excuse to play in the sun for two weeks. We learned more about how the grocery business works than I even imagined there *was* to learn. Based on what we learned, we realized that many of the assumptions we'd made about how we were going to approach Golden State's data problems were way off base. It changed how we approached virtually every process."

"Those are great points, just what I was looking for," said the Mediator. "Don't give up yet. Listen, I could tell Golden State about this, but I think it might be even more effective for you to do it. Let me see if they'd be receptive to that, and then we can all get together." He loved this coaching role, and he bounced down the hall to the other office.

———

Once they were all together again in the large conference room, the Mediator turned to Jerry and Louise and said, "As you know, I've talked to Apex about what they got out of the training, and I think it's something you should hear. But in the last few minutes, it occurred to me that it might be even more informative if you heard Daphne herself describe the training. Raj, do you think we can get her on the phone?"

"Yeah, she said she'd be available all day if we needed her input."

"Great," said the Mediator. "Let's get her on speakerphone, and we'll have a joint meeting."

Over the phone, Daphne explained the premise behind her Bahamas seminars. "I know that at first glance it seems like fun in the sun for a lot of money," she laughed, "and admittedly that's part of the appeal. A lot of trainings seem like drudgery, but at my training, students are relaxed and happy to be there. And because there's essentially nowhere else for them to be twenty-four hours a day, attendance is 100 percent, and we can accomplish an amazing amount of work. I can honestly say I've never had a complaint from students or their employers that we skimp on training. Quite the opposite, in fact. And I know what I'm talking about. I'm relatively young, I know, but I grew up in my family's grocery business, and I'm very serious about what I do. I honestly believe I know more about how to run businesses in the food industry than anyone else around."

Daphne went on to pinpoint exactly what she taught in her seminars, and her presentation—even over the phone—was impressive. The Golden State executives were riveted, clearly impressed with Daphne's knowledge and credentials. The Mediator decided that his best strategy at this point would be to just let them all keep talking.

As they heard more about the training from Apex and Daphne, the grocery executives became more and more curious about it.

"What Daphne says is quite interesting," said Jerry.

"It certainly doesn't sound like any other training I've ever encountered," said Louise. "And I mean that in a good way!"

"Yes," Jerry continued. "It's raised some issues for us that we'd like to speak about privately with the mediator."

"All right," said the Mediator. "Peter, Raj, would you excuse us for a few minutes?"

—·∞·—

"So," the Mediator asked Jerry when they were in the private office, "what do you think about what you just heard?"

"It's intriguing," replied Jerry pensively. "I never thought I'd be looking at it like this. I can see why they wanted to take this training. I still can't pay them for it; it goes against our express written policy, and the shareholders wouldn't stand for it. But Daphne's training sounds like something that's important for our industry." He paused. "I wonder if you can find out from Raj and Peter if there might be a market for similar seminars locally. Maybe we could get together on this thing."

"That's an interesting question. I'll ask them."

—·∞·—

"Raj," said the Mediator, "getting Daphne on the phone really set the wheels in motion. Jerry and Louise loved what she had to say. It's still not within their budget to pay for your training, but they're intrigued about the local market for these seminars, and they wanted me in inquire if maybe there's something Apex and Golden State could do together."

Raj and Peter looked at each other and grinned. "Funny you should ask that," said Peter. "We've actually spoken to Daphne about doing local seminars. She says there aren't any right now, but there's a real need. If somebody had the financial backing to put something together, it could be a very big business. We're not in a position to do it ourselves, but we're interested to hear more from Golden State."

The Mediator couldn't believe how well things were going. "Between the two of you, you have a wealth of knowledge and know-how. I think that if you got together on this, you might actually be able to create a new market."

"That's a great idea," said Raj. "We'd love to do this. We want to continue doing business with them. Except for this one little glitch, they've been great to work with. But do you really think they're interested?"

"I think they might be," said the Mediator. "Let me check it out."

—◦◦◦—

"Jerry," said the Mediator, "I think you and Louise really struck a nerve with that suggestion. According to Raj and Peter, there's potentially a huge market for this type of consulting locally, but no one has tapped into it yet. Apex seems interested in maybe looking into the possibility of working with you in a new market like that. What do you think?"

"I think this idea has real promise," said Jerry, "but honestly, Louise and I don't quite know how to approach it. And then there's the matter of the $30,000 they say we owe them."

"I know you can't pay them their $30,000," said the Mediator. "And they can't afford to put the kind of money into this business that is called for. But what if you were to help finance a joint company—owned by you and Apex—that offers these seminars for other retailers? You could work together to define the curriculum."

Jerry was getting excited now. "If we got together on this, there'd be no stopping us."

"Let me bring this to Apex, Jerry."

"Do it," said the Golden State VP.

—◦◦◦—

The Apex team was floored and gratified by the suggestion. "Thanks to Daphne," said the Peter, "we know enough now to help design curricula. We have staff who specialize in training; with some fine-tuning, they could be ready to go. We may as well share the wealth!"

"Let me bring you all together and we can talk about it."

"Fantastic," said Raj. "When can we get started?"

The late-afternoon joint meeting couldn't have been more differ-ent than the morning session. Instead of sitting in stony silence, the parties were energetic and cooperative.

"It's been a very interesting day," the Mediator began. "We started out talking about compensation for this training, but the conversation has transformed into a positive dialogue about cre-ating a joint venture to do these types of seminars regionally. Rather than letting the tail wag the dog by concentrating on the money, let's explore how you all can do something together."

"Look," said Louise, "Jerry and I agree that we're interested in pursuing this joint project with you. We like you, and we now see the value in the training. Still, we have a bureaucracy to deal with, and $30,000 for the training just wasn't in our budget. But if we can finance some of these seminars in the future—maybe we could put up the first $50,000 to get this started—then instead of directly reimbursing you for the training, we could get this started together."

Raj and Peter were stunned by the 180-degree turn they had witnessed that day, but they didn't waste time worrying about it. By the end of the meeting, with the help of the Mediator and the input of both parties' counsel, Apex Consulting and Golden State had a plan that satisfied both sides. They agreed to split the cost of the training in the Bahamas; Golden State wrote Apex Consulting a check for $15,000. They also added a provision to their contract that would govern any similar situations that might arise concern-ing unplanned expenses relating to consultation fees. In addition, Golden State and Apex Consulting decided to explore the possi-bility of a joint venture to provide food-industry trainings to peo-ple in the software industry locally. The parties left the meeting happy with their resolution and excited about the prospect of a new business venture. The Mediator wrote up a deal memorandum equally splitting the $30,000 and arranged for the parties to meet at a later date and start creating the new business.

But that wasn't the end of the story, and this story proved the old saying that sometimes truth is stranger than fiction. Not too many months after this meeting, Golden State suffered a series of financial setbacks and internal problems unrelated to their work with Apex. An unfortunate combination of high-level corporate expenditures and unpredictable market forces eventually led Golden State to declare bankruptcy and cease operations. But while the grocery business was going under, the training joint venture—Golden Apex Seminars—was gathering momentum. Today it is a thriving multimillion-dollar business.

WHAT HAPPENED?

At first glance, this case appeared to be about money, which usually calls for a competitive bargaining style in which the negotiator seeks to "claim" value, as in a zero-sum exchange: what you give, I take, and vice versa. However, because both parties were concerned with maintaining their business relationship, the Mediator wanted to facilitate a more cooperative approach to the negotiation that would allow the parties to "create" value. This means developing joint gains for the parties, as if they were allies. The challenge in this type of case is in managing the tension between the parties' desire to compete and their desire to cooperate.

As he listened to Apex's side of the story, the Mediator began to see that the motivating reason for attending the seminars was to improve their knowledge base, not to get a tan. On the surface, it looked like a party—at least to Golden State. But just as the captain of a North Atlantic freighter must look below the water line for hidden icebergs, the Mediator saw below the surface and recognized that more was going on here: the seminars were actually providing extra value to the company. He also saw that the two parties were basically happy with each other and just wanted to find a face-saving way to continue the relationship.

These insights allowed the Mediator to steer the negotiations onto a different and more interesting course. He decided to invest the time in the negotiation, not in finding a way to divvy up the consulting bill, but in building up the relationship between the parties. He took a creative leap and suggested that because the grocery chain knew the marketplace and the consultancy knew the technology, together they could create a third business that would capture the market. Suddenly, the money dispute that had started the mediation became secondary to the created value of a new, mutually beneficial business venture.

WHAT STRATEGIES CAN WE LEARN?

1. **When there's a choice between cooperation and competition, encourage cooperation.**

   In every negotiation, there is a tension between the desire to compete and the desire to cooperate. This mixed motive requires you to be constantly on the lookout for signals that support a cooperative environment—because that's where the most creative agreements are born. A typical competitive negotiation focuses on dividing limited resources and fails to take into consideration the potential ongoing relationships of the parties. A cooperative approach, in contrast, aims to expand resources beyond what the parties imagined when they brought their respective positions to the bargaining table. It also concentrates on joint gains as opposed to respective losses.

2. **Look beneath the surface to see what is driving each party's position.**

   After you have determined each party's perspective on the issues, consider what information is stationed behind those perspectives that might be either an impediment or a motivating force in the negotiation. Had the captain and crew of the *Titanic* known that there was a large iceberg lurking below the ocean surface, they might have been able to shift course. Test these less visible concerns to determine how important they are in the decision-making process. If they are important, consider looking at resourceful ways to develop joint gains between the parties and steer negotiations away from the typical zero-sum exchange.

3. **Decrease tensions by moving the pieces of the puzzle around.**

   People tend to get into negotiation patterns. Sometimes these patterns are good, but sometimes they lead to burnout. If you can shift patterns—by taking a time-out or having one person speak to another in a private session—you can often decrease tension and create a free flow of discussion. Under these conditions, people become willing to share information; they want to reveal true their objectives.

PART THREE

GETTING TO THE BOTTOM LINE

CHAPTER TWENTY-SEVEN

TOO MANY COOKS

"What would satisfy me?" said Roz, looking the insurance carrier's attorney right in the eye. "I think $600,000 will do it," she said, unblinking. The Mediator was enjoying watching this top Hollywood agent work the room.

"Forty thousand," the attorney for Legal Insurance Inc. shot back. "That's our offer."

"Forget it," said the lawyer representing Roz in this legal malpractice case.

"And no fees for the three stooges in the other room," Roz put in for good measure, referring to her three former lawyers, whom she was suing for malpractice.

The lawyer representing Roz's former lawyers in the fee dispute jumped into the fray: "We absolutely insist that Roz pay the $75,000 she owes my clients for the time they spent on her case," he said. "No deals."

"That's right," said Roz's second new lawyer, who was representing Roz in the case for nonpayment of fees filed against her by her former legal firm.

The Mediator sat back and watched as the roomful of lawyers tore into each other. *Too many cooks . . .* he thought to himself with a smile. *There's room for only one chef in this kitchen.* In the end, it would be up to him to make sure that all the ingredients combined to create a settlement that nourished everyone. He let the parties continue wrangling while he reviewed the three entwined cases that had started this stew bubbling.

———⁓———

The case that had started the whole thing had been brought by Brock, an aging superstar actor, against his agent, Roz, for losing out on a movie deal that he was sure could have saved his career. The case didn't have a lot of legs—Brock's star was sinking fast—so Roz felt fairly confident that she would win in court. It wasn't *her* fault the deal fell through, and she was sure that Rick, the film's producer, would back her up. But Roz relied on her regular team of lawyers—the three stooges, as she now called them—who, though skilled in many facets of the law, were not very good *entertainment* lawyers, which was what this suit called for. They had made a fatal mistake: they assumed Rick would show up in court to testify if they needed him, so they never issued Rick a subpoena. But at the crucial moment in the trial, Rick got cold feet and bailed; apparently he didn't want to lose his tenuous relationship with Brock, just in case the actor came back into favor. The lawyers called Rick repeatedly, but he never even returned their calls. When the dust settled, Brock won the case, the court ordered Roz to pay her (now ex-) client $270,000, and the three stooges billed Roz for $75,000.

Roz, incensed at being out more than a quarter of a million dollars, refused to pay her lawyers' fee and found *another* lawyer to sue them for being negligent in the way they had defended the case. Curly, Moe, & Larry, Inc. were themselves being defended by their insurance carrier, which had hired separate legal counsel to defend the legal malpractice case.

But that wasn't the end of the story. Roz's original lawyers were already unhappy that Roz had not paid their bill, and they were furious when Roz hired new lawyers to sue them for legal malpractice. So they did what came naturally: they hired a lawyer to countersue Roz for the $75,000 in fees she owed them on the original case.

As the parties argued on, the Mediator realized there were an awful lot of lawyers in the room. He reviewed the players:

In addition to being an agent, Roz herself was a lawyer.

Roz had brought two lawyers—one to demonstrate legal malpractice and one to defend against the legal fees claimed.

Roz's three original lawyers had brought two lawyers—one to defend the legal malpractice lawsuit and one to pursue their legal fees.

The claims representative for the legal malpractice insurance carrier, himself a lawyer, had his own lawyer.

Counting me, that's eleven, thought the Mediator. *Too many cooks indeed. Time to put them all in separate kitchens.*

—◦◦◦—

The Mediator decided to talk to the lawyer for the insurance carrier first, recognizing that his financial contribution to settlement would be critical to putting the pieces together.

"So what do you think of your chances in court?" he began.

"Fifty-fifty," replied the lawyer said. "I think it's clear that we're at risk here—these guys made an error in not issuing the subpoena. But we don't think the error would have made any difference in the case since it turned out that Rick was not a friendly witness. We recognize some risk here and want to pay Roz something, but certainly not anywhere close to $600,000! Her damages are only $270,000. Why would we consider anything above the damages awarded by the court? Look, our offer of $40,000 still stands. She's going to have to come down way below $270,000 before we're willing to go up. Anyway," the lawyer concluded, "we can't pay her until she settles with Curly, Moe, and Larry for the fees they're claiming."

The Mediator decided to focus on the legal malpractice lawsuit because resolution of this case would likely also lead to resolution of the fee dispute claim, and he spent the next three hours shuttling between all the parties.

—◦◦◦—

"Roz," the Mediator said, "I realize how disappointed you are in your defense team for not confirming Rick's attendance at trial. I believe the insurance company for your defense team recognizes that they have some exposure here. They're not having a problem with the concept of paying you some money to settle, but they're having trouble understanding your damages. Since the verdict was for $270,000, they're shocked at your $600,000 demand. Can you help me understand where that's coming from so I can help you pitch your case to the insurer?"

"I'm upset and angry over how they handled this," said Roz. "I really don't need this kind of aggravation—my life is already crazy enough. I just want them to pay for what I've been through."

"That's understandable, Roz," replied the Mediator. "But I'm sure your counsel has explained that the court has ruled that recovering damages for emotional distress in this type of case is not permissible."

"Yeah, that's what I've been told. I'm just so pissed off with those goons! Look, I want to get this resolved. Just tell me what you think is the best approach to dealing with the insurance company, and we'll do it."

"In my opinion, if you signaled to the insurer that you would settle under $300,000, you'd definitely get their attention."

"I'd like to get my $270,000 back," said Roz. "If I ask for $300,000, don't you think it will hurt my chances of a full recovery?"

The Mediator had to concur. "You're absolutely correct. If you really want to get a full recovery, you'll have to take the case to court. But if you want to settle this thing now, in the context of mediation, you need to know that we're going to be dealing with a risk analysis and come up with a settlement that makes *both* sides equally uncomfortable." Roz frowned. "I know that's not what you want to hear, Roz, but I figure we'd better get an understanding up front before we go down a road you don't want to take."

At that, Roz's lawyer decided to make himself heard in the discussion. "I agree with the mediator, Roz. We've got to be flexible if we want to maximize our recovery today. Remember, you and I have talked at length about doing whatever's necessary to avoid putting you through another trial."

"Fine," said Roz, looking faintly disgusted. "I give up. You can let the idiots know we'll settle under $300,000, but keep in mind I don't want to be out of pocket here. Please do your best to get back my $270,000."

—✿—

Shuttling back into the room with the insurance company for Roz's former lawyers, the Mediator decided to try a "bracketing" approach—suggesting a range that he felt would anchor the parties in a zone that had some hope of success. He began with an upbeat introduction.

"I'm happy to report that I've made good progress with Roz, and she's prepared to make a move here that you might find appealing," he said.

"If you're telling us they're coming down from $600,000 to $500,000, please tell Roz we're not interested in talking," said the insurance representative.

"Actually, I have another approach that should jump-start this negotiation. I've asked Roz to agree to negotiate under $300,000—provided you agree to negotiate above $100,000. To be perfectly frank, I'm trying to bracket this dispute in a range that makes both sides think twice about their risk. Do I have your commitment to that range?"

The defense lawyer thought for a moment. "Well, we'd feel more comfortable in agreeing to that range if we knew Roz was under $270,000. That's a high-water mark for her in this case. We just don't see this case settling north of $200,000. It will have to have a one in front of it for us to get serious."

"I'll see what I can do," said the Mediator. *Progress,* he thought.

—✿—

Out in the hallway, on his way to grab a cup of coffee between caucuses, the Mediator ran into Roz's attorney in the legal malpractice case, an old friend and colleague.

"You know," he said candidly, "I've been having second thoughts about my ability to prove this case in court. Roz is pretty hardheaded, but just between you and me, I'm pressing her to get realistic with this thing today."

"Do you think you can get her to agree to a number under $200,000?" asked the Mediator.

"That might be stretching it, but I'll see what I can do. Try to get something as close to $200,000 as possible so we can put this case to bed."

———❦———

Now the Mediator decided to press toward closure by pointing out the weaknesses of their case with the three stooges, their attorneys, and their claims adjuster.

He looked at them seriously and made his first point. "You know you lack the necessary written documentation to support your defense, don't you? Rick's testimony would have given Roz a shot at winning in court, but she never got that shot because Rick never testified. And Rick never testified because you didn't subpoena him. How would a jury be convinced that you would have won in court if you weren't even able to produce the key witness?" The three lawyers looked glum.

"Plus, as you may be aware, Roz has two witnesses—both prominent attorneys in the entertainment field—who are prepared to testify on her behalf."

"I guess this could be a problem," said the lawyers' attorney.

"Why don't you guys talk this over for a few minutes while I go back and speak with Roz?"

———❦———

Now it was time to add a little doubt to Roz's bubbling pot.

"Roz, you do have a pretty good case against your former attorneys—not issuing that subpoena to Rick was a big mistake. But, as we all know, to prove malpractice you essentially have to prove two cases at once. First, you have to prove that your original lawyers were negligent. Second, you have to prove that if Rick had been there, you would have won the underlying case against Brock. Now that's tougher. To prove that case, Rick would have to testify, and he has *no* interest in all of this. Even if you subpoena him now and he does appear, how do you think his attitude is going to play out? You also might want to consider whether or not you really want to burn your bridges; Rick's a powerful producer, and you may want to do more deals with him in the future."

"He's right, Roz," her lawyer said. "Proving two cases could be rocky."

But Roz was having a hard time letting go. "I can't believe it. This is so friggin' ridiculous! Are you sure about this?" she asked her lawyer.

"Yes. Look Roz, do you want to get out of here with some money today?"

"Yes."

"Then I strongly suggest we follow the mediator's lead here. Okay?"

Roz took a deep breath and exhaled loudly. "Okay."

"Great," said the Mediator, jumping on her agreement before she changed her mind. "Why don't you think about your options while I go back and talk with the other parties? My sense is that you're going to have to consider something under $200,000, but I'll see what I can do in the meantime."

—◦◦◦—

The Mediator was directive, suggesting numbers to each side. He felt sure that Roz would settle for around $175,000 and that she'd agree to pay the three stooges $20,000 and call it a day.

So he said to the insurance company, "I realize you don't want to pay $200,000, but if I can get the whole thing wrapped up for under $200,000, how close can you get? Would you be receptive to $190,000 or $195,000?"

"Two hundred thousand is beyond our authority on this case. I can go into the high ones, but I simply cannot get to $200,000."

"Are you saying that if I can get this thing wrapped up for $190,000 to $195,000, you would consider it?"

The insurer rubbed his jaw. "That would be stretching our limits, but we would consider it."

—◦◦◦—

"Roz, I've now spent enough time with the insurer to have a better sense of how far they will go today to settle. I don't have a specific number to offer, but I'm confident I could get you somewhere between $150,000 and $175,000, with the idea that the insurer will throw in another small amount for your former lawyers to settle their claims against you."

"Can't you get them up a little higher?" asked Roz's lawyer.

"I tried to push them to $200,000, but there was tremendous resistance. Roz, I'm taking my cues from you and your lawyer, and I understand you want this settled today. As I said earlier, if you hold out until trial you might be able to get more money, but obviously the expert costs will go up substantially as well." The Mediator waited for their response.

"What you do think?" Roz asked her attorney.

"I think it's gonna be tough to prove our case. Let's take the money and run." And to the Mediator, he said, "Do you think you can get the three stooges to take $20,000?"

"I don't know, but I'll try."

—◦◦◦—

"Look, guys," the Mediator said to the three stooges, "the most I can get you is $15,000 to $20,000."

"We'd settle for $40,000," said Curly.

"Not gonna happen, guys," said the Mediator firmly. "I'm going to step out for a few minutes to give you a chance to decide what you want to do. But recognize that I'm close to settling the malpractice case, which would leave you alone to try your case against Roz. Do you really want to put yourselves in the position of having to expose yourselves publicly for not having issued a subpoena to Rick? And consider the possibility that if you lose against Roz, she could then have a case for malicious prosecution."

"Let us talk about this for a few minutes," said Moe.

When they called the Mediator back into the room, they were ready to deal.

"We're here to finalize this once and for all," said Curly. "We decided to chalk this one up as a business loss. Get us $20,000 and we'll settle."

In the end, the deals were made and the meals were cooked to perfection: Roz went home with $195,000 from the insurance carrier to settle the legal malpractice lawsuit, and out of that she paid $20,000 to the three stooges to settle their fee dispute.

WHAT HAPPENED?

The Mediator's main problems in this case were how to manage the many participants, all relatively knowledgeable lawyers with financial stakes in the outcome, and how and in what order to resolve the interlocking cases. The Mediator decided to focus on the legal malpractice lawsuit because, in all likelihood, resolution of this portion would also lead to resolution of the fee dispute claim. Along the way, three key pieces of information came to light that had nothing to do with the facts of the case, the credibility of the parties, or the application of the law, yet everything to do with the needs of the attorneys in their respective positions.

First, the Mediator discovered that Roz's attorney was short on funds and wanted to settle the malpractice case as soon as possible. Second, the claims adjuster was reluctant to pay Roz anything over $200,000. Third, Roz's original three attorneys had made settlement of either one of the cases (legal malpractice or fee dispute) contingent on settlement of both cases. The Mediator determined that the best way to move the mediation along was to sow seeds of doubt about their options among all the participants.

Like a chef, you know that the settlement outcome will depend not only on the quality of the ingredients you're working with but also the manner in which you combine them. No matter how knotty the case or how certain or confident the parties are, there's always room for you to create doubt and thus open up some room for negotiation. In this case, the Mediator's key ingredients were the parties' own weaknesses. Identifying those weaknesses moved the parties toward settlement.

What Strategies Can We Learn?

1. **Move parties off firm positions by creating fear, uncertainty, and doubt.**

   You can transform the context of the dispute by introducing the dissonance of fear, uncertainty, and doubt. This forces the parties to think about the dispute from the point of view of their adversary. To do this safely, you must remain firm but kind and attempt it only after you have built up a reservoir of trust. You can later trade that trust for monetary concessions.

2. **Consider "bracketing" the numbers.**

   Suggest monetary ranges that you feel will anchor the parties in a zone that is worth negotiating in—a zone that has some hope of success. This usually causes the parties to come up with their own sets of reasonable ranges, which will help you figure out what their true expectations are.

3. **Try the "spinning plates" routine.**

   One of the most famous acts from the old *Ed Sullivan Show* was the guy who came on stage with a number of sticks and began spinning plates on them. In order to get all the plates to spin at the same time without breaking them, he had to start slow but spin fast. The same holds true when dealing with multiparty disputes. You must get all the parties to start moving in a direction that requires them to gain momentum, until everybody is moving faster and faster toward the same goal at the same time.

CHAPTER TWENTY-EIGHT

BOTTOM-LINE NEGOTIATING

The moment of truth had arrived: at the conclusion of a contentious business dispute, the Mediator brought all the parties back to the table to announce the termination of negotiations. The lawyers on both sides of the table were tired and aggravated by the day's work. These two hardheaded corporate counselors had simply refused to do the traditional back-and-forth negotiation dance.

As they were packing up their briefcases, Bradley, the defendant, looked at his adversary across the conference room and said, "Harris, your case is lousy. No jury in its right mind would ever see fit to award you more than the $10,000 I've offered. I'd rather pay my attorney to defend this case in court than pay you a penny more than that."

In response, Harris pounded his fist on the table and shouted, "Don't bet on it, Bradley. I can't wait to see your face when the jury returns a $150,000 verdict."

And with that, both parties and their lawyers rose and headed for the door.

"Hang on a minute," said the Mediator. It was time for a little bottom-line negotiating. "Anyone willing to place a bet on this one?"

Harris and Bradley stopped dead in their tracks, puzzled.

"You both seem certain about the value of this case. Are you willing to put a little money down?"

"What are you talking about?" Bradley asked, annoyed.

"I know it's been a long day," said the Mediator, "but I have a little proposition you may find interesting. Sit down with me here for just a few minutes, and I'll show you what I've got up my sleeve."

Clearly skeptical, Harris and Bradley took their seats. But they kept their coats on.

"Okay," said Bradley, "shoot."

"Bradley," the Mediator began, "you think there's no way a jury will award *anything*, let alone a figure over $10,000. Am I right?" Bradley nodded.

"And Harris, you think a jury would have to be out of its mind to award you anything less than $150,000, correct?"

"You've got that right," Harris replied.

"If this case goes to trial, both sides are going to spend any-where from $10,000 to $30,000 in attorney fees. Do you agree?"

"Somewhere in that range," said Bradley, and Harris nodded.

"Well then," said the Mediator, "since neither of you is willing to move off your settlement position, I propose you put your money where your mouth is. We'll agree—right here and now—that the party whose settlement position turns out to be the farthest away from the ultimate jury verdict must pay an additional $20,000—a rough estimate of the attorney fees—to the party whose last settle-ment number turns out to be closer. In other words, we'll define the prevailing party as the one who best predicts the jury verdict, and he will be entitled to $20,000 in attorney fees from the other side."

Both Harris and Bradley exchanged inquisitive looks with their attorneys. "I'll put you back in your separate rooms to discuss this with your counsel for a few moments."

———※※※———

The Mediator was fairly certain that the same conversation was tak-ing place in each room: both Harris and Bradley were seeking assurance from their counsel that they were going to win the case, yet each counsel was being noncommittal with his answer. The Mediator went into each room to speak to the parties and see how they were doing.

———※※※———

"I told Harris before the mediation that I'm not going to guaran-tee a result of $150,000 or more," Harris's attorney said. "No case is a slam dunk in court, including this one."

"I value your advice," said Harris. "That's what I pay you for. But I have a good feeling about this."

"Let me talk to Bradley and see how he's doing," said the Mediator.

—◦◦◦—

Checking in with Bradley and his counsel, the Mediator inquired, "Do you need a little more time to think this over?"

"Look," said Bradley's counsel. "My client doesn't mind gambling in court, but he's a bit gun-shy about losing the $20,000. I guess you've gotten him to consider his risk a little more closely. Give us a few more minutes to digest our options."

"Take all the time you need," said the Mediator. "I'd like to add one last twist. I suggest that you go back to your office—and I'll suggest the same to Harris, when I check back with him in a minute—and do whatever additional legal research, jury verdict research, investigation, and soul searching that you think would be helpful. When you've finished examining all the information, I'd like you to come up with a new settlement number: your best prediction of what the jury would award. It might be the same number you've already given me, or it could be a different number, just in case you decide to reconsider.

"The new number will be something you will agree to as a settlement number. I'd like you both to fax me your numbers by noon tomorrow. At that point I'll enter them into a betting agreement and circulate it for signature. I'm going to make the same proposal to Harris and his counsel in the other room."

—◦◦◦—

Even though the Mediator created a process that the parties perceived as taking them to trial, he was sure that once they really looked at their chances in court they would opt to settle. On reflection, Bradley decided he wanted the $20,000 and instructed his attorney to fax the Mediator a much more reasonable offer of $40,000. Harris also recognized that his demand was based more on posturing than on reality, and faxed in a $90,000 demand. The Mediator realized that the parties were now in a settlement range where reasonable minds might prevail. After a few telephone calls and emails, he was able to get the parties to settle at $65,000.

WHAT HAPPENED?

The Mediator saw that both Harris and Bradley thought they would be able to strong-arm the other into capitulating during the negotiation. When that failed, they were stuck in their extreme positions. The offers were too far apart for the parties to find common ground. If they continued in the direction they were going, the case would likely never settle—even though neither of them wanted to go to the expense of a trial. The Mediator needed to find a way to get them to stop posturing and start negotiating again. To do this, they would need to be a bit more realistic about what might happen at trial.

His solution was to change the context from bargaining to betting. Once Bradley and Harris perceived themselves as gamblers, they took a more realistic view of their chances. This approach encouraged, and actually rewarded, the parties to be as realistic as possible about the "trial value" of the case. By closing the gap between their original numbers, the Mediator was able to finish the job in a more traditional negotiating format.

WHAT STRATEGY CAN WE LEARN?

1. **Turn around a collapsed negotiation with a gambling reality check.**

   In a collapsed negotiation, both parties are stubbornly stuck in their positions. Usually these positions are the result of posturing rather than facts. You can provide a good reality check by offering the parties the opportunity to bet that they will be able to predict the outcome of the trial better than their opponent. For this approach to work, both parties must be willing to increase their risk at trial by expressing a willingness to lose additional money beyond the verdict. The prospect of paying off the other party, over and above the judgment at trial, gives the parties the incentive to reconsider their last settlement offers and to evaluate their cases more realistically. The case never gets to the point where the actual bet is finalized, because you are always contemplating a further negotiation after the parties have "placed their bets." This approach is really a last-ditch effort that you would use only when it becomes clear that the parties' negotiation has collapsed.

CHAPTER TWENTY-NINE

THE "FISHY CALCULATOR" METHOD

In premediation meetings, the Mediator had learned the nuts and bolts of the case. Terry had taken her daughter, Daisy, to Frankie Fish for lunch; Daisy was rarely allowed to eat at fast-food restaurants, so it was a special treat. Terry herself ate a fish sandwich with lettuce, tomato, and mayonnaise. Later that night, she experienced severe abdominal pain, cramps, and vomiting, and her husband rushed her to the hospital. The doctors diagnosed her with food poisoning. During the examination, however, she became unstable: her heart rate fluctuated wildly and uncontrollably. The doctors ordered emergency surgery to implant a pacemaker device into her heart. Terry recovered, but only after months of recuperation, suffering, and expense. Terry filed a claim against the food outlet for $250,000, and they in turn sued the four suppliers of the fish, bread, produce, and mayonnaise.

The Mediator knew that a multiparty case in which all the defendants were burying their heads in the sand could be problematic, and this one seemed to be heading in that direction. During his first private meeting with the defendants, it was clear that the parties were suspicious not only of the claim but of each other.

"No other food poisoning claims were made by anyone during this same time period," said the corporate attorney for Frankie Fish. "We sell thousands of pounds of fish items every day," he said,

---

Thanks to Robert Creo for telling me about this technique.

"and we have impeccable and elaborate food-handling procedures, which we have detailed in this DVD." He waved the disk in the air for emphasis. "It's highly improbable that any ingredient in the fish sandwich was spoiled because of our procedures. It's much more likely that the problem stems from one of our suppliers." And with that he gave each of them a meaningful look.

Predictably, each supplier argued vigorously against the responsibility of their product.

"Our fish is frozen fresh as soon as it's caught," said the lawyer for Delmonico's, the fish supplier. "Our reputation for food handling is excellent. That's why Frankie Fish has an exclusive contract with us. It's much more likely to have been one of the condiments."

"We distribute mayonnaise to hundreds of restaurants nationwide," said the attorney for the Mom's Mayonnaise. "No other allegations of spoilage have been made against any restaurant we supply. Perhaps the bread was moldy."

"There's no way our sandwich rolls could have caused this problem," the attorney for Fine Wheat Products said. "We bake our rolls and ship them out fresh every day."

"I hope you're not accusing our *lettuce* of being the culprit?" said the attorney for Amalgamated Produce Distributors.

The attorney for Frankie Fish spoke up. "I think we're all agreed that this is a spurious claim"—he looked around the table for support—"and I'd like to propose that, to make this claim go away, we each contribute a portion of our cost of defense to settle with Terry."

"That's reasonable," said the produce supplier's lawyer, "but we think Frankie Fish bears more responsibility here."

"And you think we should pay more than *you*?" asked the Fine Wheat Products lawyer.

"I didn't say that," said the Amalgamated Produce lawyer, "but since you ask, yes." Then each party in turn voiced their concern about "overpaying" with regard to the other defendants.

The Mediator cleared his throat. "I think it might be a good idea at this point to assemble a comprehensive offer. We can do this in strict confidence, so that none of you knows what anyone else is contributing."

"Why in the world would we do that?" said the Mom's Mayonnaise lawyer. "How can you possibly arrive at a fair division of responsibility?"

"I believe it's true that you've each done independent evaluations of your respective risk if this case goes to court. Is that correct?" The lawyers nodded, and the Mediator continued. "So that means you've already placed a price on settling the case, independent of each other." The lawyers sat quietly, listening. "So let's talk about how you all see the 'pecking order' of each other's liability—without discussing money, for the moment. What I recommend is that each of you list all the entities, ordered in terms of liability, from most to least. Submit the list to me, and I'll collate the information into a summary that I'll present to you in a few minutes."

After some discussion, the Mediator presented his summary, and the parties were able to agree that if there were any liability for the claim, they would view the liability in the following order:

1. Restaurant outlet
2. Fish vendor
3. Mayonnaise vendor
4. Produce vendor
5. Bread vendor

With this informal agreement in hand, they decided they were now ready to start the negotiation. They began pretty far apart: the plaintiff's initial demand was $250,000, and the combined defense offer was $35,000.

—◦◦◦—

After six hours of negotiation, there was still a significant gap between the plaintiff's final demand—$120,000—and the total proposal of the defense—$45,000.

"Do you have any flexibility on that number at all?" the Mediator asked Terry's lawyer.

"We'd like to settle this thing for six figures," he replied, "but, admittedly, my client is eager to get on with her life. If we get an offer close to six figures, we'll certainly consider it."

The Mediator understood this to mean that if Terry heard an offer in the high five figures, she'd probably go for it. He returned to the defense room with renewed purpose.

———

So far, the negotiation had been complicated by the fact that the defendants did not know how much each was contributing to the settlement. At this point, however, the Mediator felt that the gap was finally small enough to allow him to take a final stab at obtaining the full authority of each party. It was time for the "fishy calculator," a technique that ensured strict confidentiality for each party—even from the Mediator.

"Here's how it works," the Mediator said, placing a small portable calculator on the conference table so that everyone could see. The defendants and their attorneys were tired, but they were curious too. The Mediator began his explanation.

"First, I'm going to punch in a random six-digit number that only I know. Then I'll pass it to the attorney for Frankie Fish, who will key in his authority and add it to my number. He'll pass the calculator to Mom's Mayonnaise, who will key in his number and add it, and so on around the table. None of you will know my number or anyone else's number. When everyone has added his authority into the calculator, you'll pass it back to me, and I'll subtract my original six-digit number from the display total. The remaining number gives us your full authority without anyone knowing any contribution amount but his own. Sound fair?" Everyone agreed to the idea.

They passed the calculator around the table, privately keying in their authority. When it reached the Mediator again, he subtracted his secret number and arrived at the full authority: $85,000. It was certainly in the high five figures, and he was fairly sure Terry would accept the offer.

"Does everyone agree on this number as the offer?" asked the Mediator. Everyone did. "Good. Before we take this number to Terry and her attorney, I'd like to meet with each of you privately to confirm your specific contributions."

When the Mediator had confirmed the individual numbers, he took the proposal of $85,000 to Terry.

—◦◦◦—

"I'm confident that this is the full extent of the defendants' combined authority," he said.

"How can you be so sure?" asked Terry's attorney. In response, the Mediator explained how he had used the fishy calculator method to generate the proposal.

"Ingenious," said the attorney. "I've never heard of that one before. But clearly you're right—that's all they've got. Terry," he said, turning to his client, "I'm going to recommend that you accept this offer—they can't go any higher."

"I agree," she said. "You can't argue with a calculator!" Once Terry and her counsel were comfortable that no monies were left on the table, the case was settled for the $85,000 offer generated by this technique.

WHAT HAPPENED?

Trying to get a group of target defendants to cooperate in a negotiation is like herding cats. Each defendant has his own agenda, and they all tend either to point fingers at each other or to bury their head in the sand. This is because they are uncertain about what direction to go and are looking at the behavior of the others to determine what action they should take. If everyone else is evading the problem, they will evade. If everyone else is trying to solve the problem, they will go in that direction. In this case, the defendants were at each other's throats—far away from the goal of settling with Terry.

The Mediator knew that multiple defendants are generally concerned with pecking order; even though they are all in the same boat, they want to know who's going to be considered to be *more* at fault. In the case of insurance companies, this recognition allows them to put a note in the claim file stating that party A acknowledged their potential liability and put more money into the offer than party B. It's a small but symbolic point, and the Mediator saw that these lawyers were not going to be able to move on until the pecking order was determined.

In order to get the herd going in the problem-solving direction, the Mediator had to come up with some mechanism that demonstrated with certainty that their decision to follow the Mediator's suggested approach constituted correct behavior under the circumstances. Here, the Mediator came up with a two-step approach that first identified a pecking order of liability and then concealed each defendant's contribution toward settlement so that no one could point the finger at anyone else and complain that the other was not being reasonable. Each party entered a blind offer into the Mediator's calculator, giving the Mediator enough information to present a final offer of settlement to the plaintiff.

What Strategies Can We Learn?

1. **Determine a pecking order of liability among multiple defendants.**

   Ranking relative responsibility can act as a stimulant to multiple defendants who can't stop pointing fingers at each other. Ask the parties to put aside their arguments about who is at fault and have them write out an objective list of who they feel would be the most and least liable in the case. Collate that information and present to them the list they jointly devised. Before starting the negotiation, confirm that all parties agree with the final determination.

2. **Use the "fishy calculator" method to obtain combined authority from all the defendants in a multidefendant case without their having to disclose their contributions to each other.**

   The following explanation involves five parties, but this technique can be used with any number of defendants to determine combined authority. Because each party keys in their number privately and none of the other parties know what the number is, confidentiality is easily maintained. All you need is a calculator.

   1. Punch a random six-digit number, known only to you, into the calculator and pass it to party A (M = baseline mediator number).

2. Party A keys in their authority and adds it to your baseline random number. A new number $(M + A)$ is obtained.
3. Party A passes the calculator to party B, who keys in their own final number and adds it to the number in the display. A new number $(M + A + B)$ is displayed. Party B does not know the amounts keyed in by either you or party A.
4. Party C follows the same procedure and types in their own number. The new display number is now $(M + A + B + C)$. The calculator is passed to party D.
5. Party D follows the same procedure and keys in their own authority. The new number on the display is now $(M + A + B + C + D)$. Party D passes the calculator to the final defendant, party E.
6. Party E keys in their number and adds it to the total. The new display number is $(M + A + B + C + D + E)$. The calculator is passed back to you.
7. Subtract the original M baseline from the display total and obtain the full authority without any party's knowing any contribution amount but their own.

CHAPTER THIRTY

THE CROSSOVER

This was a big one—a whistleblower case in the drug industry—and the Mediator was expecting to put in a very long day. Amanda Jones, a relatively low-level researcher for Phrick Pharmaceuticals, had accidentally discovered that Phrick's popular painkiller, Headocaine, could cause potentially life-threatening side effects. She immediately told her supervisor, but he informed her that the company knew all about it; they had decided to withhold that information from the public and leave Headocaine on the shelves until they had sold out their inventory. Amanda took her complaint to human resources, and a few days later she was escorted out of the building—terminated. Furious, she filed suit against Phrick for unspecified damages. Now the whole world would know about Phrick's duplicity.

The case had already been heavily litigated—both sides had taken many depositions, both sides had big-gun attorneys—and the case was barreling full speed ahead toward court. In fact, articles about the case were still making the papers on an almost daily basis, so the Mediator had been a little surprised when Phil, the lawyer for the researcher and a long-time colleague, had called to set up a mediation. The Mediator was preparing for a grueling negotiation that might go on for days, but he was in for a surprise.

In the late afternoon on the eve of the mediation, Phil called. "I'm in a little bit of trouble here," he admitted. "If this thing doesn't settle out of court, it's going straight to trial. I'm a good lawyer—in fact, I'm a damn fine trial lawyer—but I've never handled a case with the potential public ramifications this one is likely to generate. I've called in Oscar Rank to help in that eventuality, but I'd really like to work this out before that whole ball gets rolling."

The Mediator was impressed. "Oscar Rank! Mr. Court TV himself." Oscar Rank, a well-known celebrity lawyer, was a celebrity in his own right and a powerhouse in court. "You're really getting out the big guns for this one, Phil."

"Rank has been through this a million times," Phil explained. "I'm not above admitting when I'm in over my head. If I need help, I need help. But I really don't want it to get that far."

A few hours later, the Mediator got another call—this time from the defense lawyer, who had been hired by Phrick's insurance carrier. "Hi, Hal," said the Mediator. "What's up?"

"Look," said Hal, "I'm just going to lay it all out for you. We're coming in tomorrow to talk to you, and I really want to get this case settled. I just heard that the plaintiff is planning on pulling in Oscar Rank to try this thing, and that's just going to turn into an enormous media circus. Frankly, I don't want to go there. And I'm concerned that my carrier is going to mess up this negotiation by low-balling the offer, which will cause Rank to bolt the mediation and go to court, where he loves to be anyway." He paused, clearing his throat.

"Look—you know how to put deals together, so I need your advice. *I don't want this case to go to a jury.*" He paused, waiting.

"What are you telling me, Hal?" asked the Mediator, waiting for the other shoe to drop.

"I'm telling you that I'm hiring you for your expertise in negotiating deals. I'm afraid our normal approach will crater this case. I thought I would just tell you what they'll pay and let you deal with the negotiation. Look, I know that the insurance company batted around something in the range of $2 million." He paused again.

"So you're telling me they might settle for up to $2 million?" The Mediator's heart was racing.

"Yes," said Hal, "but they'll never tell you to your face. I just wanted you to know. Naturally, they would be delighted to settle much lower."

"Okay," said the Mediator. "Thanks for that information. I'll see you in the morning."

———※———

At eight the next morning, the Mediator had a full conference table. The plaintiff's side was represented by Amanda Jones; her lawyer, Phil; and Oscar Rank, looking appropriately serious. On the defense side sat the insurance representative and Hal. The Mediator had already decided to hold his information close to his chest and see where the negotiation went. "Phil," he said, "why don't you begin by telling us what brings you here today?"

For the next twenty minutes, the group listened as Phil explained Amanda's discovery of the drug's side effects, the concern that had led her to confront the company with her findings, and what he termed their retaliatory termination of her employment. For another twenty minutes, they all listened as Hal outlined Phrick's case, which consisted mainly of emphatic denial of wrongdoing. It was all pretty much what the Mediator expected to hear, but he knew it was important to let each side have the opportunity to make its case. After all, that was the ritual they expected and part of the reason they were here.

When Hal had finished, the Mediator said, "Thanks to both of you. There are some issues I would like to clarify. Right now, I'd like to break up into separate rooms. I'll meet with the plaintiff side first."

———⚬⚬⚬———

"Oscar," he began, "what's your assessment of this case? I know you walked into a hornet's nest here."

"This is a really good case," replied Rank with a smile. "I'd say it's easily worth $800,000, maybe $1 million for settlement purposes. We could do even better in court, but the client is here to resolve the case."

The Mediator nodded impassively, but his mind was racing: Phrick was willing to go as high as $2 million to settle, and Rank was expecting only $1 million. *Oh man*, thought the Mediator, *this case is already settled.* But they'd been there less than an hour, and both parties were expecting a tough negotiation. The Mediator was in a bind. *If I close it down now, they're both going to wonder what happened, and if they could have gotten more.*

It was a classic "crossover": the defendant was willing to pay more than the plaintiff was hoping to get. And because the Mediator had this information before negotiations had even begun, it was also an ethical challenge: he had to make the case come out so that both parties felt they'd gotten their money's worth—and a fair deal. The Mediator decided that his only choice here was to allow the process to play itself out as usual, and try to maneuver both sides toward the middle of a range they didn't even know existed. "Okay," he said. "Let me speak to the other side and see what they say." But rather than do that—after all, he already knew the answer—he took a walk outside, trying to get his thoughts together and determine the best approach.

Then, instead of going to the other side, he instead went back into the plaintiff's room. He said, "Listen, I think they're looking to you to make a demand for settlement. Have you given much thought to where you would like to start?"

"We're thinking of demanding $1.5 or $2 million," said Rank.

The Mediator thought hard and pragmatically. He was in a position of complete control. *How will I be viewed by the insurance company when it comes to my relationship with them in the future? If I settle this case for $1 million right now, when they're willing to go up to $2 million, they'll think I'm God. On the other hand, it's not fair to the plaintiff to have her leave money on the table.* But he knew he had to remain fair, so he decided to nudge the plaintiff's offer up a notch.

"Listen, you told me you value the case in the $800,000 to $1 million range, so why don't you make a demand that's a little higher—maybe something north of $2 million?"

Rank leaped on it. "Sure, if you think that'll fly. How much?"

"How about $2.5 million?" the Mediator replied, planning to work down to a number between $1 million and $2 million.

"Sure," said Rank, "go ahead!" And the Mediator went to see the defense, leaving Amanda Jones and her two lawyers smiling.

———✑✑———

"The plaintiff is asking for $2.5 million," he told the defense. He could practically see a thought balloon forming over Hal's head that said *Wow! The case is settled! We're almost there!*

The insurance representative, clearly surprised, said, "Really? That's very interesting."

"What would you like to offer?" asked the Mediator.

"I don't know," he replied. "What do you suggest?"

"Well," said the Mediator, pretending to think, "how about $400,000?"

—◅◌◌◌▻—

The Mediator went back and forth between caucus rooms for the next six hours, letting them play it out. Finally, he had maneuvered them into position by creating an artificial impasse between a demand for $2 million and an offer of $1 million.

But Rank threw a curve. "Great! Tell them we'll take the $1 million."

The Mediator was exhausted with the effort of pushing the plaintiff toward $1.5 million—what was this guy's problem? Didn't he want to go higher? "Oscar, I think you should play hardball here," he said. "Ask for more and see what happens. My experience and instinct tells me you've got a chance."

"Well," Rank said doubtfully, "if you think so. I don't want to blow it for Amanda here. If anyone ever deserved a good payday for a good deed, she does."

"Trust me," said the Mediator, and he went off to close the deal.

—◅◌◌◌▻—

"Listen," the Mediator said to the defense, "I've got an idea. You're offering $1 million; they want $2 million—allow me to recommend to each side that we meet in the middle. What if I can get the plaintiff to accept $1.5 million? Will you make that offer?"

And with that, the case was settled in five minutes, and everybody went home happy.

WHAT HAPPENED?

The Mediator found himself in an interesting and somewhat unusual (but certainly not unheard of!) predicament: he knew from the outset where both parties wanted to end up. This presented him with something of an ethical dilemma. He had to maintain the confidentiality of the information he received from the defense counsel about how high his principal would go to settle the case, so he could not just say to the plaintiff, "They're willing to give you $2 million. I think you should ask for it." At the same time, he was bound to protect the evaluation of the plaintiff's new counsel that his case was worth between $800,000 and $1 million. The Mediator could not have told the defense, "They're expecting to walk away with only $1 million. You can get off for a lot less than you planned!" Fortunately, he had already formulated an ethical fallback stance for such situations: whenever he encountered an overlap or crossover situation like this, his practice was to gently guide the parties to a number in the middle that both sides would find to be a fair settlement.

The key was timing: although from the outside his approach seemed somewhat manipulative, he made sure the negotiation lasted for a standard amount of time. Both sides were expecting to have to negotiate; if they reached agreement too easily and too quickly, they would both wonder if they had the "winner's curse," the feeling that they could have done better in a longer negotiation.

As was true in this case, mediators sometimes have a lot of control over the outcome. An ethical mediator is scrupulous about not favoring one side or the other, but rather strives to find a middle ground that leaves both sides equally happy.

WHAT STRATEGIES CAN WE LEARN?

1. **In case of crossover in offer and demand, strive to find middle ground between the two figures.**
   When you have a situation in which the demand and the offer overlap, guide the parties to a number that is exactly in the middle of their respective positions. Each side will feel a sense of fairness and will leave the process uplifted. Resist the temptation to short-circuit the negotiation process, or the parties will feel that they either left some money on the table or paid too much.
2. **Don't rush the dance.**
   Pacing and timing can be crucial; artificially pushing the pace of negotiations to the conclusion you want everyone to reach is never a good idea. Resist the temptation to use

the confidential information you obtain to accelerate the negotiations. Instead, set the pace of the negotiations such that each caucus generates movement, and the parties have a sense of progress. To reinforce the idea that progress toward settlement is indeed being made, remind them of specific gains they have already attained. Next, use language that sets up a response pattern and causes the parties to nod in agreement with your positive assessments. Finally, reinforce the idea that even though the negotiation is taking time, it is moving steadily toward an outcome that will be fair for everyone.

3. **Avoid the "winner's curse."**

When one party feels that the deal was too easy, a kind of "buyer's remorse" can set in that leaves them with second thoughts about the outcome. It is therefore critical for the parties to go through a thorough negotiation process even when the settlement number is fairly easy to achieve.

PART FOUR

THE MEDIATOR'S HIP-POCKET GUIDE TO STRATEGY

No two cases are exactly alike, and every moment in a mediation presents an opportunity to prevent an impasse, remove an emotional impediment to negotiation, or move out of deadlock. As the mediator, you make the call: there are no definitive rules, just the opportunity to call on all your skills and improvise in the moment. You'll draw on your intuition and sense of timing and on what you've gleaned from personal experience—both from the case and from life itself. You can also pick and choose from the skills in this section, a summary of some of the many improvisational options available to mediators. Keep these tricks and techniques in your hip pocket and pull them out when needed.

GETTING THE BALL ROLLING

These options are the first tools to choose from when dealing with a logjam in the negotiation of a case. They can stimulate conversation, close a gap, and get the parties moving in a good direction.

Brainstorming. Brainstorm (either separately or with all parties) to increase the list of settlement options from which to choose. The basic rule is that you all agree to brainstorm without censoring options; postpone any evaluation of an option until the very end of the brainstorming session. No decisions are made at the brainstorming session. They are made after you synthesize the information and have had a chance to discuss the options with each party separately.

Broader View of Resources. Explore *what* can be distributed, *when* it can be distributed, *by whom* it would be distributed, and *how much* of it could be distributed. This is particularly helpful when the parties are discussing both monetary and nonmonetary solutions, and the opportunity to find a creative solution arises.

Conditional Offer.   A conditional offer is one that you disclose only if a certain condition is met. You can use this as a tool to close the gap between the parties. For example, if party A authorizes you to offer x and party B is seeking $x + y, then you are authorized by party A to disclose an increased settlement offer if party B meets a certain condition, such as decreasing its demand by z.

Controlled Sharing.   Use one set of numbers for the negotiation and another set of numbers for behind-the-scenes discussions. For example, if a party reveals what they want to settle the case, but doesn't want to offer the final settlement amount all at once, they might offer half their money with the idea of negotiating up to their reserve point.

Decision Tree.   Use this four-step method to create a basis for assessing risk and a quantifiable value or range of settlement: (1) list various possible events that might occur in the litigation (or beyond); (2) consider the costs or gains associated with each possibility (expressed in dollars); (3) estimate the probability of each possibility (the likelihood that it will occur, expressed as a percentage); and (4) evaluate the overall picture by multiplying each possibility by its probability.

Goodwill.   Encourage trust by building rapport early. Speak about topics unrelated to the dispute, such as recent travel, sports, the news, or whatever is of interest to the parties. When parties and counsel see you early on as a person they can relate to, you can draw on this goodwill to become directive later in the negotiation.

Inventory.   When parties seem to be tiring during long negotiations, stop and take a verbal inventory of progress so far, concentrating on the opportunities that have been created. This reminds the parties that the day hasn't been wasted and that although they have not yet reached settlement, with a bit more work they will succeed.

Neutral Evaluation.   Make a candid (sometimes written, sometimes verbal) assessment of the dispute as to its likely outcome or the value of a legal claim or defense if it were adjudicated. The parties can use this evaluation to conduct a further risk analysis as to what might happen in court.

People Mover.   Physically move people into different combinations or breakout meetings to find common ground for settlement—for example, a meeting between you and one counsel only, a meeting between you and both counsel only, and so on. You might also move the parties to a different and less formal physical location, such as a coffee shop or bar.

Reality Television.   Mirror back to the parties the current state of negotiations in real time—saying, for example, "So here's where I think we stand now . . ." Then explore what might happen under certain conditions, such as if negative evidence were presented against the parties' positions. This will help you determine how far they are prepared to go before finalizing the deal.

Role Play.   Ask the party to play the role of the other side for a moment and to act out the other party's point of view on the case. Use this method when parties are unable to see things from any perspective but their own.

Serving the Parties.   Use this skill to gently redirect parties who want to negotiate themselves toward what you perceive as a minefield. First, remind them that you are there to serve them and will do anything they want you to do. Then remind them of your experience in negotiations, and caution them that if you obediently follow their direction with respect to the next move, they might not like the outcome.

Speaking the Client's Language.   While speaking to the lawyer about the settlement numbers, make sure you use language that is geared to the client's ears and interests. This helps the client understand what's going on with the negotiation and gives the attorney an excuse to talk to the client privately about what you just said.

Storytelling. Tell the parties a story about another case or a similar situation. Use this technique to create an emotional connection you can build on during the negotiation, or to give them a reflection (positive or negative) of how their case might turn out.

Transparency. There is always a gap between what you as mediator are thinking and what you actually say. Sometimes you want to keep your thoughts to yourself, but at other times it pays to be *transparent:* to tell the parties *what* you are going to do and *why* you are going to do it. This transparency can help ensure that the parties are clear about the process, the goals, and their roles; it offers you immediate feedback about strategic decisions, reducing delays created by uncertainty; and it creates trust by giving the parties a glimpse of your thinking, analysis, and process decisions.

Two-Step Offer. Obtain two offers from a party at one time: an offer you can disclose to the other party immediately and an offer you can disclose *only* if it will unequivocally settle the case.

Whole into Parts. Break the issues down into smaller parts, isolating the demanding pieces and reserving them for later. This sets the stage for agreement on the easier parts and creates a more flexible mind-set for negotiation on the more difficult ones.

SECOND LINE OF DEFENSE

You can often hit a standstill in negotiation after considerable effort has been devoted to settlement. You know the parties are quite invested in reaching a conclusion, but they are getting tired, dragging their feet, or digging in their heels. Use the tools in this section to help wake them up and get them moving again.

The Apology. Sometimes a simple apology from the defense is all it takes to remove the plaintiff's emotional impediment to negotiation. This is a powerful option in employment and probate cases.

Avoiding the Winner's Curse. We all have an inner clock, and parties have an internal sense of how long a negotiation should take. If things move too quickly, the parties will be left with the feeling of "the winner's curse"—that if things had moved more slowly, they might have cut a better deal. Even when you know you can wrap things up quickly, it's to everyone's advantage to keep the negotiation proceeding normally, for a reasonable amount of time, before the inevitable settlement.

Balancing the Books.   If party A says they won't pay more than party B, have party B commit (in private caucus) to a significant number. Then work on party A to balance the books.

Bathroom Move.   Often lawyers will not reveal to you, in the client's presence, how far their client is willing to go in a negotiation. If you can speak to the lawyer in a less formal moment—in the restroom, for example—you can use that opportunity to learn the true story. (This only works if you and lawyer are the same gender.) This move is something to improvise rather than plan. It's a real opportunity to take advantage of the moment!

Best Settlement Offer.   Obtain in confidence what the party thinks is their best settlement offer. In the case of a defendant, for example, you're looking for the number that is the maximum they will accept in terms of negotiation—the point at which they feel they would rather go to trial than pay a penny more. Get their permission to float the number to the other party as something coming from you rather than them. This allows them to test the waters before committing and allows you to try a different approach if this fails.

Bracketing.   Establishing a high and low end for offers and demands can help stabilize a negotiation. Suggest monetary "ranges" for offers that you feel will anchor the parties in a zone that is worth negotiating in. This generally causes the parties to come up with their own ranges, which helps you figure out where they are willing to settle.

Counterintuitive Thinking.   Sometimes the shortest distance between two points is not a straight line. When your usual procedure just doesn't work or the parties seem to need a jump-start, consider recommending the *opposite* of what's expected or what naturally comes to mind.

Culling the Herd.   In a multiparty case, the parties tend to have a herd mentality: they move together, and it may not be the direction you had in mind. Bringing several defendants together in the same room will almost invariably cause them to discuss ways to pay less—not something you want to encourage. The solution is to keep them separated as much as possible.

Currency.   The medium of exchange in negotiations can come in many forms—and not always monetary. When there's not enough money in the pot, consider using another form of currency—shares of stock, free vacations, continued health benefits, and so on—to make up the difference.

Decoy.   In a multiparty setting, force a party's hand by using the possibility that another party (or parties) will settle. This tends to stir up the mix because one party generally doesn't want to be left standing alone.

Divide and Conquer.   In multiparty cases in which the negotiation is locked up, try splitting the defendants up into separate caucus rooms and determining the feasibility of direct individual deals with the plaintiff.

Double-Bracketing.   In this transparent approach to negotiation, ask each side to bracket a range of settlement amounts that comes as close to the insult zone as possible, without their actually giving you a number that is insulting. Having to quantify their range focuses their thinking and also allows room to move into a more reasonable negotiating zone. Make the bracketing confidential.

Expert Opinions.   When disagreement about a particular issue has caused an impasse and neither side is willing to budge, explore their willingness to obtain a neutral expert opinion on the issue to settle the disagreement.

Face-to-Face.   When the parties have an ongoing relationship, the presence of lawyers may actually inhibit reconciliation. Bringing the parties together for a face-to-face meeting—without counsel, but in your presence—may serve as an icebreaker. Note that you must first get permission from the lawyers to do this.

"Final Jeopardy" Mediation. Ask the parties to write down (and show you) what they think their adversary's offer is or will be. What they write down reveals a tremendous amount about what they are thinking and possibly expecting in settlement.

Fireworks. In cases where the parties seem set and immovable, you can create little explosions—by dropping unexpected information "bombs," shaking up normal procedure, or reacting unpredictably—that blow them out of their comfort zones and send them scurrying around in directions they didn't expect. When they all settle down again, they may be in a better position to negotiate.

Floater. Float a trial balloon—a number or range of numbers—that you think might get a reaction from the party. Make sure they understand that this number is coming from you, not from the other side. This is another way to get a party to reveal how much they are willing to spend or receive in settlement.

The Headline. Ask the party to play the role of news editor and come up with the headline if the evidence is presented against their interest. This transitional move serves as a reality check that can persuade the party to reduce their expectations.

Hit the Marker. Identify goals in a negotiation and encourage the parties to "hit" them. For example, get party A to commit to taking the negotiation to a different level if it becomes clear that party B is willing to move into a certain range, such as six figures.

Let's Make a Deal, aka the Monty Hall Approach. At the conclusion of a negotiation, when you are close to a deal but not there yet, offer three choices to the party: door number 1, door number 2, or door number 3. Door number 1 is a guaranteed amount in response to a competitive offer. Door number 2 is a range or bracketed amount. Door number 3 is your proposal of a specific number. This works because people like options, particularly in a distributive negotiation where money is the only currency.

The Mario Clinco.   In a highly emotional case involving a monetary negotiation, your allowing offers to be transmitted between the parties may cause reactive devaluation (whereby a party automatically rejects a proposal by an adversary simply because it was made by the adversary). Instead, make a hypothetical proposal, asking, "How would you respond if . . . ?" Then, when the timing is right, make a recommendation. (The late Mario Clinco was a trial judge in Santa Monica, California, who was renowned for using this technique.)

Mirror.   People often make statements early in the mediation that they later regret. Make a mental note of these potentially useful statements. You can pull them out later, during a stuck point in the negotiation, to remind parties of their previous commitment.

Overlap.   Ask the defendant if they would consider offering a sum that you know is more than what the plaintiff would accept. Tell them you will not offer it at this time but that you just want to get a sense of how far you need to go with the negotiation. Having this information allows you to test the other party to determine their reserve number.

Slow Drip.   You may have access to strategic information that will prevent a traditional negotiation. You don't want to hit the uninformed party over the head with this information all at once. Get permission from party A to slowly reveal small portions of the information to party B in an attempt to condition party B to shift positions.

You Pick the Music.   Sometimes party A insists on a traditional negotiation and party B hates to negotiate, but both parties have come to the dance. In this case, allow party B to "pick the music" they will dance to by developing the negotiation agenda. This gives party B a feeling of holding some power; a sense of powerlessness is probably the root of the party's disinclination to negotiate.

EXTREME IMPROVISATIONAL NEGOTIATION

The hours have dragged on and on, and the parties have had just about all they can stand of each other and the negotiation process.

You have exhausted virtually every option, and the only person demonstrating any energy to keep going is the mediator—you. Here are some skills to pull out when all else fails.

Adjournment v. Termination.   To avoid giving up altogether and sending a case to court, consider adjourning the process for the moment, but leave open the possibility of reconvening at a later date or following up by telephone.

Blind Bid.   When two or more parties are negotiating over the same object, such as an art piece, a restaurant, or some other property, have them give you their last best confidential offers to buy the object. The highest bidder wins. No need to negotiate!

Contingent or Partial Deal.   When you are unable to settle the entire case, consider resolving some but not all of the issues (or parties, in a multiparty case). This allows the door to remain open for further discussion after the dust has settled and the decision makers have a chance to reconvene.

The Double-Blind Proposal.   In confidential caucus with each side, propose a possible solution that you feel may be acceptable. Stress that this is not your opinion of value; rather, it is your *best judgment* of an acceptable point of agreement. Write down the proposal on a piece of paper and ask the parties to respond yes or no to the proposal. If both parties say yes, you will announce a settlement. If either party says no, then there will be no deal. If one or both parties say no, you will not reveal who (if either) was willing to accept the deal. This protects the party from exploitation in a later negotiation. This technique works best when you have established trust early on.

Good Timing.   Delay proposals to the point of no return—when instinct tells you that they have the greatest probability of acceptance—then make a recommendation.

I Have a Plane to Catch.   When negotiations seem to be grinding to a halt or moving at the pace of molasses, accelerate the discussion by highlighting the value of limited time: "I'm sorry to rush you, but I've got a plane to catch at eight o'clock."

The Mediator's Hip-Pocket Proposal. Before making a double-blind proposal (whereby you give each side a number and ask them to respond yes or no), make sure you have obtained agreement from one side that the anticipated proposal will be acceptable. Keep this agreement in your hip pocket and pull it out when you need it.

Net to Client. On a whiteboard or chalkboard, provide a dual financial overview of what the settlement value looks like to the party: (1) how it looks today, without risk, before court costs and expert fees are incurred, versus (2) how it would look if the party were to go to court without certainty of outcome. This usually provides a needed reality check that shocks the party into making an effort to settle the case.

One-Text Approach. Use this to foster discussion and guide the parties toward resolution. Prepare a "draft" agreement using the ideas and proposals of both parties and circulate it to them for comments and criticism. Repeat the process until you feel that no further revisions can be made. Then ask the parties to accept or reject the proposed settlement as outlined in the draft.

The Vin Scully. On September 9, 1965, Sandy Koufax pitched his fourth no-hitter, a perfect game. For thirty-eight seconds after the final pitch, instead of commenting on Koufax's performance, sportscaster Vin Scully let the radio audience listen to the crowd's celebration as they joyfully threw seat cushions, programs, and hats into the air. Scully's decision to step back made a lasting impression on a generation of sports fans. The lesson is that sometimes it's more useful to allow the parties to tell their stories without interference, direction, or narration.

ABOUT THE AUTHOR

Jeffrey Krivis has been a successful mediator and a pioneer in the field for fifteen years, and has served as the president of the International Academy of Mediators and the Southern California Mediation Association. He has been recognized by the *Daily Journal,* the leading legal newspaper in California, as one of the top twenty mediators in the state and as one of the top fifty neutrals in the state. He has been honored as one of the "Super Lawyers" in California by *Los Angeles Magazine* and *Law and Politics Media.*

After graduating from Southwestern University School of Law in 1980, Krivis began his legal career as a trial lawyer, and helped found the firm of Krivis & Passavoy in 1985. In 1990 he founded First Mediation Corporation, which serves as the administrator of his practice and as a resource for clients and colleagues in the field of alternative dispute resolution.

Krivis is on the board of visitors of Pepperdine Law School and has served as an adjunct professor of law at the Straus Institute for Dispute Resolution since 1994, where he has taught various courses and workshops, including Specialized Mediation (employment, personal injury, and medical malpractice), the Dispute Resolution Clinic, Advanced Mediation, and Mediating the Litigated Case.

Krivis has mediated thousands of cases in a wide variety of areas, including class action, business, mass tort, employment, professional liability, entertainment, securities, catastrophic injury, toxic torts, construction defect, and insurance (life, health, and disability). In 1993 he received the Dispute Resolution Lawyer of the Year Award from a publicly traded corporation. He is also on the editorial board of the CPR Institute for Dispute Resolution and serves on the board of directors for the Los Angeles County Bar Association Dispute Resolution Services. He has achieved an "AV" rating by Martindale-Hubbell.

Krivis is the author of numerous articles and guides in the area of alternative dispute resolution; they can be found on his Web site, www.firstmediation.com.